Henry James at Home

by the same Author

The Rise of Castlereagh
The Empress Catherine and
    Princess Dashkov
Londonderry House and its
    Pictures
Princess Lieven
Judge Jeffreys
Mexican Empire
John Law
A Victorian Historian: Letters
    of W. E. H. Lecky
Privacy and the Press
Trials of Oscar Wilde
Mr and Mrs Beeton
Simla and the Simla Hill States
    Under British Protection
A History of Pornography
Cases That Changed the Law

Carson
Trial of Craig and Bentley
United in Crime
The Strange Death of
    Lord Castlereagh
Sir Patrick Hastings:
    His Life and Cases
Trial of Sir Roger Casement
The Quiet Canadian:
    The Secret Service Story of
    Sir William Stephenson
Oscar Wilde: The Aftermath
Norman Birkett
Cynthia
Lord Reading
The Story of Lamb House
Strong for Service: The Life of
    Lord Nathan of Churt

with the Marchioness of Londonderry, D.B.E.

The Russian Journals of Martha
    and Catherine Wilmot

More Letters from Martha
    Wilmot: Impressions of Vienna

with G. R. Falkiner Nuttall

Air Defence and the Civil
    Population

with John Kisch

An International Case Book of
    Crime

HENRY JAMES IN 1912

From the charcoal drawing by John Sargent in the Royal Collection in Windsor Castle.

By gracious permission of Her Majesty Queen Elizabeth II

HENRY JAMES AT HOME

H. Montgomery Hyde

Farrar, Straus & Giroux   New York

for John and Holly

'I am not a writer of the Gladstonian postcard – I mean I can do little with *that*.'

Henry James to Miss Bethem-Edwards, June 12th, 1913
Ashley MSS: British Museum (Add. 4860).

❦ Acknowledgements

I wish to thank my cousin, Mr John S. R. James, trustee of the James estate and controller of the copyright, for permission to quote from the voluminous notebooks and unpublished correspondence of Henry James and other members of the James family, preserved in the Houghton Library of the Harvard University and other libraries and private collections. For making this material available to me, I am particularly indebted to Dr William H. Bond, Librarian of the Houghton Library; Mr William H. Runge, Curator of Rare Books in the University of Virginia; and the staffs of the Brotherton Library in the University of Leeds; Trinity College, Cambridge; the Department of Manuscripts in the British Museum, and the National Trust.

I am likewise indebted to Professor J. C. Waterlow (on behalf of his mother Lady Waterlow) and to the late Dr John D. Gordan, Curator of the Berg Collection in the New York Public Library, for allowing me to see and use the unpublished diary of Sir Sydney Waterlow, the copyright in which belongs to Lady Waterlow. I also have to thank the Astor, Lenox, and Tilden Foundations of the Library for their part in allowing the quotation of passages from this remarkable diary, besides authorizing my access to it.

For permission to quote from the writings and recorded recollections of the late Miss Theodora Bosanquet, my thanks are due to her literary executrix, Professor Theresa J. Dillon.

I am under an especial sense of obligation to Miss C. F. Kingdon for giving me extracts from the diary kept by her mother when she was Henry James's amanuensis.

Readers of Dr Leon Edel's volumes of the life of Henry James will recognize my debt to his researches. I acknowledge in particular the assistance which I have derived while writing the first two chapters of this book from *Henry James: The Conquest of London*; *Henry James: The Middle Years*; and the Introduction ('The Dramatic Years') to his edition of *Guy Domville*. At the same time I should record that my discovery of the MS of the Waterlow diary, the location of which was previously unknown to Dr Edel in the New York Public Library, has enabled him to make exhaustive use of it in the account of Henry James and Sir Sydney Waterlow which he has recently given in *The Times Literary Supplement* (August 8th, 1968).

I am grateful to the British Broadcasting Corporation for kindly supplying me with a copy of the script of *Recollections of Henry James in his Later Years*, first broadcast in 1956.

The Appendix ('The Lamb House Library') was originally published in *The Book Collector*, and I am obliged to the editor for consenting to its republication here.

For their continuous and ever ready help and interest over the years in enabling me to assemble my Henry James collection, without which it would have been impossible to write this book, I am under a great debt of gratitude to Mr John S. Van E. Kohn and Mr Michael Papantonio of the Seven Gables Bookshop, New York.

I must also thank the following, who have helped me with their personal memories of Henry James and in other ways: Miss M. Elizabeth Barber, Mr C. Waller Barrett, Mrs Millicent Bell, Mr Victor Bonham-Carter, Mr Lew D. Feldman, Mr Roger Frewen, Sir Rupert Hart-Davis, Professor Richard H. Logsdon, the late Mr Percy Lubbock, Sir Compton Mackenzie, Mr Burgess Noakes, Mr Simon Nowell-Smith, Viscount Simon, Mr Roger Senhouse, Mr George F. Sims, and Mr Peter Warren.

The frontispiece portrait of Henry James by John Sargent is reproduced by gracious permission of Her Majesty Queen Elizabeth the Second. Sources of the other illustrations with the necessary acknowledgements similarly appear beneath each illustration in the text.

ACKNOWLEDGEMENTS

Finally, I thank my wife for her inexhaustible patience and good humour in typing the frequently confusing and illegible manuscript of these pages as a labour of love.

Westwell House,   H.M.H.
Tenterden, Kent.
January, 1969.

❦ Preface

Thanks to the National Trust, I have been able to compose this book in the serene atmosphere of the house where Henry James spent most of the last eighteen years of his life, and which he regarded, from the time he bought it, as 'my home for the rest of my days.' It has been an inspiration, as well as a privilege for me as his kinsman, to have worked in the room where he wrote *The Wings of the Dove* and his other novels of the later period, as well as preparing the Collected Edition of his *Novels and Tales*, and also to have had daily access to his library and the various association items and Jamesiana now preserved in Lamb House. I take this opportunity of expressing my appreciation to the Trust for its confidence in allowing me to occupy this historic dwelling.

✿ Contents

❧ Illustrations

Henry James at Home

One ❧ Mayfair

In 1876, American-born Henry James, then aged thirty-three and on the threshold of his career as a writer, decided to settle in England, which was to become his permanent home. He had spent the previous twelve months in France, mostly in Paris, having arrived there from New York with the object of finding the literary world with which he felt that he had the strongest affinity. But, although he met Ivan Turgeniev, who addressed him as '*mon cher ami*' and through the Russian novelist was introduced to the circle of Gustave Flaubert which included Edmond de Goncourt, Alphonse Daudet, Maupassant, Zola and others, Henry soon came to realize that Paris was not the place for him. For one thing, he found the literary fraternity too exclusive and impervious to foreign influences. 'I don't like their wares, and they don't like any others', he told his friend, William Dean Howells, editor of the *Atlantic Monthly*, in which Henry's novel *The American* was being serialised at this time.[1] To his brother William, who had twitted him on employing 'French tricks' in his letters, he confessed that his 'last layers of resistance to a long-encroaching weariness and satiety with the French mind and its utterance' had fallen from him 'like a garment'.

I have done with 'em, forever, and am turning English all over. I desire only to feed on English life and the contact of English minds – I wish greatly I knew some. Easy and smooth-flowing as life is in Paris I would throw it over to-morrow for an even very small chance to plant myself for a while in England. If I had a single good friend in London I

1

would go thither. I have got nothing important out of Paris
nor am likely to . . . A good deal of Boulevard and third-rate
Americanism: few retributive relations otherwise.[2]

Nor was he in sympathy with the Puritan outcry against
Zola's novel of the evils of drink and sex, *L'Assommoir*, although
personally he found it 'devilishly dirty'. This had resulted in
the dropping of its serialisation half way through the story in
Le Bien Public, a magazine owned by Menier, the chocolate
manufacturer. Of course, he himself was unlikely to offend in
this way. 'Among your tribulations as editor, I take it that this
particular one is not in store for you', Henry wrote to Howells,
after a discussion with Flaubert about Zola's 'catastrophe'.
(Howells had just asked James to prolong the instalments of
The American). 'On my way down from Flaubert's I met poor
Zola climbing the staircase, looking very pale and sombre,
and I saluted him with the flourish natural to a contributor
who has just been invited to make his novel last longer yet.'[3]
Henry left Paris for good early in December 1876, and
crossed the channel to take up residence in London. Although
he knew virtually no one there, he was not a complete stranger
to the sights and sounds of the English capital. As a boy of
twelve, he had spent a winter with his parents and two of his
brothers in furnished houses which they took, the first, a small
house, 3 Berkeley Square, where they spent a month, and the
other at 10 Marlborough Place, St John's Wood, a much larger
house, rented for £250 a year. 'We are delightfully situated
here, and shall be tomorrow even more so in all probability,'
his father had written home as they were about to move from
Mayfair to St John's Wood at the end of their first month.
'Our circle of acquaintances is extending among very nice
people, too, literary some of them and others well worth
knowing. The boys have a capital tutor, and were never so
sweet and good, all of them . . . We have a home-feeling in
London that is very agreeable, and you do not feel yourself so
constantly cheated as you are apt to in Paris.'[4] This was the
London of Dickens and still more of Thackeray, but when
Henry tried to recall it twenty years later, 'it had turned to grey,

like faded ink.' However, when he came in old age to compose his fragmentary autobiography, he was to recall the view from the house in St John's Wood across a large green expanse where ladies and gentlemen practised archery, so utterly different from anything that could be seen from the family home in New York City. ('It was such a whiff of the old world of Robin Hood as we could never have looked up from the mere thumbed "story", in Fourteenth Street at any rate, to any soft confidence of'.)[5] Henry's recollections of his next visit, as a young man of twenty-five, were more vivid. This time he was on his own. The initial impression of the cheerless lodging in 7 Half Moon Street, where he spent some weeks in the spring of 1869, remained with him long afterwards. He had arrived from Liverpool on a cold, March afternoon and having attended to the distribution of his luggage sat down to consider his habitation.

It was on the ground floor, and the fading daylight reached it in a sadly damaged condition. It struck me as stuffy and unsociable, and its mouldy smell and its decoration of lithographs and wax flowers – an impersonal black hole in the huge general blackness. The uproar of Piccadilly hummed away at the end of the street, and the rattle of a heartless hansom passed close to my ears.

A sudden horror of the whole place came over me, like a tiger-pounce of homesickness which had been watching its moment. London was hideous, vicious, cruel, and above all overwhelming; whether or not she was 'careful of the type', she was indifferent as Nature herself to the single life.

In the course of an hour I should have to go out to my dinner, which was not supplied on the premises, and that effort assumed the form of a desperate and dangerous quest. It appeared to me that I would rather remain dinnerless, would rather even starve, than sally forth into the infernal town, where the natural fate of an obscure stranger would be to be trampled to death in Piccadilly and have his carcass thrown into the Thames. I did not starve, however, and I eventually attached myself by a hundred human links to the dreadful, delightful city.[6]

Henry summoned up courage to inquire of the landlord, whose name was Lazarus Fox, where he could best betake himself most regularly for his dinner. Mr Fox was a pensioned-off servant from an aristocratic household, who kept the establishment in Half Moon Street for the purpose of letting rooms to bachelor gentlemen. 'Well,' said the landlord as he surveyed the newest arrival, 'there is the Bath Hotel, sir, a very short walk away, where I should think you would be very comfortable indeed. Mr So-and-So dines at his club, sir – but there is also the Albany in Piccadilly to which I believe many gentlemen go.'

For his first night Henry had not fancied sitting in lone state at the heavy mahogany of the stodgy little hotel that in those days and for long afterwards occupied the north-west corner of Arlington Street, on the site of the present Ritz, although in common with many of his compatriots he was to resort to it repeatedly during the years following. Instead he fell back on the Albany, 'a small eating-house of the very old English tradition,' which like the Bath Hotel has long since disappeared. It was situated a little further east, on the opposite side of Piccadilly to the more famous set of 'chambers' of the same name. Henry had never seen anything like it before. One sat in 'small compartments, narrow as horse-stalls, formed by the high straight backs of hard wooden benches and accommodating respectively two pairs of feeders, who were thus so closely face to face as fairly to threaten with knife and fork each others' more forward features. The scene was sordid, the arrangements primitive, the detail of the procedure, as it struck me, well nigh of the rudest; yet I remember rejoicing in it all . . . There were restaurants galore even at that time in New York and in Boston, but I had never before had to do with the eating-house and had not yet seen the little old English world of Dickens, let alone of the ever-haunting world of Hogarth, of Smollet and of Boswell, drenched with such a flood of light.'[7]

Although he made several interesting acquaintances on this trip, including William Morris and his wife, Ruskin, John Morley and Leslie Stephen, it had not been a particularly enjoyable visit for Henry. Besides feeling acutely homesick,

4

he had suffered from various ailments, which were said in his letters to his brother William to be '*private* and not fit for the family circle'. They seem to have consisted of a combination of backache and constipation, which had impelled him to seek relief in a hydropathic establishment at Great Malvern, there to undergo a severe regimen of injections, douches and mechanical appliances. He had complained too of the lack of intellectual companionship among his fellow patients. 'Never from a single Englishman of them all have I heard the first word of appreciation and enjoyment of the things here that I find delightful', he had written to his brother. 'To a certain extent this is natural: but not to the extent to which they carry it. As for the women, I give 'em up in advance. I am tired of their stiffness and tastelessness – their dowdy beads and their lindsey woolsey trains.' In particular, the women lacked what he called 'intellectual grace' and 'moral spontaneity', unlike his beloved American cousin Minnie Temple or his Boston friend 'Clover' Hooper.

They live wholly in the realm of the cut and dried. 'Have you ever been to Florence?' 'Oh, yes.' 'Isn't it a most peculiarly interesting city?' 'Oh, yes, I think it's so very nice.' 'Have you read *Romola*?' 'Oh, yes, I think it is so very clever.'

The English have such a mortal distrust of anything like criticism or 'keen analysis' (which they seem to regard as a kind of maudlin foreign flummery) that I rarely remember to have heard on English lips any other intellectual verdict (no matter under what provocation) than this broad synthesis – 'so immensely clever'. What exasperates you is not that they can't say more, but that they wouldn't if they could.

Yet, in spite of their faults in his eyes, he had qualified this somewhat harsh appraisal to the effect that the women were 'well enough' and that the English as a whole were 'a great people for all that'.[8]

In 1872, he had passed through London again on the Grand Tour of Europe he made with his sister Alice and his aunt Kate Walsh to collect material for *Transatlantic Sketches*, the travel

articles which he originally wrote for the American *Nation*.
But on this occasion he had been as little enamoured of the
English capital as before. 'Oh, the grimness of London!' he had
exclaimed. 'And, oh, the cookery of London!'

Now, four years later, he was back in London again. On
December 12th, 1876, two days after leaving Paris, he found
rooms within a stone's throw of his first lodgings in Half Moon
Street. His new abode, now demolished, where he was to spend
most of the next decade, was at 3 Bolton Street, just off Piccadilly.

What he thought of the place and its surroundings and indeed of London generally at this stage of his career he was to set
down in his journal on returning to his parents' home in Boston
for a short holiday after five years' residence in Bolton Street.

I have *lived* much there, thought much, learned much,
produced much; the little shabby furnished apartment ought
to be sacred to me. I came to London as a complete stranger,
and today I know much too many people. *J'y suis absolu-
ment comme chez moi.* Such an experience is an education –
it fortifies the character and embellishes the mind . . .

. . . for one who takes it as I take it, London is on the
whole the most possible form of life. I take it as an artist
and a bachelor; as one who has the passion of observation
and whose business is the study of human life – the most
complete compendium of the world. The human race is
better represented there than anywhere else, and if you
learn to know your London you learn a great many things. [9]

[TWO]

Henry's rooms, for which he paid two-and-a-half guineas
(slightly less than $16) a week, were on the first floor of the
small four-storied Georgian house at the Piccadilly end of
Bolton Street. His sitting-room, where he ate and worked, had
a balcony, from which he could catch a sideways glimpse of the
trees in Green Park. It was a most respectable thoroughfare,
which had an eighteenth-century air about it. Fanny Burney
had lived a few doors away at No. 11, the 'Old Pretender' had
once lodged there, while in a later period Lord Melbourne had

6

been noted for the 'little dinners' he gave in Bolton Street. Opposite the window where his writing table was placed, Henry's gaze met the blank wall of a big house, not a very inspiring view for literary labour, it is true, though it came to have for him what he called a 'a vast convenient neutrality'. This wall was part of Bath House, the town house of Lord Ashburton, of the rich banking family of Baring, once much frequented by Thackeray and Carlyle.

The day after he installed himself in No. 3 Bolton Street, Henry wrote to his sister Alice:

> I have an excellent lodging in this excellent quarter, a lodging whose dusky charms – including a housemaid with a prodigious complexion but a demure expression and the voice of a duchess – are too numerous to repeat. I have just risen from my first breakfast of occasional tea, eggs, bacon and the exquisite English loaf, and you may imagine the voluptuous glow in which such a repast has left me. *Chez moi* I am really well off – and it's a rare pleasure to feel warm in my room, as I sit scribbling, a pleasure I never knew in Paris. But after that charming city London seems almost superficially horrible, and general unaesthetic cachet. I am extremely glad, however, to have come here and feel completely that everything will improve on acquaintance.

The front door of the lodging was usually opened by a slender, tall, rather pretty girl. She was not a servant, but a relation of the landlady. 'She's an English character,' Henry remarked to an American friend when he got to know her. 'She's what they call in England a "person". She isn't a lady and she isn't a woman; she's a person'. One thing about her Henry always remembered. The smallest witticism on his part produced uncontrollable fits of laughing. 'Oh, please don't, Mr James!' she would giggle, 'It's quite too funny!'[10]

Then there was Louisa, the dark-faced maid with the ducal voice, who brought him his first breakfast. She would also bring him other meals if he needed them, but these usually consisted of a chop and boiled potatoes. The maid helped in the kitchen, and once, without apparent success, Henry tried to get her to introduce a little variety into the cooking of the potatoes. He described the conversation in a letter to his sister Alice in Cambridge, Massachusetts:

H.J. (to the maid): Can't you do anything in the world with potatoes but drearily boil them?

THE MAID: Oh dear yes, sir, certainly, we can *mash* them!

H.J: That comes to the same thing. No other way?

THE MAID: I don't think we have heard of any other way, sir.

H.J: You can't fry them?

THE MAID: I don't think we could do that, sir? Isn't that French cookery, sir?

Eventually the maid left to marry a deformed cobbler, whose acquaintance she had made in the neighbourhood. When her successor arrived, Henry asked her what her name was.

'Well, sir, it might be Maria.'

'It *might* be?' Henry queried in surprise.

'Well, sir, they calls me Maria,' the newcomer admitted.

'Isn't it your name?'

'My name's Annie, sir, but Missus says that's too familiar.'

So Henry 'compromised' and called her Annie-Maria. 'It is part of the British code that you can call a servant any name you like', he explained for the benefit of the family in Cambridge, 'and many people have a fixed name for their butler, which all the successive occupants of the place are obliged to assume, so that the family needn't change its habits.'

A propos of which a lady told me the other day that on his return from the U.S. the Dean of Westminster told her that in America there were no perceptible servants at all. 'Haven't you really any *somewhere?*' she asked me. This was at dinner, and there were half a dozen footmen behind our chairs. 'Yes,' said I, 'but at dinner, for instance, they get under the table!'[11]

For the first time in his life, Henry James began to enjoy London. 'I had very few friends, the season was of the darkest and wettest,' he was to write in the retrospective passage in his journal already quoted; 'but I was in a state of deep delight. I had complete liberty, and the prospect of profitable work; I used to take long walks in the rain. I took possession of London; I felt it to be the right place. I could get English books: I used to read in the evenings, before an English fire. I can hardly say how it was, but little by little I came to know people, to dine out, etc. I did, I was able to do nothing at all to bring this state of things about; it came rather of itself.'[12]

It probably began with George Smalley, the London correspondent of the New York *Tribune*, on whom as a contributor he called and introduced himself. Smalley, who 'has a pretty house and wife is very civil', passed him on to various friends, besides putting him up as a temporary member of the Savile Club, then in Piccadilly and only a short distance from Bolton Street. In this way he was gradually introduced into London literary life, making friends amongst others with Andrew Lang, the poet and classical scholar, and Frank Hill, the editor of the *Daily News*, whose wife reviewed books. When his card for the Savile ran out, John Lothrop Motley, the historian of the Dutch Republic and former United States Minister to the Court of St James's, 'on whom I had no claim of *any* kind, sent me an invitation to the Athenaeum, which was renewed for several months and which proved an unspeakable blessing'. This was indeed so, since in addition to being able to extend the circle of his acquaintances very considerably, he had the use of what was undoubtedly the best London club library in most congenial surroundings. Here he would repair to dine after a hard day's writing in his lodgings, an additional advantage, since the dinner was 'good and cheap' in comparison with the London restaurants, 'whose badness is literally fabulous'. For Henry the Athenaeum was 'the last word of a high civilization'.

Henry had brought with him a few letters of introduction to local notabilities. Of these the most important was from his Boston friend, Henry Adams, who had married 'Clover' Hooper, to the Liberal peer, Lord Houghton, formerly Mr

Richard Monckton Milnes. Nicknamed 'the cool of the evening', the eccentric and dilettante 'Dicky' Milnes at this time fancied himself with some truth as 'the first wit in London'; he was sixty-eight and nearing the end of his life. 'A word from him went far,' wrote the author of *The Education of Henry Adams*. 'An invitation to his breakfast-table went farther. Behind his almost Falstaffian mask and laugh of Silenus, he carried a fine, broad, and high intelligence which no one questioned . . . Socially, he was one of two or three men who went everywhere, knew everybody, talked of everything, and had the ear of Ministers; but unlike most wits, he held a social position of his own which ended in a peerage, and he had a house in Upper Brook Street to which most people were exceedingly glad of admission. His breakfasts were famous, and no one liked to decline his initiations, for it was more dangerous to show timidity than to risk a fray. He was a voracious reader, a strong critic, an art connoisseur in certain directions, a collector of books, but above all he was a man of the world b rofession, and loved the contacts – perhaps the collisions of iety.'[13]

Before he had time to present his letters of introduction Henry was supposed to receive an invitation to one of the celebrated Saturday breakfasts, no doubt at the suggestion of some mutual acquaintance. He came through the ordeal successfully and the invitation was renewed soon afterwards. ('He invites me most dotingly.') The other guests on the second occasion included Goldwin Smith, whom he found 'pleasanter than my prejudice against him,' and John Morley, who had 'a most agreeable face', though he hardly opened his mouth. ('He is, like so many of the men who have done much here, very young-looking.') At this time Morley was reader for the publishing house of Macmillan and he also edited the *English Men of Letters* Series for that firm. He was to commission *Nathaniel Hawthorne* from Henry. On the other hand, Morley was to advise against the publication of Henry's *French Poets and Novelists*, which he characterized in a confidential report to the firm as 'mediocre . . . honest scribble work and no more'. Incidentally, Macmillan's rejected their reader's advice and brought out the work, as they seem to have been anxious to secure an option on Henry's future writings. The instantaneous success of *Daisy Miller*, which they were to publish eighteen months later, amply justified their confidence in the young American writer.

Lord Houghton was a great bookman and his library was particularly rich in choice and rare erotica, which he had assiduously collected for many years, mostly with the help of Paris agents. Henry was to see some of the choicer specimens when he visited the eccentric peer's country place in Yorkshire a little later. Meanwhile it is doubtful if they formed a topic of breakfast-time conversation. His host is more likely to have discussed the French poets and novelists about whom Henry was currently writing, since Houghton mentioned that he was going over to Paris shortly and Henry offered to provide him with introductions to Turgeniev and also to Flaubert, whom he described as 'an excellent and interesting fellow, well worth knowing and worth all the others a hundred times over – both in genius and personal nature'. Houghton politely accepted the offer, and the introductions duly arrived with a covering letter from Henry, who was careful to observe the etiquette in the matter of introductions. ('I have left the note pen, according to the rules of American civility – which has more rules than are commonly supposed.')[14]

Houghton, who had taken a fancy to the young American, next invited him to a dinner which he gave in his town house and to which Lord Tennyson, the Poet Laureate, Mr Gladstone, the Liberal Leader of the Opposition in the House of Commons, and Dr Henry Schliemann, the German archaeologist, were also bidden. The meal was fixed for the unusually early hour of seven o'clock to suit Tennyson's expressed wish and the fact that, as the host explained, 'all society has to submit to this idiosyncrasy of the poetical digestion'.[15]

Henry gave an account of the evening in a letter which he wrote next day to his brother William.[16]

Athenaeum Club, Pall Mall. March 29, 1877. . . .
Yesterday I dined with Lord Houghton – with Gladstone,

Tennyson, Dr Schliemann (the excavator of old Mycenae, etc.) and half a dozen other men of 'high culture'. I sat next but one to the Bard and heard most of his talk, which was all about port wine and tobacco: he seems to know much about them, and can drink a whole bottle of port at a sitting with no incommodity. He is very swarthy and scraggy, and strikes one at first as much less handsome than his photos: but gradually you see that it's a face of genius. He had I know not what simplicity, speaks with a strange rustic accent and seemed altogether like a creature of some primordial English stock, a thousand miles away from American manufacture.

Behold me after dinner conversing affably with Gladstone – not by my own seeking, but by the most importunate affection of Lord H. But I was glad of a chance to feel the 'personality' of a great political leader – or as G. is now thought here even, I think, by his partisans, ex-leader. That of Gladstone is very fascinating – his urbanity extreme – his eye that of a man of genius – and his apparent self-surrender to what he is talking of, without a flaw. He made a great impression on me – greater than anyone I have seen here: though 'tis perhaps owing to my naïveté, and unfamiliarity with statesmen.

Dr Schliemann told me one or two curious things. First, he is an American citizen, having lived some years in America in business. Second, though he is now a great Hellenist, he knew no word of Greek until he was 34 years old, when he learned it in six weeks (!!) at St Petersburg. *A que c'est être Allemand!**

The other men at Houghton's dinner were all special notabilities. Next me sat a very amiable Lord Zouche – noted as the unhappy young peer who a short time since

---

* Schliemann was 55 at this time. The son of a poor pastor in Mecklenburg, he made a fortune as a military contractor during the Crimean War, on which he retired to devote the remainder of his life to archaeological research in Greece. His theory that Hissarlik was the site of Homeric Troy gained the enthusiastic support of Gladstone. Happening to be in California when the latter was made a state of the Union, in 1850, he became and remained an American citizen. Most of his books, including *Troy and its Remains* (1875) and *Mycenae* (1877) were first issued in English.

married a young wife who three or four months after her marriage eloped *bel et bien* with a guardsman.*

By upbringing and indeed personal conviction Henry was a Liberal sympathiser, and his letters at this period abound in sentiments of opposition to the Conservative policies of Disraeli, particularly in the Near East.

I am not one of the outsiders who thinks that the 'greatness' of England is now exploded, [he wrote at this time] but there mingles with my interest in her prospects and doings in all this horrible Eastern question a sensible mortification and sadness. She has not resolutely played a part – even a wrong one. She had been weak and helpless and (above all) unskilful; she has drifted and stumbled and not walked like a great nation. One has the feeling that the affairs of Europe are really going to be settled without her. At any rate the cynical, brutal, barbarous pro-Turkish attitude of an immense mass of people here (I am no fanatic for Russia, but I think the Emperor of R. might have been treated like a gentleman!) has thrown into vivid relief the most discreditable side of the English character.[17]

Incidentally, the prevalent feeling that Gladstone's political career was virtually finished was to be most forcefully contradicted by events. In fact, the Liberal leader – he was 68, the same age as Lord Houghton – was to be Prime Minister three times more and to continue to lead his party in the House of Commons for the next seventeen years.

There was another side to the British social coin which intrigued Henry. How did the British, outwardly so proper in their churchgoing and public behaviour, cope with what he

* Robert 15th Lord Zouche (1872–1914) was the son of the well-known Victorian traveller and bibliophile Robert Curzon, whose *Visit to the Monasteries in the Levant* (1849) has been described as one of the most charming books of travel ever written. In 1875, he married the Hon. Annie Fraser, daughter of the 17th Lord Saltoun, whom he divorced a year later. He never remarried. Parham, his property near Pulborough, is one of the best and most interesting Elizabethan houses in the country. His father's great collection of Oriental manuscripts was deposited by him in the British Museum.

euphemistically called their 'fermenting idiosyncrasies'? One obvious answer was supplied by the young women of easy virtue, who frequented Piccadilly and, as Henry put it, were 'too addicted to violent forms of coquetry'. But the question went deeper than this, into the worlds of W. T. Stead's *Maiden Tribute of Modern Babylon* and the anonymous *My Secret Life*. Henry was dimly aware of them beneath the surface of well-ordered Victorian living, and like others he was to be sharply reminded of them when some of their features were on occasion publicly manifested in such affairs as the Dilke divorce, the Cleveland Street scandal, and the Oscar Wilde trials.

He was struck too by the appalling poverty, which contrasted strongly with the life in the clubs and the middle and upper class drawing-rooms, to which he was being invited more and more. There were too many gin-shops and too many miserable women at their door-steps, with hordes of dirty-faced children sprawling between one's legs. One cold, foggy night, he stumbled across 'a horrible old woman in a smoky bonnet, lying prone in a puddle of whisky'. On another occasion, when he was walking with a member of the American Legation staff, he was stopped by a street urchin, a little girl, who held out a grubby hand for alms. He gave her something and then turning to his companion remarked with feeling: 'They imitate so well the tones of wretchedness!'

He watched the Oxford and Cambridge University boat race from Barnes Bridge, where he stood in the midst of 'a dingy British mob, with coal smoke ground into its pores'. For two minutes he found it a supremely beautiful sight, when the two 'great white water-swimming birds, with eight feathered wings' came in view, but for those two minutes he complained at having to wait a horribly, bleak hour and a half, shivering, in mid-Thames, under the sour March wind. What Henry saw, or partly saw, was certainly unique, since it was the only contest in the history of the gruelling four-and-a-half mile race from Putney to Mortlake in which the rival crews finished in a dead heat.

By the end of his first London 'season', Henry confessed that he felt more at home in London than anywhere else in the world, so much so that he felt his 'sense of peculiarities' and his appreciation of people and things might be losing its edge. Yet he had formed no friendships which might be described as intimate. Least of all did he propose to take a wife. For the time being, at least, he felt wedded to his work and his bachelor apartment in Bolton Street.

'I have taken a great fancy to the place,' he wrote at this time; 'I won't say to the people and things; and yet these must have a part in it. It makes a very interesting residence at any rate; not the ideal and absolutely interesting – but the relative and comparative one . . . So my interest in London is chiefly that of an observer in a place where there is most in the world to observe. I see no essential reason however why I should not some day see more of certain Britons and think that I very possibly may. But I doubt if I should ever marry – or want to marry – an English wife!'[18]

[THREE]

By the end of his second year in Bolton Street, Henry had become a literary 'lion'. This was largely due to the success of his short novel *Daisy Miller* – 'a really quite extraordinary hit', as he described it to his mother – which first appeared in the summer of 1878 in two instalments in the *Cornhill Magazine*, then edited by Leslie Stephen. Stephen had accepted the story 'with effusion' after it had been turned down by *Lippincott's* in America without comment as being, Henry presumed, 'an outrage on American womanhood'. *Daisy Miller* was followed in the *Cornhill* at the end of the same year by *An International Episode*, a beautifully balanced little tale of an American girl who during the summer in Newport meets the aristocratic Lord Lambeth, who is obviously attracted by her, and then comes to London only to reject him when he proposes marriage. In one review, written by Mrs Hill, wife of the *Daily News* editor, the author was criticised for representing Lord Lambeth and his cousin Mr Beaumont as almost cockney types. As a rule Henry ignored reviews, but since he had met

15

Mrs Hill socially, he felt justified in defending himself in a spirited letter.

Amongst other points, Mrs Hill had taken him to task over the number of times he made Lord Lambeth exclaim, 'I say'. He replied that he had recently spent six months as a member of the aristocratic St James's Club where 'the golden youth of every description used largely to congregate', and that he had certainly heard more 'I says' than he had ever heard before, notwithstanding that nineteen out of twenty of the young men in the place had probably been to a public school.

However, this detail is not of much importance; [he went on] what I meant to indicate is the (I think) incontestable fact that certain people in English society talk in a very offhand, informal, irregular manner, and use a great many roughnesses and crudities. It didn't seem to me that one was bound to handle their idiosyncracies of speech so very tenderly as to weigh one idiom very long against another. In a word, the Lord Lambeths of the English world are, I think, distinctly liable, in the turn of their phrases, just as they are in the gratification of their tastes – or some of them – to strike quite conservative people like your humble servant as vulgar . . . Trollope, Thackeray, Dickens, even, with their big authoritative talents, were free to draw all sorts of unflattering English pictures, by the thousand. But if I make a single one, I am forthwith in danger of being confronted with a criminal conclusion – and sinister rumours reach me as to what I think of English society . . . Meanwhile I shall draw plenty of pictures of disagreeable Americans, as I have done already, and the friendly Briton will see no harm in that! – it will seem to him a part of the natural fitness![19]

During the winter and spring of 1878–79, which saw the publication in combined book form of *Daisy Miller* and *An International Episode*, Henry was greatly in demand by London hostesses. By the end of the first week of June 1879, he had dined out 107 times, a considerable gastronomic feat. 'You will simply wonder what can have induced me to perpetrate such a folly, and how I have survived to tell the tale!' he told his Cambridge friend Grace Norton. 'I admit that it is enough for the present, and for the rest of the summer I shall take in sail.'[20] Nevertheless he accepted thirty-three more dinner invitations before the end of the season. 'I couldn't keep out of it (I had become a highly developed diner-out),' he afterwards wrote in his journal, 'and its interruptions, its repetitions, its fatigues, were horribly wearisome and made work extremely difficult.'[21]

He recorded this reflection during a brief visit he made to America three years later, but on his return to Bolton Street he felt impelled to continue his dining-out habits, though he never exceeded the record he had established in '78 and '79. Edmund Gosse, who called to see him about some literary work soon after he got back, recalled that he found him stretched on a sofa and apologizing for not rising to greet his visitor. Noting the look of surprise on Gosse's face, Henry hurriedly explained that he was not an invalid, but that a muscular weakness of the spine obliged him, as he said, 'to assume the horizontal posture' during some hours every day in order to bear the almost unbroken routine of evening engagements. Gosse also recalled his appearance, seen then for the first time in daylight. 'There was something shadowy about it, the face framed in dark brown hair cut short in the Paris fashion, and in equally dark beard, rather loose and "fluffy". He was dressed in deep mourning for his mother, who had died a few months previously.' His manner appeared to Gosse to be 'grave, extremely courteous, but a little formal and frightened, which seemed strange in a man living in constant communication with the world'. After their business had been concluded – Gosse wanted an article from him on George du Maurier and his drawings – Henry talked 'with increasing ease, but always with a punctilious hesitancy, about Paris, where he seemed, to Gosse's 'dazzlement', to know an even larger number of persons of distinction than he knew in London.[22]

Henry would work on an average for six or seven hours a day. In spite of his succulent first breakfast in Bolton Street, he usually forewent this meal unless he had guests, as he some-times did. He would lunch alone in his rooms and usually work on for several hours in the afternoon. He would occasionally go out to tea with friends, but he did not accept any luncheon invitations except on Sundays. If he were not dining out in a private house, he would have his evening meal at his club and afterwards read or write letters or go for a walk before return-ing to Bolton Street about eleven o'clock or later. Early in his residence he found that a club was 'indispensable'. After enjoy-ing the temporary shelter of the Savile, the Travellers, the Athenaeum and the St James, he was eventually, in 1878, elected to the Reform, then a Liberal stronghold. 'This was an excellent piece of good fortune,' he was to write some years later in his journal, 'and the Club has ever since been, to me, a convenience of the first order. I could not have remained in London without it, and I have become extremely fond of it; a deep local attachment.'[23] It was to remain for him 'the most comfortable corner of the world'. His election to the Reform was considerably helped by Sir Charles Dilke, the rising Liberal politician, then in his middle thirties and 'only now emerging', in Henry's words, 'much less radical than he began from his early cloud, his having attacked the Queen and cremated his (deceased) wife'. Other leading Liberals, with whom he became closely acquainted at this period, included Lord Rosebery, Sir William Vernon Harcourt and the veteran John Bright, besides the Irish Nationalist M.P. and journalist Justin M'Carthy.

It is from Justin M'Carthy's pen that we get a clear picture of Henry's success in having 'thoroughly domesticated himself in London Society' at this period.

No man is more popular in London dining-rooms and drawing-rooms than Henry James, and a first night at a theatrical performance would seem incomplete if his familiar figure were not to be seen in the stalls or in one of the boxes. Henry James, too, has an interest in political life, and dines with leading public men in the London clubs which repre-sent the one side in politics and the other. He is a delightful talker, and in his talk can develop his views and ideas about

every passing subject which can clothe even the trivial
topics of the day with intellectual grace and meaning. Every
now and then some vivid saying or some sparkling epigram
comes in, and indeed, there is only, so far as I know, one
thing which Henry James never could do in any conversation – he never could be commonplace. [24]

Among the callers at Bolton Street was the brilliant 'doctri-
naire radical' Henry Bryce, who had been appointed Regius
Professor of Civil Law at Oxford at the age of thirty-two.
(Henry pronounced him 'distinctly able'.) He carried Henry
off to Commemoration at this University, and along with
Dilke they also visited Cambridge for May Week, where Henry
dined as the guest of an inter-university club in Trinity.

Charles Dilke, an old Cambridge man (when I say old I
mean he is only my age) took me very fraternally, by the
arm, and walked me over the whole place: showed me its
lovely picturesqueness in detail. I think it beats Oxford,
though inferior in *ensemble*.

Dilke is a very grand fellow, and a specimen of a fortunate
Englishman: born without exceptional talents to a big
property, a place in the world, and a political ambition
which, resolute industry in the form of social circumstances
aiding, he is steadily *en train* to realize. And withal not a
grain of genius or inspiration.

The first Secretary of the American Legation in London at
this time was William Jones Hoppin, an elderly bachelor,
who had practised law for many years in New York before
rather late in life joining his country's diplomatic service. He
was well read, wrote verse, translated plays from the French
and was interested in the arts. He had arrived in London about
the same time as Henry and by reason of his position was
naturally invited out a good deal to diplomatic parties. Yet he
was not a social success like Henry, and this gave him considerable cause for concern. Hoppin would make new acquaintances, but they never blossomed into friendships. He would
meet a woman at dinner, talk to her as pleasantly as he could,

and afterwards hear that she had spoken of him as 'agreeable'.
Yet, although he knew that she had enjoyed his talk, she never
asked him to her receptions or dinners or even to visit her.
'I am satisfied that youth and personal appearance have a
good deal to do with such matters', was Hoppin's conclusion.
'An old fellow with an unprepossessing exterior has but a small
chance.' There was not time to '*grow* into favour' in London.
'You must strike for it at once.' As for Henry James, he had
youth, good looks, good manners, and above all literary popularity on his side. 'People read his books and their curiosity is
piqued to know him. I don't think he talks remarkably well. I
believe he keeps his most piquant ideas for his novels – but he
has that dash of cynicism which is in fashion.'

Although Hoppin was to revise his opinion of Henry's table
talk, which he subsequently described as 'pleasant', he did not
perhaps quite appreciate the reason for Henry's success with
women to the extent that his Legation colleague Ehrman
Syme Nadal did. Nadal was Second Secretary and a Vir-
ginian, who had been a journalist, unlike the Yankee Hoppin,
whose junior he was by twenty years or so and who considered
him something of a lightweight. Yet Nadal's appreciation went
deeper than Hoppin's. Besides the attractions enumerated by
Hoppin, women liked Henry 'especially for his sympathetic
and delicate discernment of their own nice qualities', according to Nadal. 'He seemed to look at women rather as women
look at them. Women look at women as persons; men look at
them as women. The quality of sex in women, which is their
first and chief attraction to most men, was not their chief
attraction to James . . . I think he liked a pronounced and perhaps somewhat conscious refinement in women. There was an
English woman, a spinster, who was and always remained one
of his most intimate and devoted friends, and whom I knew.
She was rather pretty, and you needed only to glance at her to
see that she was especially what you call "nice". This lady had
the somewhat extreme refinement I am speaking of. I recall
one characteristic remark of hers: she once asked me if I did
not think it was vulgar to take offence.'

Also, Henry had an unerring sense of what was 'done' and

what was 'not done' in English society. He never put a foot
wrong socially. 'You never make a fool of yourself, do you?'
Nadal once asked him, when they were dining together in the
Café Royal. 'Never by any chance', was the confident reply.
To the easy-going southerner, he seemed to think a great deal
about 'a correct and respectable deportment'. On one occasion after they had been dining together at the St James's
Club, Nadal took Henry to see some people in Kensington. The
diplomatist got out of the hansom first and, going up the
steps, took hold in the dark of the servants' bell, which he proceeded to pull. 'What,' said Henry in a shocked voice, 'you
haven't rung the servants' bell?' The point was, of course, that
after-dinner calls were not made except if the caller knew the
people well, which in this case Nadal did, so that the mistake
really made no difference. But Henry still thought he should
have rung the visitors' bell and not the servants'.

In his talks with Nadal, Henry made no secret of his social
aspirations. The diplomatist, on the other hand, did not think
it was really worth while, particularly if the social aspirant
was snubbed on the way up. Once, when Nadal spoke disap-
provingly of some other Americans who had been treated like
this in the pursuit of social success, Henry commented: 'I
don't agree with you. I think a position in society is a legiti-
mate object of ambition.' He told his fellow countryman that
he wanted 'to be taken seriously' by the English; it was a
phrase he often made use of in conversation with Nadal. For
Henry particularly detested what he called 'that excluded
feeling'. 'I don't think he wanted to be in smart English
society because he really preferred the company of smart
people', Nadal remarked of him. 'It was rather that he did
not like to feel that he was shut out from that or any other
kind of company . . . I dare say also that he wanted to be
enough in smart society to know what it was like. He wished
to be an international novelist, and desired to know that as
well as other parts of English life. Then he knew that it is perhaps truer of England than of any other country that "a box
ticket takes you through the house". Other people, whose
company I dare say he really preferred, artists, and people of

letters, etc., would think all the more of him if he were about in the world of fashion.'[25]

[FOUR]

In those days there were no autumn sittings of Parliament to bring the country members to town. The period between the rising of both Houses in August, which marked the end of the London season, and the reassembly of Parliament in the following February was the time when the big landowners busied themselves on their estates and when country house parties were most fashionable. In his early days in England, Henry participated in a good deal of country house entertaining, with its hunting and shooting and other open air sports. 'It is certainly a thing they have brought to great perfection,' he told Grace Norton, 'and if you can stand the occasional dullness and the superabundance of poor unanimated talk, one can get much that is entertaining and interesting out of it.'

In the autumn of 1878, Henry paid his first visit to Scotland, 'a most beautiful and admirable little country', where he stayed with Sir John and Lady Clark, 'than whom there could not be a more tenderly hospitable couple', at Tillypronie, Aberdeen. 'Sir John caresses me like a brother, and her ladyship supervises me like a mother.'* Every day 'brought with it some pretty entertainment', which Henry described in a letter to his sister Alice.

On the first day I went to some Highland sports, given by Lord Huntly, and to a sumptuous lunch, in a coquettish marquee, which formed an episode of the same. The next day I spent roaming over the moors and hills, in company with a remarkably nice young fellow staying in the house, Sidney Holland, grandson of the late Sir Henry. . . . Nothing can be more breezy and glorious

---

* Sir John Forbes Clark (1821–1910), 2nd Baronet, married Charlotte daughter of Mr Justice Coltman. He had formerly served in the diplomatic service and was a substantial landowner.

than a ramble on these purple hills and a lounge in the sun-warmed heather. The real way to enjoy them is of course supposed to be with an eye to the grouse and partridges: but this is, happily, little of a shooting house, though Holland keeps the table – one of the best in England (or rather in Scotland, which is saying more) – supplied with game. The next day I took part in a cavalcade across the hills to see a ruined castle; and in the evening, if you please, stiff and sore as I was, and am still, with my exploits in the saddle, which had been sufficiently honourable, I went to a ball fifteen miles distant.

The ball was given by a certain old Mr Cunliffe Brooks, a great proprietor hereabouts and possessor of a shooting-lodge with a ball-room; a fact which sufficiently illustrates the luxury of these Anglo-Scotch arrangements.* At the ball was the fabulous beauty Mrs Langtry, who was staying in the house and who is probably for the moment the most celebrated woman in England. She is in sooth divinely handsome and it was 'extremely odd' to see her dancing a Highland reel (which she had been practising for three days) with young Lord Huntly, who is a very handsome fellow and who in his kilt and tartan, leaping and hooting and romping opposite to this London divinity, offered a vivid reminder of ancient Caledonian barbarism and of the toughness which lurks in all British amusements and only wants a pretext to explode. We came home from our ball (where I took out two young ladies who had gone with us for a polka apiece) at four a.m., and I found it difficult on that morning, at breakfast to comply with that rigid punctuality which is the custom of the house.

To-day our fine weather has come to an end and we are

---

* William Cunliffe Brooks (1819–1900) a rich Manchester industrialist and M.P. was created a baronet in 1886. He was said to have given his daughter a dowry of £200,000 when she married the 11th Marquess of Huntly in 1869. Lord Huntly (1847–1937), Premier Marquess of Scotland, was seriously in debt at this time, largely the result of losses on the turf and shortly afterwards Sir John Clark told Mr and Mrs Henry Adams, who were staying with him that 'the sheriffs were camping in Aboyne Castle, which waved its proud old flag at us as we drove by'. In 1882, Huntly, who had been a Lord-in-Waiting to Queen Victoria, was charged with obtaining money by false pretences from a bill broker: *The Letters of Mrs Henry Adams*, ed. Ward Thoron, 324.

closely involved in a ferocious wet tornado. But I am glad of the rest and quiet, and I have just bolted out of the library to escape the 'morning service', read by the worthy Nevin, the American episcopal chaplain in Rome, who is staying here, to which the dumb and decent servants are trooping in. I am fast becoming a good enough Englishman to respect inveterately my own habits and do, wherever I may be, exactly what I want. This is the secret of prosperity here – provided of course one has a certain number of sociable and conformable habits, and civil inclinations, as a starting point. After that, the more positive your idiosyncrasies, the more positive to convenience.[26]

He spent Christmas in one Yorkshire country house, with the Milnes Gaskells, and saw in the New Year at another, Lord Houghton's, Fryston Hall, where his Lordship's 'immense library', consisting largely of erotic books, had been 'thrown into hopeless confusion at the time of the partial burning of his house two years ago, and is now scattered all over the place', so he told his sister Alice.

Lord H. has just come into my room to know why I haven't come down to afternoon tea, and plumping himself into my armchair is apparently lapsing into sociable slumber. He is a very odd old fellow, extremely fidgety and eccentric; but full of sociable and frendly instincts, and with a strong streak of humanity and democratic feeling. He has begun to snore violently and I must finish my letter as I can.

Henry's principal complaint about the 'Yorkshire climate' was that it had given him back the chilblains of infancy.

There were other visits, less agreeable. One which Henry did not repeat was to Eggesford Manor, Lord Portsmouth's place in North Devon. He found the 'local gentlefolk' who were staying in the house 'of no distinctive qualities' and 'the whole thing is dull', for which the beauties of the countryside apparently offered no adequate compensation. Lord Portsmouth was simply a great hunting and racing magnate, 'who keeps the hounds in this part of the country and is absent all day with them'. Apart from 'a big cold library of totally unread books', where Henry sat disconsolately waiting for his host to show him the stables and kennels, there was 'nothing in the house but pictures of horses – and awfully bad ones at that'. He escaped from this uncongenial atmosphere as quickly as he decently could. ('I don't think I could stick out a Sunday here.') But not before he inspected the stables and kennels with about forty hunters and a wonderful pack of foxhounds 'lodged like superior mechanics'.[27]

The peak of country house splendour, which Henry had to endure, was reached at Mentmore, the Rosebery's 'huge modern palace' in Bedfordshire, where he was a guest on several occasions. Here too there was the inevitable visit to the stables, this time in the more congenial company of Sir John Millais, the painter, to see 'three winners of the Derby trotted out in succession'. On the occasion of his first visit, in November 1880, when the veteran radical M.P. John Bright was also a guest, Henry wrote an informative account to his mother.

I have spent a good deal of the time in listening to John Bright, whom, though I constantly see him at the Reform Club, I have never met before. He has the repute of being often 'grumpy'; but on this occasion he has been in extremely good form and has discoursed uninterruptedly and pleasantly. He gives one the impression of sturdy, honest, vigorous, English middle-class liberalism, accompanied by a certain infusion of genius, which helps one to understand how his name has become the great rallying point of that sentiment. He reminds me a good deal of a superior New Englander – with a fatter, damper nature, however, than theirs. . . .

They are at afternoon tea downstairs in a vast, gorgeous hall, where an upper gallery looks down like the colonnade in Paul Veronese's pictures, and the chairs are all golden thrones, belonging to ancient Doges of Venice. I have retired from the glittering scene, to meditate by my bedroom fire on the fleeting character of earthly possessions, and to commune with my mammy, until a supreme being in the shape of a dumb footman arrives, to ventilate my shirt and turn my stockings inside out (the beautiful red ones imported by Alice – which he must adore so much, though he doesn't venture to show it), preparatory to dressing for dinner.

Tomorrow I return to London and to my personal occupation, always doubly valued after 48 hours passed among *ces gens-çi,* whose chief effect upon me is to sharpen my desire to distinguish myself by personal achievement, of however limited a character. It is the only answer one can make to their atrocious good fortune. Lord Rosebery, however, with youth, cleverness, a delightful face, a happy character, a Rothschild wife of numberless millions to distinguish and demoralize him, wears them with such tact and bonhomie that you almost forgive him. He is extremely nice with Bright, draws him out, defers to him etc., with a delicacy rare in an Englishman.[28]

Henry's return from the magnificence of Mentmore to the comparative shabbiness of Bolton Street marked almost exactly four years' residence in England. It had been four years of progressive achievement both in his chosen profession as a writer and as a social figure. When he looked out of the balcony window of his sitting-room, or surveyed the rows of invitations on his mantelpiece, it was as a person of some consequence. Indeed that very month the incoming Lord Mayor of London had invited him to the traditional banquet in the Guildhall, where he rubbed shoulders with Cabinet Ministers and the diplomatic corps and listened to Mr Gladstone, once more at the head of a Liberal Government, discoursing at length on foreign affairs. He had a word with the new American Minister, James Russell Lowell, the ex-college professor, poet and humourist from Boston who knew his family well. Lowell had come from the American Legation in Madrid, where, without bothering to consult Henry, he had asked the State Department to appoint his young fellow-countryman secretary of legation. When he heard about it, Henry had been worried lest he should get the appointment, which he did not want, and he was greatly relieved when he learned that the suggestion had been turned down in Washington. Henry liked Lowell, who had made a good initial impression in London, in spite of the handicap of an invalid wife. 'He is universally liked and appreciated, his talk enjoyed (as well it may be, after some of their own!) and his poor long-suffering wife is doing very well.' Henry hoped that the new Republican President, James A. Garfield, who was full of ideas for reforming the United States Government Service, would leave Lowell at his post, 'It will be in the highest degree indecent to remove him,' Henry noted at this time; 'though I wish he had a pair of secretaries that ministered a little more to the idea of American brilliancy. Lowell has to do that quite by himself.'[29] So much for Hoppin and Nadal. As for the President, whatever plans he may have had for removing Lowell were frustrated by an assassin's bullet after only four months at the White House. Lowell's appointment was reconfirmed by Garfield's Vice-President and successor, Chester Arthur, much to Henry's delight, and Lowell continued to serve until the Democrats won the Presidency with the ungracious Grover Cleveland four years later.

With the passing of another year, Henry decided that the time had come for him to leave Bolton Street to return to America on an extended visit for six months or so. His parents were getting old and he felt that he should not defer the visit any longer if he was to see them alive. But he had every intention of returning to London, being as he put it 'at least now a thoroughly naturalized Londoner – a cockney *"convaincu"*', and he kept on his rooms. 'I am attached to London in spite of the long list of reasons why I should not be,' he told the Harvard University President Charles Eliot Norton; 'I think it on the whole the best point of view in the world. There are times when the fog, the smoke, the universal uncleanness, the combined unwieldiness and flatness of much of the social life – these and many other matters – overwhelm the spirit and fill it with a yearning for other climes; but nevertheless one reverts one sticks, one abides, one even cherishes! Considering that I lose all patience with the English at least fifteen times a day, and vow that I renounce them for ever, I get on with them beautifully and love them well.'[30]

Very early in his London years Henry had reacted vigorously against 'the Anglo-Saxon incapacity for emotional expression', as his nephew Henry James Junior later described his attitude at this time. 'At times it seemed as if he regarded himself as a sort of champion of another school of manner and as having a mission to show by example that the expressive habit was good and right. The thing grew on him and I know that it excited surprise and remark.' A story in point which Henry used to tell with great enjoyment concerned an occasion on which he went to see James Russell Lowell off on a steamer voyage in New York. Some French or Spanish friend of the Ambassador's also appeared and Lowell and the Latin embraced each other at the foot of the gang plank. Henry was much amused at hearing an Englishman standing nearby remark to his wife, 'Look at those two dirty Frenchmen kissing each other.'

'Uncle Henry would gladly have shocked the Englishman himself and I have no doubt tried it', was his nephew's comment on this incident. 'Considering what British manners and prejudices are, there was something almost splendid in his disregard of bystanders and listeners when he cared to express his goodwill to anyone of whom he cared at all.'[31]

[FIVE]

New Year, 1882, found Henry in Washington, paying his respects to his friends the Henry Adamses at their house in H Street. Mrs Marian Adams, whom he remembered in his youth as 'Clover' Hooper and had nicknamed 'Voltaire in petticoats', still had a touch of acid in her remarks. 'The young emigrant has much to learn here', she wrote of Henry during this visit. 'He is surprised to find that he can go to the Capitol and listen to debates without taking out a license, as in London. He may in time get into the "swim" here, but I doubt it. I think the real, live, vulgar, quick-paced world in America will fret him and that he prefers a quiet corner with a pen where he can create men and women who say neat things and have refined tastes and are not nasal or eccentric.'[32]

Clover Adams also disapproved of the company he kept, particularly Representative George Robeson of New Jersey, who with his wife was prominently entertaining Oscar Wilde, then on a lecture tour, and the corrupt Republican ex-Secretary of State, James G. Blaine, who invited Henry to a dinner party which he gave in honour of President Arthur. The company included the new British Minister, Sir Lionel Sackville-West, who had come from Spain with his 'delightful little foreign daughter, who is the most perfect *ingenue* ever seen in America', as Henry called the offspring of the Minister and his Spanish dancer mistress Pepita. The local press, which printed the list of guests in full, described Henry James as 'that eminent novelist and anglicized American'.[33]

Henry called on Oscar Wilde, as he felt he must, Wilde having referred to him and W. D. Howells as the only American writers worth reading. But their meeting was hardly felicitous. When Henry told the apostle of the aesthetic movement that he was homesick for London, Oscar dismissed him as provincial. 'Really! You care for *places*,' he exclaimed. 'The world is my home!' Henry subsequently referred to him as 'an unclean beast', 'a fatuous fool', and 'a tenth rate cad'.[34]

Henry's Washington visit was suddenly interrupted by the news that his mother was seriously ill with bronchial asthma in the family home in Quincy Street, Cambridge.* It took him thirty-six hours to make his way there in a blinding snow storm, only to find her dead from heart failure when he arrived. 'The sweetest, gentlest, most natural embodiment of maternity', was how he described her to his friend and publisher Edwin Godkin, editor of the *Nation*.

I knew that I loved her, [he wrote in his notebook at the time] but I didn't know how tenderly till I saw her lying in

---

* Mrs Mary Robertson James (1810–1882) was the daughter of James and Elizabeth (Robertson) Walsh of New York City and was descended from Hugh Walsh who emigrated from the north of Ireland, as did her father-in-law William James. Her brother, a classmate of Henry James, Sr, at Princeton Theological Seminary, had shared his religious doubts and had with him turned his back on the ministry and left the seminary.

her shroud in that cold North Room, with a dreary snow-storm outside, and looking as sweet and tranquil and noble as in life. . . . It is impossible for me to say – to begin to say – all that has gone down into the grave with her. She was our life, she was the house, she was the keystone of the arch. She was patience, she was wisdom, she was exquisite maternity. Her sweetness, her mildness, her great natural beneficence were unspeakable, and it is infinitely touching to me to write about her as she *was*. When I think of all that she had been, for years, – when I think of her hourly devotion to each and all of us – and when I went to Washington the last of December I gave her my last kiss, I heard her voice for the last time, – there seemed not to be enough tenderness in my being to register the extinction of such a life. But I can reflect, with perfect gladness, that her work was done – her long patience had done its utmost . . . Thank God one knows this loss but once; and thank God that certain supreme impressions remain![35]

Henry took rooms in Boston, at 102 Mount Vernon Street, on Beacon Hill, so as to be near his father, whom he described as 'infirm and rather tottering'. The rooms were bare and ugly, but they were comfortable and, in a certain way, pleasant, and Henry made a gallant attempt to recreate in them the atmosphere of Bolton Street. 'I used to walk out, and across the Common every morning, and take my breakfast at Parker's' he noted afterwards. 'Then I walked back to my lodgings, and sat writing till four or five o'clock; after which I walked out to Cambridge over that dreary bridge whose length I had measured so often in the past, and four or five days in the week, dined in Quincy Street with Father and Alice. In the evening, I walked back, in the clear, American starlight. I got in this way plenty of exercise. It was a simple, serious, wholesome time. Mother's death appeared to have left behind it a soft beneficent hush in which we lived for weeks, for months, and which was full of rest and sweetness. I thought of her, constantly, as I walked to Boston at night along those dark vacant roads, where, in the winter air, one met nothing but the coloured lamps and the far-heard jingle of the Cambridge horse-cars. My work at this time interested me, too, and I look back upon the whole three months with a kind of religious veneration. My work interested me even more than the importance of it would explain – or than the success of it has justified. . . .'

If I can only *concentrate* myself: this is the great lesson of life. I have hours of unspeakable reaction against the smallness of production; my wretched habits of work – or of un-work; my levity, my vagueness of mind, my perpetual failure to focus my attention, to absorb myself, to look things in the face, to invent, to produce, in a word. I shall be 40 years old in April next: it's a horrible fact! I believe however I have learned how to work and that it is in moments of forced idleness, almost alone, that these melancholy reflections seize me. When I am really at work, I'm happy, I feel strong, I see many opportunities ahead. It is the only thing that makes life endurable. I must make some great efforts during the next few years, however, if I wish not to have been on the whole a failure. I shall have been a failure unless I do something great![36]

It was his father's insistence that he should resume his literary work in England that led Henry to stick to his sailing date, as originally planned, in the spring. On the eve of his embarkation, he received a parting letter from his father with the premonition of approaching death.

And now, my darling boy, I must bid you farewell. How loving a farewell it is, I can't say, but only that it is most loving. All my children have been very good and sweet from their infancy, and I have been very proud of you and Willy. But I can't help feeling that you are the one that has cost us the least trouble, and given us always the most delight. Especially do I mind mother's joy in you the last few months of her life, and your perfect sweetness to her. I think in fact it is this which endears you so much to me now. No doubt the other boys in the same circumstances would have betrayed the same tender and playful love to her, only they

were not called upon to do so. I am in no way unjust to
them, therefore, but I feel that I have fallen heir to all dear
mother's fondness for you, as well as my proper own, and
bid you accordingly a distinctly widowed farewell ...
Good-bye then again, my precious Henry! .... We shall each
rejoice in you in our several ways as you plough the ocean
and attain to your old rooms, where it will be charming to
think of you as once more settled and at work.[37]

The elder Henry James survived his wife by less than a year.
After the younger Henry's departure for Europe, he and
Alice, who was able to keep house for him, moved from Cambridge to Boston, where they found a house in Mount Vernon
Street, not far from the temporary lodgings occupied by the
younger Henry. Here the old man died a week before Christmas, 1882 while his second son Henry was still at sea vainly
hoping to reach his bedside before the end. Henry Junior
reached Boston too late even for the funeral, but he learned all
the details from Alice and Aunt Kate, which he relayed to
William, who was on a trip to Europe and whom he had left
behind in Bolton Street.

131, Mt. Vernon St, Boston, December 26, 1882. ...
He prayed and longed to die. He ebbed and faded away,
though in spite of his strength becoming continually less, he
was able to see people and to talk. He wished to see as
many people as he could and he talked with them without
effort. ... Alice says he said the most picturesque and
humorous. He knew I was coming and was glad, but not
impatient. He was delighted when he was told that you
would stay in my rooms in my absence, and seemed much
interested in the idea. He had no belief apparently that he
would live to see me, but was perfectly cheerful about it.
He slept a great deal, and, as Aunt Kate says, there was 'so
little of the sick-room' about him. He lay facing the windows, which he would never have darkened – never pained
by the light.
I am writing this in his room upstairs, and a cast which
Alice has taken from his head, but which is very satisfactory

and represents him as terribly emaciated, stands behind me on that high chest of drawers ... The house is so *empty* – I scarcely know myself. Yesterday was such a Christmas as you may imagine – with Alice at K. Loring's, me ill in bed here, and Aunt Kate sitting alone downstairs, not only without a Christmas dinner but without any dinner, as she doesn't eat, according to her wont![38]

Henry James, Senior, was certainly an eccentric theosophist. Asked by his daughter Alice during his last days what he wished the minister of religion to say at his funeral, he replied, after some reflection: 'Tell him to say only this. "Here lies a man who has thought all his life that the ceremonies attending birth, marriage, and death were all damned nonsense." Don't let him say a word more!' Alice James lamented that 'there was no Unitarian even elastic enough for this'. ('What a washed-out, cowering mess humanity seems beside a creature like that!') It was to remain for the elder brother William to edit his father's literary remains and make an adequate appreciation of his theological writings, of which the best known was *The Secret of Swedenborg* ('and he kept it!' William Dean Howells complained).

From Henry's rooms in Bolton Street, William had written his father a fond letter of farewell, which ended with these words:

As for the other side, and Mother, and our all possibly meeting, I can't say anything. More than ever at this moment do I feel that if that *were* true, all would be solved and justified. And it comes strangely over me in bidding you good-bye how a life is but a day and expressly mainly but a single note. It is so much like the act of bidding an ordinary good-night.

On the last day of 1882, a Sunday morning, Henry went out to Cambridge cemetery. 'I stood beside his grave for a long time,' he told William, 'and read him your letter of farewell – which I am sure he heard somewhere out of the depths of the still bright winter air. He lies extraordinarily close to Mother, and as I stood there and looked at this last expression of so many years of mortal union, it was difficult not to believe that they were not united again in some consciousness of my belief.'[39]

Henry lingered in Boston until the late summer of 1883 in order to settle his father's affairs. In the resulting distribution he found his income augmented by some $1300 a year, which he handed over to Alice, as he was now well able to maintain himself by his pen, although this was not always to be so. He spent his fortieth birthday in New York on a visit to a friend in East 25th Street. 'I never return to this wonderful city without being entertained and impressed afresh,' he wrote to the artist George du Maurier, who had done the illustrations for his brilliant short novel *Washington Square*. 'New York is full of types and figures and curious social idiosyncrasies, and I only wish we had someone here, to hold up the mirror, with a fifteenth part of your talent. It is altogether an extraordinary growing, swarming, glittering, pushing, chattering, good-natured, cosmopolitan place, and perhaps in some ways the best imitation of Paris that can be found (yet with an originality of its own).'[40]

Henry returned to Bolton Street at the beginning of September, 1883, 'and that', as he told his friend du Maurier, 'will be for a long day.' Indeed he was not to see his native America again for over twenty years, although he was to become increasingly involved with attachments in the European continent, particularly in Italy. He now began to look round for a new place in which to live, where he could spread himself and which he could furnish to his own taste. His inquiries gave rise to rumours among several of his female friends that he was contemplating marriage, but he quickly disabused them of any such intention on his part. 'Sooner or later I shall take a house,' he told one of them at this time, 'but there is no hurry, and when I do a conjugal Mrs H. is not among the articles of furniture I shall put into it. . . . I find life quite interesting enough as it is, without such complicated and complicating appendages.' He made it clear to his friends that he had never regarded marriage as a necessity, but only as the last and

THE LONDON OF HENRY JAMES

'I take it as an artist and a bachelor; as one who has the passion of observation and whose business is the study of human life – the most complete compendium of the world. The human race is better represented here than anywhere else, and if you learn to know your London you learn a great many things.'

From the photograph by Alvin Langdon Coburn in the New York edition of The Golden Bowl

highest luxury. 'I shall never marry,' he confessed to Grace Norton; 'I regard that now as an established fact, and on the whole a very respectable one; I am both happy and miserable enough, as it is, and don't wish to add to either side of the account. Singleness consorts much better with my whole view of existence (of my own and that of the human race) my habits, my occupations, prospects, tastes, means, situation "In Europe" and absence of desire to have children – fond as I am of the infant race.'[41]

He spent much of the autumn and winter house hunting. He began in St John's Wood, where he had stayed as a boy with his parents in '58 and which evoked vivid memories. Eventually he discovered a seemingly ideal dwelling in Elm Tree Road, which had belonged to an artist and possessed a commodious studio, converted into a dining-room, and a pleasant garden. But on reflection he decided that the place was too far from his clubs and the theatres for his convenience. He felt a 'sudden sense of being very well off where I am', and in spite of their shabbiness and darkness he decided to say on in the Bolton Street lodgings for the time being. In fact he was to remain in Bolton Street for two more years before he found what he wanted.

His social life now underwent a perceptible change. 'I, at the age I have reached, have purposes far too precious to put the rest of my years to, to be able to devote long days sitting about and twaddling in even the most gracious country houses', he told Grace Norton. Nor was he any longer the inveterate diner out. 'My quietness (comparative of course) is my solemn choice, and means that I have been dining out much less than at most former times, for the sacred purpose of getting my evenings to myself. I have been sitting at the British festive board for so many years now that I feel as if I had earned the right to give it up save in the most seductive cases. You can guess the proportion of these! It is the only way to find any time to read – and my reading was going to the dogs. Therefore I propose to become henceforth an occasional and not a regular diner, with the well-founded hope that my mind, body, spirits, temper and general view of the human understanding and of the conversational powers of the English race, will be the gainers by it.'[42]

During this period, 'the middle years', as he called them, Henry turned from the more or less ephemeral acquaintances of English drawing-rooms and country houses to the cultivation of sincere and lasting literary and artistic friendships in England and on the Continent. These included Edmund Gosse and his wife, the du Maurier family, Robert Louis Stevenson, Mrs Humphry Ward, John Sargent, Paul Bourget, Fanny Kemble, Constance Fenimore Woolson, and Violet Paget, who wrote under the name 'Vernon Lee'. ('She satirized me in *Vanitas*,' he wrote; 'she is a tiger cat.') He still regarded himself as the external observer of the English scene, but he was no longer the slightly rebellious immigrant. From now on he was to experience a deep sympathy with England and things English, in spite of being still capable of 'raging against British density in hours of irritation and disgust'. He took an increasing interest in the English political scene and hoped that the English race would continue to stand high in the world, in spite of current prophecies of the coming downfall of Britain's Empire. This was the period, too, of the maturer novels, *The Bostonians* and *Princess Casamassima* and shorter tales like *The Aspern Papers* and *The Lesson of the Master*.

Of his many English friends, perhaps his closest was Edmund Gosse, who was really half-American, since his mother came from Boston. An accomplished linguist as well as poet and literary critic, Gosse was employed at this time as a translator in the Board of Trade at a salary of £400 a year, a dreary job which fortunately left him with plenty of time for his literary interests. Soon Henry was sending him critical essays for comment and help. For instance, he was writing to Gosse at the end of 1883:

I am glad you find the paper on Turgenev something of a picture. He was a noble really inspiring model, and I almost feel as if what I had *not* managed to say in my article was the most essential and characteristic thing. But if it has an aroma of tenderness, it has some justification.

36

He was a pure delightful mind; and I have never known anyone who made upon me the same kind of impression.[43]

A long and intimate correspondence gradually developed between the two writers, covering the widest range of topics, literary, social and political.* Each would consult the other with considerable freedom, for both had literary problems and troubles, and looked to each other for consolation and support. This link was strengthened by the sympathy Henry showed Gosse when the latter was severely attacked for alleged inaccuracies in a series of lectures he delivered at Trinity College, Cambridge, in 1886, and afterwards published under the title *From Shakespeare to Pope*. 'I am delighted the air of your life is clear again,' Henry wrote to him when the furore generated by the attack had abated. 'I *did* foresee it would be. One has only to hold fast, and it always is.'[44]

Henry's peculiar literary position, after his return from the United States in 1883, was well summarized by Gosse in a review which he wrote of Percy Lubbock's edition of *The Letters of Henry James* nearly forty years later.[45]

When he returned to Bolton Street. . . . he had broken all the ties which held him to residence in America, a country which, as it turned out, he was not destined to revisit for more than twenty years. By this means Henry James became a homeless man in a peculiar sense, for he continued to be looked upon as a foreigner in London, while he seemed to have lost citizenship in the United States. It was a little later than this that that somewhat acidulated patriot, Colonel Higginson, in reply to someone who said that Henry James was a cosmopolitan, remarked, 'Hardly! for a cosmopolitan is at home even in his own country!' This condition made James, although superficially gregarious, essentially isolated, and though his books were numerous and were greatly admired, they were tacitly ignored alike

---

* Over 250 letters from James to Gosse and members of the Gosse family are preserved in the Brotherton Collection in the University of Leeds. Of these, only about thirty have hitherto been published, mostly in Percy Lubbock's edition of *The Letters of Henry James* (1920).

in summaries of English and of American current literature. There was no escape from this dilemma. Henry James was equally determined not to lay down his American birthright and not to reside in America. Every year of his exile, therefore, emphasized the fact of his separation from all other Anglo-Saxons, and he endured, in the world of letters, the singular fate of being a man without a country.

But fundamentally his character remained unchanged. 'Harry is as nice and simple and amiable as he can be,' wrote William during one of his visits to London at this period. 'He has covered himself, like some marine crustacean, with all sorts of material growths, rich seaweeds and rigid barnacles and things, and lives hidden in the midst of his strange heavy alien manners and customs; but these are all but 'protective resemblances', under which the same dear old, good, innocent and at bottom very powerless-feeling Harry remains, caring for little but his writing, and full of dutifulness and affection for all gentle things.'[46]

Two ❧ Kensington

[ONE]

It was not until the end of 1885, after he had completed nine years residence in Bolton Street, that Henry at last decided to make a move. He found the ideal unfurnished flat in Kensington, 13, De Vere Mansions, situated at 34, De Vere Gardens, just off Kensington Road and a few minutes' walk from Kensington Gardens and the Albert Hall. De Vere Mansions had recently been built in response to the increasing demand for self-contained sets of apartments. No 13 was at the south-west end of De Vere Gardens. Henry's new habitation was on the fourth floor – 'my chaste and secluded Kensington *quatrième*', he used to call it – and it had an elevator, *anglice* lift, then quite a novelty in London. He gave his publishers as a reference, the landlord seemingly never having heard of Henry James, and he signed a twenty-one year lease to run from December Quarter Day. However, two months went by before the place was ready for his occupation and he had collected sufficient furniture.

There was a large drawing-room, which he used as a library, and a smaller sitting-room for receiving visitors, as well as a dining-room, a guest bedroom, servants' quarters and 'the usual offices'. The colour scheme for the sitting-room was a combination of Whistlerian blues and yellows, while he had the library decorated in the 'richest crimson'. The furniture was solid and utilitarian, no Chippendale and nothing original, he assured his friends, just 'expectedness everywhere'. He moved in on March 6th 1886. 'The place is excellent in every respect,' he wrote to William after h had been in residence for three days, 'improves on acquaintance every hour and is, in particular, flooded with light like a photographer's studio. I

39

commune with the unobstructed sky and have an immense bird's-eye view of housetops and streets. My rooms are very pretty as well as very convenient, and will be more so when little by little I have got more things. When I have time I will make you a diagram and later, when the drawing-room (or library: meantime I have a smaller sitting-room in order) is furnished (I have nothing for it yet), I shall have the place photographed. I shall do far better work than I have ever done before.' A month later he wrote: 'My flat is perfection, and ministers, more than I can say, to my health, my spirits and my work. There is unfortunately still a great deal to be done in the way of fitting it up. It is large enough to swallow up a good deal of furniture without showing it much.'[1]

He engaged a married couple called Smith as servants on living-in board wages of £10 a month, the man as butler-valet and the wife as cook. Mrs Smith was a rather frightened looking creature, who would interview the master every morning, in a large white apron, to get her 'orders for the day'. Unfortunately, as will be seen, Smith developed into a heavy drinker and eventually had to be got rid of. Henry regarded him as 'an excellent fellow', at least in the early days, although the butler's intellectual qualities do not seem to have been particularly brilliant. 'When I gave him an order,' Henry told his friend Edmund Gosse, 'he had to go through three successive mental processes before he could understand what I was saying. First he had to register the fact that he was being spoken to, then to assimilate the meaning of the order given to him, and lastly to think out what practical consequences might be expected to follow if he obeyed it.' On the other hand, as Mrs Wharton dryly observed, perhaps these mental gymnastics were excusable in the circumstances.[2]

As he grew older, Henry felt more and more the need for intellectual companionship. 'Could you by a miracle,' he wrote to Edmund Gosse, shortly after he had established himself in De Vere Mansions, 'if you are not afraid of a very modest dinner, come and break bread with me tonight at the primitive hour of seven? I am alone, and there is a solitary fowl. But she shall be dressed with intellectual sauce . . . I am famished for a little literary conversation. In this city of 5,000,000 souls, but not, alas brains, I find *none*.'[3]

The Gosses set aside one evening a week when they were 'at home' to Henry after dinner in their house in Delamere Terrace. Edmund's son Philip has recalled how 'at the stroke of nine by the clock in the drawing-room any Monday evening, we would hear the front-door bell ring, and after a short spell of muffled conversation in the hall, Mr Henry James – in those days wearing a beard – would be ushered in by the parlour maid.' Sometimes the Gosses would have other visitors on these occasions. Once Henry wrote to Edmund Gosse in pleasurable anticipation at the prospect of meeting that prolific novelist whom Max Beerbohm described as 'one of the miracles of modern literature' – 'Ouida' (Maria Louise Ramé). 'Your bell pull will on Thursday night next vibrate to my touch even as the neighbouring minster steeple vibrates, as usual to the stroke of nine. The prospect of a whole evening with dear proud Ouida attracts me beyond all things.'[4]

Sometimes Henry and Edmund Gosse would join others like-minded on a working holiday. For instance, in the late summer of 1886, they went to the picturesque Worcestershire village of Broadway where they would foregather each day in the home of Frank Millet, the American painter, along with several other artists, including Edwin Abbey, John Sargent and Alfred Parsons. Gosse has given a vivid glimpse of the party:

> The Millets possessed, on their domain, a medieval ruin, a small ecclesiastical edifice, which was very roughly repaired so as to make a kind of refuge for us, and there, in the mornings, Henry James and I would write, while Abbey and Millet painted on the floor below, and Sargent and Parsons tilted their easels just outside. We were all within shouting distance, and not much serious work was done, for we were in towering spirits and everything was food for laughter. Henry James was the only sedate one of us all – benign, indulgent, but grave, and not often unbending beyond a genial chuckle. We all treated him with some involuntary respect, though he asked for none. It is

remembered with what affability he wore a garland of flowers at a birthday feast, and even, nobly descending took part one night in a cake-walk. But mostly, though not much our senior, he was serious, mildly avuncular, but very happy and unupbraiding.

In those days Henry James wore a beard of vague darkish brown, matching his hair, which had not yet withdrawn from his temples, and these bushy ornaments had the effect of making him in a sense shadowy. Almost every afternoon he took a walk with me, rarely with Sargent, never with the sedentary rest; these walks were long in time but not in distance, for Henry was inclined to saunter. He had not wholly recovered from that weakness of the muscles of his back which had so long troubled him, and I suppose that this was the cause of a curious stiffness in his progress, which proceeded rather slowly. He had certain preferences, in particular for the level road through the green landscape to the ancient grey village of Aston Somerville. He always made the same remark, as if he had never noticed it before, that Aston was 'so Italian, so Tuscan.'

His talk, which flowed best with one of us alone, was enchanting; with me largely it concerned the craft of letters. I remember little definitely, but recall how most of us, with the ladies, spent one long rollicking day in rowing down the winding Avon from Evesham to Pershore. There was much 'singing in the English boat,' as Marvell says, and Edwin Abbey 'obliged' profusely on the banjo. Henry James I can still see sitting like a beneficent deity, a sort of bearded Buddha, at the prow, manifestly a little afraid that some of us would tumble into the river.[5]

From Broadway Henry went on to Leighton Buzzard to stay *en famille* with the Rosebery's, since he still indulged in a certain amount of country house visiting. The only other guest was Gladstone's former private secretary Edward Hamilton, whose services in this 'strict and severe office' the Liberal leader had called 'simply indescribable'. In an interesting unpublished passage from his personal diary, Hamilton recorded his impressions of the occasion:

Mentmore. Sunday 10 October, 1886. Came down yesterday afternoon. Only Henry James (American) here – the
nicest type of American man I know – pleasant and accomplished! I am ashamed to say I have never read any of his
books.

Rosebery was delightfully agreeable last night at dinner,
and displayed very freely that talent for versatility of
conversation which he possesses as much I think as Mr
G[ladstone]. The society of men of letters like H. James is I
believe the society which Rosebery in his heart of hearts most
enjoys. The era in which he would have preferred living was
last century; and he selected Italy as his ideal abode without
any hesitation. He had been reading through *John Inglesant*
again. He had been bored and yet fascinated in a manner for
which he could not quite account. It was the book of a man
steeped in the 17th century but possessing no *art*. H. James
agreed and attributed the success of the book in great part
to Mr G[ladstone]'s advertisement of it. He extolled R.
Stevenson's books which are now quite the rage, *Kidnapped*
being the latest which greatly pleased Mr G. Marie Antoinette
and Carlyle also formed topics of conversation.

. . . We all agreed that the most interesting time to
have lived in would have been from about 1760 to 1830.
In that period one might have seen by far the most
remarkable agglomeration of notabilities. Who was the per-
sonage during that era whom we should most liked to have
seen. Rosebery said Napoleon; H. James, Byron; myself,
Pitt.[6]

There was, of course, some variation in the intellectual
quality of Henry's table talk. E. S. Nadal recalled lunching
with Henry on one occasion in De Vere Mansions, when his host
sat with a Dachshund bitch 'of beautiful appearance' called
Tosca on his lap for most of the time. They were speaking of
sex in women and were comparing European with American
women in this regard. Nadal had the notion that 'American
women had less of this quality than European women, that in
many American women it was negative, and in European
women positive, and that many American girls looked like

effeminate boys.' Henry, who was stroking his Dachshund's head, commented, with a nod in the dog's direction: 'She's got got sex, if you like, and she's quite intelligent enough to be shocked by this conversation!'[7]

Although Henry himself almost certainly never enjoyed sexual relations either with a member of the opposite sex or with his own, he was nevertheless profoundly interested in the subterranean manifestations of contemporary sexual morality, which showed that Victorian men were neither as respectful of female virtue, nor the women themselves as virtuous, as they were both commonly represented in the novels issued by the popular circulating libraries. At the time of Henry's move from Piccadilly to Kensington, what he described as 'the everlasting and most odious Dilke scandal' was nearing its sordid climax. Henry confessed to Grace Norton that the divorce proceedings brought by Mr Donald Crawford, M.P. against his wife, citing Sir Charles Dilke as co-respondent, had a certain 'low interest' for him, since he had the 'sorry privilege' of being acquainted with most of the individuals involved in the suit. 'Dilke's private life won't (I imagine) bear looking into,' he wrote at the time, 'and the vengeful Crawford will do his best to lay it bare. . . . For a man who has had such a passion for keeping up appearances and appealing to the said middle class, he has, in reality, been strangely, reckless. His long, double liaison with Mrs Pattison and the other lady [Christina Rogerson], of a nature to make it a duty to marry *both*(!!) when they should become free, and the death of each husband at the same time – with the public watching to see *which* he *would* marry – and he meanwhile "going on" with poor little Mrs Crawford, who is a kind of infant – the whole thing is a theme for the novelist – or at least for *a* novelist.'

To his brother William, he enlarged upon this unsavoury theme:

Dilke is decidedly, and most deservedly ruined – as any man must be who sits and hears so foul a tale told of him as was told by Donald Crawford at the trial and is unable, and afraid (that he should be cross-examined) to raise the least whisper to contradict it. He has behaved throughout with strange pusillanimity and want of judgment and tact; and the thing is too bad for him to get over. That is, if he does, the 'moral tone' of London will show itself worse even than it has hitherto appeared, though I have never thought it very high.

I am sorry to say that my old friend Mrs Rogerson has been much mixed up with the whole business, though rather by her misfortune than by her fault. Enough, however, to have been both made temporarily insane (she seems better now) and virtually ruined by it.

A collection of episodes more hideous and abominable in all their ramifications, it would be impossible to conceive, but I won't infect the pure air of Cambridge with them – though I have profited by them much as a novelist.

It was scarcely surprising that Dilke's political career, like Parnell's a few years later, was irreparably ruined, for on top of the other complications in the case, Mrs Crawford's mother had once been Dilke's mistress. He lost his seat at the next General Election, and although he was eventually to return to Parliament for another constituency he never again held political office. Incidentally, Henry was just as fascinated by the Parnell scandal and the Irish Nationalist leader's relations with Kitty O'Shea. He even attended the trial of the O'Shea divorce petition, which he called 'thrilling' and 'throbbing'.

In spite of his interest in sex matters, there was a strong vein of Puritanism in Henry's make-up, which tended to prudery. For instance, while he admired Guy de Maupassant's narrative gifts, he strongly disapproved of the Frenchman's attitude towards women as exemplified in both his writings and his private life. When he had read *Bel-Ami*, he described the story as 'the history of a Cad, by a Cad – of Genius!' Maupassant paid a visit to London in August, 1886, and one evening Henry took him out to dinner in a restaurant at the nearby Earl's Court Exhibition. After they had been seated at their table for a short time, Maupassant looked round the room and said to his host, 'There's a woman sitting over there whom I would like to have. Go over and get her for me.'

Henry looked rather shocked. 'My dear friend, I cannot possibly do that, she may be perfectly respectable. In England you have to be careful.'

A few minutes later Maupassant spotted another woman. 'Surely you know her at least? I could do quite well with her, if you would get her for me.' Then, after a sigh, he added, 'If only I knew English!'

When Henry had refused for about the fifth time, Maupassant observed sulkily, 'Really you don't seem to know anybody in London!'[8]

On the other hand, human relationships of a 'nefarious' and 'abnormal' character exercised a curious fascination for him. For instance, he wanted to know more about the reasons for Byron's quarrel with his wife and the poet's suspected incestuous connection with his sister, 'the sole *real* love, as he emphatically declares, of his life'. Henry showed a lively curiosity about the Byron papers which threw light upon these relationships, and some years later he was able to examine the documents along with the young Scots writer John Buchan, whose wife's aunt was the widow of Byron's grandson and possessed the papers in question. What they actually revealed is a matter of conjecture, possibly that Byron had sodomized his wife. At all events, Buchan was to put it on record that he and Henry spent a summer week-end 'wading through masses of ancient indecency, and duly wrote an opinion.' Buchan added that 'the thing nearly made me sick', but that his colleague 'never turned a hair'. His only words for 'some special vileness' were 'singular', 'most curious', and 'nauseating, perhaps, but how quite inexpressibly significant'.[9]

There was indeed a Rabelaisian side to Henry's character, which none of his previous biographers nor the discreet editor of his *Letters* has hinted at. But it was well known to his more intimate friends. Hugh Walpole, for instance, commented upon it in two letters to Edmund Gosse, hitherto unpublished.[10] 'How he adored an "eccentric" and abnormal story and wanted it from every possible view!' wrote Walpole. 'I shall never forget his minute and luscious account of A. C. B[enson] caught unawares and helpless in a Brothel!'* Pressed by Gosse for details, Walpole replied that he could not possibly give all the story on paper but that he would tell it to him in detail when they next met. However, he did give Gosse a summary of it.

It began with a secret raid on the part of three friends who thought the victim needed education. The unfortunate one was kidnapped, taken to a certain house of resort, stripped, and left alone with a lady previously selected because of her passion for [The] Upton [Letters] and [From a] College Window. Followed Horror of Victim, Seduction by Siren, Victim gradually tempted into bed, Siren quoting Upton and asking questions à la Church Fam[ily] News. Victim gradually forgets where he is, is slowly and skilfully beguiled, finally as he enumerates with high-voiced pride the numbers of subscribers to Church Fam[ily News] and the virtue of Reginald Smith† unexpectedly falls.

There was of course much more – and I will tell you later what I can – but of course the thrill was in the slow emptying of H.J.'s imagination and his own chuckling and monkey-like surprise at what came!

On the subject of homosexual relationships Henry seems to have held an open mind. He had at least one friend, whose defence of it was known to him. This was John Addington Symonds, then trying to cure himself of tuberculosis in the Swiss Alps. Henry greatly admired his writings on Italy, and their acquaintanceship began when Henry sent him an essay on Venice which he had written for the Century. This evoked a

---

* Arthur Christopher Benson (1862–1925) second son of Edward White Benson, Archbishop of Canterbury. For twenty years he was a schoolmaster at Eton, which he left to devote more time to writing. In 1904 he was elected a Fellow of Magdalene College, Cambridge, and eleven years later was elected Master. He was a close friend of Henry James, whose letters to him were subsequently published by his brother E. F. Benson. See Letters to A. C. Benson and August Monod. Edited by E. F. Benson (1930).

† Reginald John Smith (1857–1916), director of the publishing firm of Smith, Elder, which published many of Benson's books.

friendly letter from Symonds which Henry answered in like vein. 'I nourish for the said Italy an unspeakably tender passion,' he wrote, 'and your pages always seemed to say to me that you were one of a small number of people who love it as much as I do – in addition to your knowing it immeasurably better. I wanted to recognize this (to your knowledge); for it seemed to me that victims of a common passion should sometimes exchange a look, and I sent you off the magazine at a venture.'

The subject of Symonds had come up in conversation with Edmund Gosse, and what Gosse had said had given Henry the idea for a short story. Henry noted in his journal how it originated:

March 26, 1884. Edmund Gosse mentioned to me the other day a fact which struck me as a possible *donnée*. He was speaking of J.A.S. the writer (from whom in Paris the other day I got a letter), of his extreme and somewhat hysterical aestheticism, etc.: the sad conditions of his life, exiled to Davos by the state of his lungs, the illness of his daughter, etc. Then he said that, to crown his unhappiness, poor S's wife was in no sort of sympathy with what he wrote; disapproving of its tone, thinking his books immoral, pagan, hyper-aesthetic, etc. 'I have never read any of John's works. I think them most *undesirable.*'

It seemed to me *qu'il y avait la un drame – un drame intime*; the opposition between the narrow, cold Calvanistic wife, a rigid moralist; and the husband impregnated – even to morbidness – with the spirit of Italy, the love of beauty, of art, the aesthetic view of life, and aggravated, made extravagant and perverse, by the sense of his wife's disapproval....[11]

The result had been *The Author of Beltraffio*, which Henry had written in a week or so in Bolton Street and which was published in the *English Illustrated Magazine* in June and July, 1884. 'I am told that my *Author of Beltraffio* is a living and scandalous portrait of J. A. Symonds and his wife whom I have never seen,' he later wrote to his brother. Indeed Symonds was plainly recognized as the novelist Mark Ambient, on the whole a sympathetic portrayal, although Henry had tilted at some of the more extravagant features of the aesthetic movement in the character of the novelist's sister. Mrs Ambient also accorded closely with what Henry had heard of Catherine Symonds, since she was made to declare, 'I consider his writings most objectionable'.

After the first instalment had appeared, in June, 1884, Gosse wrote Henry a letter of congratulation, which drew forth this reply despatched by hand:

I am delighted you see some life in it and have an appetite for the rest. Of course it is tragic – almost (I fear) repulsively so. But the 2nd part is better written than the first, and I agree with you in thinking the thing is more solid than many of my things. I feel it is more *packed* – more complete. But I shall do better yet! Meanwhile you obey a very human inspiration when you murmur *bravo!* in the ear of the much attempting, slowly-composing, easily-discouraged and consistently dissatisfied fictionist. . . .

P.S. Perhaps I *have* divined the innermost cause of J.A.S.'s discomfort – but I don't think I seize, on p. 57, exactly the allusion you refer to. I am therefore devoured with curiosity as to this further revelation. Even a post-card (in covert words) would relieve the suspense of the perhaps-already-too-indiscreet-H.J.

Such was the extent of Henry's prurient interest that he instructed the messenger conveying the note to Gosse's house to 'wait answer'. Further details have not apparently survived.[12]

Some years later, in 1891, Symonds produced his remarkable investigation into the causes of homosexuality with revolutionary proposals for changes in the law under the title *A Problem of Modern Ethics*. The work was privately printed and limited to fifty copies, one of which reached Henry's hands through Edmund Gosse, to whom it had been sent by the author.* Henry's reaction to 'those marvellous outpourings', as he described the book, was again one of sympathy, although he naturally did not dare to come out publicly in defence of the Symonds thesis. 'J.A.S. is truly, I gather, a candid and consistent creature, and the exhibition is infinitely remarkable,' he wrote to Gosse. 'It's, on the whole, I think, a queer place to plant the standard of duty, but he does it with extraordinary gallantry. If he has, or gathers, a band of the emulous, we may look for some capital sport. But I don't wonder that some of his friends and relations are haunted with a vague malaise. I think one ought to wish him more humour – it is really *the* saving salt. But the great reformers never have it – and he is the Gladstone of the affair.'[13]

Gosse also lent Henry the MS of Symonds' autobiography which by a coincidence Henry read at the height of the Oscar Wilde scandal. His 'fond out-pourings', as Henry described the author's uninhibited homosexual experiences, seem to have made a considerable impression on him.† 'It always seemed as if I *might* know him and of few men whom I didn't know has the image so much come home to me,' wrote Henry when the news of Symonds' 'so brutal and tragic extinction' reached him. 'Poor much-living much-doing passionately out-giving man!'[14]

Another letter to Gosse, written three days after Oscar Wilde's arrest on homosexual charges in April 1895, showed how the dramatist's downfall exercised a curious fascination for Henry.

---

* Gosse sympathized with Symonds, since at one time he also had homosexual leanings. This is confirmed by a revealing letter from Gosse to Symonds, which Dr Phyllis Grosskurth quotes in her recent biography of Symonds. 'I know of all you speak of – the solitude, the rebellion, the despair,' Gosse wrote after reading the text of the *Problem*. 'Yet I have been happy, too; I hope you also have been happy, – that all with you has not been disappointment and the revulsion of hope? Either way, I entirely and deeply sympathize with you. Years ago I wanted to write to you about all this, and withdrew through cowardice. I have had a very fortunate life, but there has been this obstinate twist in it! I have reached a quieter time – some beginnings of that Sophoclean period when the wild beast dies. He is not dead, but tamer; I understand him and the trick of his claws.'
Phyllis Grosskurth. *John Addington Symonds* (1964), 280–1.

† Complete publication of the MS of the autobiography, which is now preserved in the London Library, is restricted until 1976.

(Above) EDMUND GOSSE
'I am delighted the air of your life is clear again . . . One has only to hold fast and it always is.'

From a photograph by courtesy of the Radio Times Hulton Picture Library

(Below)

EDWARD COMPTON

in the title role of *The American*
'. . . the gratified Compton publicly pressed one's hand, and one felt that, really, as far as Southport could testify to the circumstance, the stake was won!'

From a photograph by courtesy of Sir Compton Mackenzie

HENRY JAMES IN 1894
'... used to be taken for a sea-captain ...'
From the original painting by Sir Philip Burne-Jones in Lamb House

It has been, it is, hideously dramatic and really interesting; – so far as one can say that of a thing of which the interest is qualified by such a sickening horribility. It is the squalid gratuitousness of it all – of the mere exposure – that blurs the spectacle. But the *fall* from nearly 20 years of a really unique kind of 'brilliant' conspicuity (wit, 'art', conversation – 'one of our 2 or 3 dramatists', etc.) to that sordid prison cell and this gulf of obscenity over which the ghoulish public hangs and gloats – it is beyond any utterance of irony or any pang of compassion! He was never in the smallest degree interesting to me – but this hideous human history has made him so – in a manner.[15]

'You ask of Oscar Wilde,' he wrote to his brother at the same time. 'His fall is hideously tragic, and the squalid violence of it gives him an interest (of misery) that he never had for me, in any degree, before. Strange to say, I think he may have a future, of a sort, by reaction, when he comes out of prison, if he survives the horrible sentence.'

Three weeks later, when Wilde stood in the dock for the second time – the jury had been unable to agree on a verdict at the first trial – and the despicable perjured blackmailers called by the prosecution were telling their sordid stories, Henry wrote again to Gosse on the subject:

34 De Vere Gardens, S.W. Sunday [April 29, 1895]
These are the days in which one's modesty is, in every direction, much exposed, and one should be thankful for every veil that one can hastily snatch up or that a friendly hand precipitately muffles one withal . . .
Did you see in last evening's half-penny papers that the wretched O.W. seems to have a gleam of light before him (if it really counts for that!) in the fearful exposure of his (the prosecution's) little beasts of witnesses? What a nest of almost infant blackmailers![16]

The 'gleam of light' proved deceptive, and Wilde duly received the maximum sentence of two years imprisonment with hard labour, which he served without any remission. Attempts were made by his friends, both in England and France, to petition Queen Victoria for his earlier release, but without success. The petition in France was drawn up by Stuart Merrill, an American poet who lived in Paris and wrote in French. Merrill asked another American writer, Jonathan Sturges, who lived in London and knew Henry, to solicit his support. On November 27th 1895, Sturges wrote to Merrill: 'Henry James came in to see me yesterday, and I communicated that part of your letter which concerned him. He will write to you himself in a few days, but I do not think he will sign the petition, though I know that he feels sorry for Oscar. . . . James says that the petition would not have the slightest effect on the *authorities* here who have the matter in charge, and in whose nostrils the very name of Zola and even of Bourget is a stench, and that the document would only exist as a manifesto of personal loyalty to Oscar by his friends, of which he was never one.'*

Among the new books which Wilde asked his friend Robert Ross to send him in his lonely exile was *The Two Magics*, which contained *The Turn of the Screw*. 'I think it is a most wonderful, lurid, poisonous little tale, like an Elizabethan tragedy,' Wilde told his friend when he had read it. 'I am greatly impressed by it. James is developing, but he will never arrive at passion, I fear.'[17]

It may be noted here that Henry was a contributor from the first to the penultimate number of the celebrated quarterly publication which was mistakenly associated in the public mind with Oscar Wilde. At the time of the latter's arrest, the newspaper headlines stated 'YELLOW BOOK UNDER HIS ARM.' The book in question was *Aphrodite* by Pierre Louÿs and happened to have a yellow cover. It was generally believed that the volume Wilde was carrying was *The Yellow Book*, the *avant-garde* periodical which had been launched in the previous

---

* Although never a personal friend of Wilde's, Henry James did have some regard for him as a fellow writer, at least in his earlier days. In 1888, when Wilde was up for election to the Savile Club, he was among the thirty-one members who supported his candidature by signing their names in the Candidates' Book – the others included Edmund Gosse, Rider Haggard, W. E. Henley, Walter Besant and J. W. Mackail. But owing to opposition the candidature was not proceeded with.

year by the publisher John Lane with Henry Harland as
literary editor and Aubrey Beardsley as art editor. Under this
erroneous impression an angry crowd demonstrated outside
the publishing offices at The Bodley Head, and broke the
windows. 'It killed *The Yellow Book*,' Lane used to say, 'and it
nearly killed me.' In fact, Wilde had no connection with the
journal and never contributed anything to its pages, although
he would probably have been only too glad to do so if he had
been asked. The Wilde scandal gave Lane a pretext for dismissing Beardsley, whose daring drawings with their scarcely
veiled indecencies embarrassed both publisher and readers.
But this move did not save *The Yellow Book*, although it
lingered on for two more years.

Henry was the first contributor commissioned by the editor,
and a short story by him appeared at the beginning of the first
number in April 1894. Yet he felt uncomfortable when he saw
it in print. 'I haven't sent you *The Yellow Book* – on purpose,'
he wrote to his brother from Rome at the end of May; 'and
indeed I have been weeks and weeks receiving a copy of it
myself. I say on purpose because, although my little tale
which ushers it in ("The Death of the Lion") appears to have
had, for a thing of mine, an unusual success, I hate too much
the horrid aspect and company of the whole publication. And
yet I am to be intimately, conspicuously associated with the
2nd number. It is for gold and to oblige the worshipful Harland
(the editor).' Besides another short story ('The Coxon Fund'),
the second number contained a portrait of Henry by his
American compatriot John Sargent.

Henry contributed twice more to *The Yellow Book*, on both
occasions after Beardsley's dismissal, and his continued appearance caused a reader of another journal to complain that 'of
late' Henry James had 'been in bad company', having 'become
one of the Yellow Book clique!' of decadents. That he thus
exposed himself may be put down to his regard for the editor,
to whom he was '*mon maître*' and the 'supreme prince of short
story writers.' 'I hope you read and like Henry James?' Harland asked another of his contributors. 'To me he seems the
only master of considered prose we've got. Ah, but you're not

mad about style, as I am. Besides, by the bye, he's one of the two or three "good" men I know.'[18]

[TWO]

Although Henry's mode of living in De Vere Mansions with a butler and cook suggested the prosperous author, and although his working conditions were more comfortable and congenial than they had been in Bolton Street, in fact he earned progressively less. He could still command reasonable sums for serialization, particularly in the American reviews and *The Yellow Book* also paid well, at least in the first lush year of its production, but the sales of his books in England were not encouraging. Frederick Macmillan, the English publisher, lost money over the two long novels, *The Bostonians* and *Princess Casamassima* which Henry wrote at this time and in which he departed from the theme of so many of his earlier and successful stories of the adventures of American girls and their suitors in Europe. The author was eventually pulled up with a jolt when negotiating for the sale of his next novel, *The Tragic Muse,* and his English publisher offered him an advance of only £70 instead of the usual £200 or £150. Macmillan was quite willing to go on publishing Henry in the circumstances, but at this the author jibbed strongly, 'I would rather not be published at all than be published and not pay – other people at least,' he told Macmillan, adding that unless he could put the matter on a more remunerative footing all round he would give up his English 'market' ('heaven save the market!') and concentrate on his American. 'But I must experiment a bit first – and to experiment is of course to say farewell to you. Farewell, then, my dear Macmillan, with great regret – but with the sustaining cheer of all the links in the chain that remain still unbroken.'

Macmillan eventually did bring out *The Tragic Muse,* so that Henry must have pocketed his pride and either accepted the reduced advance or agreed to some form of compromise. However, the threatened break took place, and Henry's next books in England came out under the imprint of William Heinemann.

Meanwhile he set about looking for a new means of making some money. Fortunately, so it seemed, the means was at hand in the shape of a letter to him from a theatrical producer called Edward Compton. The producer's wife was an American actress, who performed under the name of Virginia Bateman, and she happened to have read an article in some theatrical journal suggesting that Henry James's novel *The American* would make a good play. Compton accordingly wrote to inquire whether the author would care to adapt the work for the stage. 'Of how little money the novel makes for me I needn't discourse here', Henry noted in his journal at this time. 'The theatre has sought me out – in the person of the good, the yet unseen, Compton. I have listened and considered and reflected, and the matter is transposed to a minor key. To accept the circumstances, in their extreme humility, and do the best I can *in* them: this is the moral of my present situation.'[19]

Compton gave the author £250 as an advance to dramatize *The American*, and having disposed of *The Tragic Muse*, Henry set to work. After the first draft had been completed, the two men met to discuss it in De Vere Gardens. The producer brought along his 7-year-old son Monty, the future Sir Compton Mackenzie, who remembered that Henry had a fairly full dark brown beard and that he betrayed a slight restless anxiety in his manner. 'He may have been embarrassed by the presence of a small boy,' noted young Monty. It is more likely that Henry's apparent nervousness was due to his apprehension of Compton's criticism of his first dramatic effort.

While his seniors were gravely talking, the boy had an opportunity of looking around the room. What he called 'the variety of the great novelist's accommodation for his work' was of considerable interest to the young embryo novelist.

On the right of the window was a desk at which he could write, standing; along the wall on the left was a day bed with a swivel-desk attached on which he could write, lying; in front of the window was a large knee-hole desk at which he could write, sitting. Observing my eyes wandering round these engines of his craft, Henry James explained to me with elaborate courtesy their purposes.

Compton Mackenzie produced his birthday book, which he asked 'the great novelist' to inscribe on the date on which he was born. Henry obligingly did so adding to his autograph, in the space for his birthday – April 15th – the date on which he wrote it – May 5th, 1890. Each entry was embellished with a quotation of the Poet Laureate Lord Tennyson, but unlike another novelist, Thomas Hughes, author of *Tom Brown's Schooldays*, who had also written his name in the book, Henry made no comment on the particular quotation which appeared opposite his name; it was from *Maud* and read, 'A stony British stare' – not perhaps an altogether happy omen for the would-be dramatist.[20]

Author and producer parted on the understanding that the play, which was now finished, should go into rehearsal in the autumn and be produced in the current winter provincial repertory, after which Compton hoped to bring it to London. Compton would play the name part himself. His offer of a ten per cent royalty on the gross box office receipts held out a vision to the author of £80 a week in the provinces and rather more in London. Henry was also much encouraged by the favourable reaction of his sister Alice who read the play on her sick bed. It made him feel 'as if there had been a triumphant premiere', he told her, 'and I had received overtures from every managerial quarter and had only to count my gold'.[21]

After considerable cutting, a process carried out by Mrs Compton – 'my wife is good at cutting', the actor-manager told the author who had protested at 'this monstrous piece of surgery' – *The American* had its opening performance at the Winter Gardens Theatre in Southport, the Lancashire watering place, on January 3rd, 1891. Henry was present in a state of tense nervous excitement. 'In heaven's name, is it *going*?' he asked, as he flung himself on Compton at the end of the first act. 'Going?' was the comforting reply. 'Rather! You could hear a pin drop.' The delighted author took a bow before the curtain, 'while the applausive house emitted agreeable sounds before a kind of gas-flaring indistinguishable dimness and the gratified Compton publicly pressed one's hand and one felt that, really, as far as Southport could testify to the circumstance, the stake was won'. Of course, it was only Southport, as Henry reflected, but he had larger hopes, 'inasmuch as it was just the meagre provincial conditions and the limited provincial interpretation that deprived the performance of all adventitious aid'.[22]

The provincial tour was reasonably successful. At all events, it encouraged Compton, who had taken a long lease of the Opera Comique Theatre in London, to put the piece into rehearsal there with the actress Elizabeth Robins as the heroine and Compton still playing the hero. Meanwhile Henry busied himself in De Vere Gardens with planning more 'theatricals'. 'Don't be hard on me,' he wrote to R. L. Stevenson. 'Simplifying and chastening necessity has laid its brutal hand on me and I have had to try to make somehow or other the money I don't make by literature. My books don't sell, and it looks as if my plays might. I have, in fact already written two others than the one just performed; and the success of the latter pronounced – really *pronounced* – will probably precipitate them.' At the same time, he told his brother that he felt at last as if he had found his real form, which he was capable of carrying far, and for which 'the pale little art of fiction, as I have practised it, has been, for me, but a limited and restricted substitute'.[23]

Every day, while *The American* was being rehearsed, Henry would drive to the theatre from De Vere Gardens, bringing with him a hamper of sandwiches and other delicacies for the caste. No other playwright, in Miss Robins's tolerably wide experience, had ever thought of feeding the company, and the kind gesture made an agreeable impression in the theatre. The play opened on September 26th, 1891, with an impressive first-night audience which included the American Minister, Robert Lincoln, and a representative gathering of the London literary world. The author turned up with his brother William and his Boston friend, Grace Norton, and at the end took a curtain call. The notices, however, were very mixed. 'My own suspense has been and still is great, though the voices of the air, rightly heard, seem to whisper *prosperity*', Henry wrote to Edmund Gosse, after the play had been running a week. 'The papers have been on the whole quite awful – but the audiences are altogether different. The only thing is that these first three or four weeks *must* be up-hill: London is still empty, the whole enterprise is wholly new – the elements must assemble.'[24]

The theme of the play, which closely followed the book, was the action of a successful Californian company promoter in search of a bride among the French aristocracy. Unfortunately Elizabeth Robins was miscast in the part of the prospective bride; the public associated her with Ibsen's *avant-garde* plays and may have suspected that Henry was imitating the shocking Norwegian dramatist. After some weeks, when the play was visibly dragging, it received a fillip when the Prince of Wales announced his intention of attending a performance, which he did in a house specially 'dressed' for the occasion. The play was also helped by some revisions to the script which the author provided in time for the fiftieth performance. But neither royal patronage nor these alterations could save *The American* and Compton had to withdraw it after seventy nights. 'Honor is saved,' wrote Henry, 'but I grieve to say nothing else, for the piece made no money.' It was never revived, though Compton put it on again in the provinces for which the author rewrote the fourth act with a happy ending. 'But oh,' he confessed to Mrs Compton, 'I do indeed want to try to do something that of a Saturday night in crowded provincial cities will help to make all our fortunes, and I mean to tackle this question in right earnest. The trouble is that I can only work interruptedly. But I see what is wanted – I think I may say that.'[25]

Alas for such vexatious strivings. Of the five plays which Henry wrote at this period, besides *The American*, only one reached the stage, after nearly three years of irritating and frustrating negotiations and delays. This was *Guy Domville*, a costume piece set in the eighteenth century on the conflicting demands of the world and the cloister for a member of an old English Catholic family. Compton, to whom the author first offered the scenario of this play, turned it down. It was eventually produced by another actor-manager, George Alexander, with the result that the disappointed and disillusioned author abandoned the theatre for ever as a means of livelihood.

Indeed Henry's unhappy experience on the first night may well have contributed to his decision to leave London and make his principal home in the country.

The son of a Scots commercial traveller, named Samson, George Alexander had recently become the lessee of the St James's Theatre, which he was to make famous by the long series of artistic and financial successes which he produced and in which he acted for over a quarter of a century. A singularly handsome man, and something of a dandy, still in his thirties, Alexander had a fine figure and stage presence which made him a matinée idol, and though never a brilliant actor he possessed a certain distinction and charm of manner which gained him a steady following at the box office. Henry had been greatly impressed by his production of Arthur Pinero's *The Second Mrs Tanqueray* in May, 1893, and had sought a meeting with the young actor-manager, whom he was convinced would take a serious play from him. Several ideas were discussed. The one which appealed most to Alexander was the drama which took shape as *Guy Domville* and after many delays and cuts ('Oh, the mutilated, brutally simplified, massacred little play!') at last went into rehearsal in the final weeks of 1894. The cast was a good one and in addition to Alexander in the name part included Herbert Waring, H. V. Esmond, Franklyn Dyall, Marion Terry and Irene Vanbrugh. For their use the author had a few copies printed 'in intense secrecy' – they are now extremely rare and valuable collectors' items.* The period costumes and stage sets were elaborate and expensive. 'My only anxiety is how Alexander will carry the weight of his own part, which is a very beautiful and interesting one,' Henry wrote to his brother. 'So awfully much depends on him.'[26] He was deeply occupied with rehearsals when he learned a few days before Christmas of the sudden death following a stroke of his friend Robert Louis Stevenson in the Pacific island of Samoa where he had settled with his family. The news stunned him, and he poured out his feelings to Gosse.

---

* One recently fetched £320 at public auction in London. This copy is now in the Bodleian Library. Only five other copies are known to be extant.

... of what can one think, or utter or dream, save of this
ghastly extinction of the beloved R.L.S.? It is too miserable
for cold words – it's an absolute desolation. It makes me
cold and sick – and with the absolute, almost alarmed sense,
of the visible material quenching of an indispensable light.
That he's silent forever will be a fact hard, for a long time,
to live with. Today, at any rate, it's a cruel, wringing emotion. One feels how one cared for him – what a place he took;
and as if suddenly *into* that place there had descended a
great avalanche of ice. I'm not sure that it's not for *him* a
great and happy fate; but for us the loss of charm, of sus-
pence, of 'fun' is unutterable.

Stevenson was the second literary friend he had lost within
a few months. Earlier that year, Constance Fenimore Woolson, grand-niece of James Fenimore Cooper and 'a friend of
many years with whom I was extremely intimate and to whom
I was greatly attached', whose short stories Henry had praised
for their minuteness of observation and tenderness of feeling,
had committed suicide by jumping out of a window of her
house in Venice; like Mrs 'Clover' Adams she suffered from
chronic melancholia. With the dead woman's sister, Mrs Clara
Benedict, Henry spent five weeks in Venice going through
Miss Woolson's voluminous literary and other remains. Later
he used to recount with a certain wry humour his experience
when he took her extensive wardrobe of clothes out into the
lagoon in a gondola and reverently cast them upon the waters.
He had neglected to attach any weights to the clothes, which for
the most part consisted of various black dresses. The result was
that they became inflated with air and soon he was surrounded
by a series of 'horrible black balloons'. The more he retrieved
them and repeated the operation, the more inflated they
became, until he finally gave up the task in despair and went
back to his hotel.

Like Stevenson's, the image of Constance Woolson long continued to haunt Henry. But he found it a relief to be able
to write to Gosse. He could barely keep his mind on the
theatre. 'That business becomes for the hour tawdry and heartless to me.'[27]

[THREE]

Saturday, January 5, 1895, was appointed for the opening performance of *Guy Domville*. As the night drew near, the author's nervous anxiety increased. He spent much of the Saturday restlessly walking in Kensington Gardens, after which he returned to his flat and dashed off a series of letters to various friends. 'I am counting on some psychical intervention from you,' he told his brother. 'This is really the time to show your stuff.' And to his friend Edward Warren, the architect, he wrote: 'I am in a state of trepidation out of all proportion (I won't say) to my possible fate, but to the magnitude of the enterprise of the work. Unfortunately, however, one can have a big danger, in the blessed theatre, even with a small thing; whereas I am not sure one can have a success on anything like the same scale. Still, the omens are as good as omens can ever be. . . .'[28]

One omen which manifested itself was far from propitious. Even as Henry sat at his writing desk in De Vere Mansions, an unsigned telegram addressed to George Alexander at the theatre was handed in by two ladies at Sloane Square Post Office. It read: 'With hearty wishes for a complete failure.' The senders' identities were never established, though it was thought that the two ill-wishers were actresses who had hoped to get parts in the production and had been disappointed. At all events, it seems to have been directed against the producer rather than the author. Alexander duly received the message, which he mercifully withheld from the author until after the performance.

Henry felt far more nervous and excited than he had been on the first night of *The American*. He had long made up his mind that he could not sit through the performance and that he would only put in a brief appearance at the end. However, there was the question of how to employ the intervening time. Edmund Gosse had suggested that he should beguile the 'tremulous' hours in a nearby pub. In the event, the author had 'the luminous idea of going to see some other play'. His choice fell on Oscar Wilde's *An Ideal Husband,* which had opened two nights previously at the nearby Theatre Royal, Haymarket. Henry's choice could scarcely have been less fortunate. He had never cared much for Wilde and the rapture with which Wilde's epigrams liberally sprinkled throughout this brittle comedy were received with waves of laughter by the Haymarket audience further unnerved him. 'I sat through it,' he told his brother afterwards, 'and saw it played with every appearance (so far as the crowded house was an appearance) of complete success, and *that* gave me the most fearful apprehension. The thing seemed to me so helpless, so crude, so bad, so clumsy, feeble and vulgar, that as I walked away across St James's Square to learn my own fate, the prosperity of what I had seen seemed to me to constitute a dreadful presumption of the shipwreck of *Guy Domville*, and I stopped in the middle of the Square, paralysed by the terror of this probability – afraid to go on and learn more. "How *can* my piece do anything with a public with whom *that* is a success?" It couldn't – but even then the full truth was, "mercifully", not revealed to me; the truth that in a short month my piece would be whisked away to make room for the triumphant Oscar.'[29]

A few minutes before the final curtain, Henry entered the St James's Theatre by the stage door and immediately went back-stage, where the cast, no doubt hoping to spare his feelings, gave him reassuring but misleading accounts of how the performance had gone. Act I had been received well enough, but after the first interval the gallery had turned restive and unruly and thereafter things had gone from bad to worse. Rude remarks had been made at one of the actresses, whose ornate plumed headgear provoked a line from the current song hit, 'Where did you get that Hat?' Finally, when George Alexander began his moving speech towards the end with the words, 'I'm the last, my lord, of the Domvilles,' a rough shouted back, 'It's a bloody good thing y'are!'

When the curtain at last came down, there was an outburst of well-bred applause – for the fashionable first night audience contained many of the author's friends and others to whom he was well known – mingled with some boos. In response to several calls from the front of the house for the author,

Alexander took Henry by the hand and led him before the foot-lights. This time the applause was completely drowned by the jeers. Among those present on this baleful occasion was young H. G. Wells, then starting his career as a dramatic critic; he later recorded in his autobiography that he never heard any sound more devastating than the crescendo of booing that ensued. 'For a moment or so James faced the storm, his round face white, his mouth opening and shutting', seemingly unable to believe his ears. Then with a deprecatory shrug of the shoulders, he turned and fled to the wings followed by Alexander, whom Wells felt must have been seized by 'a spasm of hate for the writer of those fatal lines' to have exposed him to such an ordeal.[30]

Pandemonium broke out. The artist Philip Burne-Jones, who had recently painted the author's portrait and occupied a box, turned in the direction of the booers and applauded loudly. This set up a further round of booing, accompanied by hisses, which lasted for the best part of a quarter of an hour. Alexander now practically lost his head and went on to the stage where he made a speech in effect apologizing to the audience for having produced the play at all. 'T'aint your fault, gov'nor,' another voice shouted, 'it's a rotten play!'

Four days later, when he could bring himself to put on paper what had happened, Henry wrote to his brother:

34, De Vere Gardens, W. January 9, 1895. . . .
Even now it's a sore trial to me to have to write about it – weary, bruised, sickened, disgusted as one is left by the intense, the cruel ordeal of the first night that – after the immense labour of preparation and the unspeakable tension of suspense – has, in a few brutal moments, not gone well. In three words the delicate, picturesque, extremely human and extremely artistic little play was taken profanely by a brutal and ill-disposed gallery which had shown signs of malice prepense from the first and which, held in hand till the end, kicked up an infernal row at the fall of the curtain. There followed an abominable quarter of an hour during which all the forces of civilization in the house waged

a battle of the most gallant, prolonged and sustained applause with the hoots and jeers and catcalls of the roughs,
whose *roars* (like those of a cage of beasts at some ir fernal
'zoo') were only exacerbated (as it were) by the conflict.
It was a cheering scene, as you may imagine, for a nervous,
sensitive, exhausted author to face. . . .

Everyone who was there has either written to me or come
to see me – I mean everyone I know and many people I don't.
Obviously my little play, which I strove to make as broad,
as simple, as clear, as British, in a word, as possible, is over
the heads of the *usual* vulgar theatre-going London public –
and the chance of its going for a while (which it is too early
to measure) will depend wholly on its holding on long enough
to attract the *unusual*. I was there the second night (Monday,
7th) when, before a full house – a remarkably good 'money'
house, Alexander told me – it went singularly well. But it's
too soon to see or to say, and I'm prepared for the worst. . . .

Don't worry about me: I'm a Rock. If the play has no
life on the stage I shall publish it; it's altogether the best
thing I've done.*

You would understand better the elements of the case if
you had seen the thing it followed (*The Masqueraders*)† and
the thing that is now succeeding at the Haymarket – the
thing of Oscar Wilde's. On the basis of *their* being plays, or
successes, my thing is necessarily neither. Doubtless,
moreover, the want of a roaring actuality, simplified to a
few big *familiar* effects, in my subject – an episode in the
history of an old English Catholic family in the last century –
militates against it, with all usual theatrical people, who
don't want plays (from variety and nimbleness of fancy) of
different *kinds,* like books and stories, but only of one kind,
which their stiff, rudimentary, clumsily-working vision recognizes as the kind they've had before. And yet I had tried so
hard to meet them! But you can't make a sow's ear out of a
silk purse.[31]

---

* Apart from the few privately printed acting copies *Guy Domville* never
appeared in the author's lifetime. It was first published in *The Complete Plays
of Henry James* (1949), edited by Leon Edel.

† By Henry Arthur Jones.

'The poor little play', was taken off after thirty-one per-
formances – 'the horridest four weeks of my life', as the author
called them – in spite of some favourable notices from the
critics, including William Archer and Bernard Shaw. 'I haven't
been near the theatre since the second night,' Henry wrote to
his brother on February 2nd, 'but I shall go down there late
this evening to see it buried and bid good-bye to the actors . . .
The money disappointment is of course keen – as it was wholly
for money I ventured. But the poor four weeks have brought
me $1,100 – which shows what a tidy sum many times four
weeks would have brought; without my lifting, as they say,
after the first performance, a finger.' On the other hand,
Alexander lost heavily – the equivalent of almost $9000, or
£1873, to be precise.[32]

Then, irony of ironies, Henry's play was withdrawn to
make way for another of Wilde's, the brilliantly witty light
comedy, *The Importance of Being Earnest*. 'There is nothing, fortunately so dead as a dead play – unless it be
sometimes a living one,' wrote Henry to his brother envi-
ously. 'Oscar Wilde's farce which followed *Guy Domville* is, I
believe, a great success – and with his two roaring successes
running now at once he must be taking in the profits.' But
not for long. Within barely 'a short month', the 'triumphant
Oscar' was to be arrested and both his successes were
to disappear from the London theatre, never to be revived in his lifetime – after Alexander had pasted strips
of paper over the author's name on the playbills in a desperate attempt at prolonging the life of the money-spinning
comedy.

It took Henry a long time to get over his bitter sense of
disappointment. To the sympathetic Mrs Compton, who suggested that he might now do something else for her husband's
company, he wrote that the failure of *Guy Domville* had completely sickened him of the theatre and that he felt like wash-
ing his hands of it forever. 'It had every advantage of production I could have hoped for, and yet proved simply the most
horrible experience of my life. As I walked home, alone, after
that first night, I swore to myself an oath never again to have

anything to do with a business which lets one into such traps, abysses and heart-break.'[33]

[FOUR]

In an attempt to take his mind off the 'unmitigated disaster' of *Guy Domville* Henry sought a complete change from the London scene, by accepting an invitation from Lord Houghton, the son of the first Lord, who had befriended him when he first settled in London, to stay with him in Dublin. On becoming Liberal Prime Minister for the fourth time in 1892, Gladstone had appointed 'poor young Lord Houghton', as Henry called him – he was 34 at the time of his appointment – to be Lord Lieutenant or Viceroy of Ireland, an office which John Morley, who was his Chief Secretary, described as 'the most thankless office that any human being in any imaginable community could undertake.' Besides the task of trying to govern a country whose people were virtually ungovernable, it involved giving a series of balls, levées and receptions in Dublin Castle during the 'season'; for this purpose the Lord Lieutenant moved from the more comfortable Viceregal Lodge in Phoenix Park to the seat of the Irish administration in the historic Castle. Henry, who was lodged there with the other specially invited guests, found the whole atmosphere artificial and uncongenial.

My six days at the Castle were a gorgeous bore, and the little viceregal 'court' a weariness alike to flesh and spirit. Young Lord Houghton, the Viceroy, 'does it', as they say here very handsomely and sumptuously, (having inherited just in time his uncle Lord Crewe's great property) but he takes himself much too seriously as a representative of royalty and his complete Home Rule – or rather anti-Home Rule boycotting by the whole landlord or 'nobility and gentry' (including all Trinity College, Dublin) leave his material for a 'court' or for entertaining generally in a beggarly condition.

He had four balls in the six days I was there and a gorgeous banquet every night, but the bare official and military class peopled them, with the air of a very dull and second-rate, though large, house-party from England. His English friends fail him and won't come because they know to what he is reduced; and altogether he is quite pathetic and desolate and impossible – from the constant standing in a cloud of aide-de-camps, on one's hind legs, from whom I was devoutly thankful to retire. He means well, but he doesn't matter; and the sense of the lavish extravagance of the Castle, with the beggary and squalor of Ireland at the very gates, was a most depressing haunting, discomfort.

From the Castle Henry went on to the Royal Hospital in the suburb of Kilmainham to become

domesticated with very kind and valued old friends, the Wolseleys – Lord W. being commander of the forces here (that is, head of the little army of occupation in Ireland – a five years appointment) and domiciled in this delightfully quaint and picturesque old structure, of Charles II's time – a kind of Irish Invalides or Chelsea Hospital – a retreat for superannuated veterans out of which a commodious and stately residence has been carved. We live side by side with the 140 old red-coated cock-hatted pensioners – but with a splendid rococo hall separating us, in which Lady Wolseley gave the other night the most beautiful ball I have ever seen – a fancy [dress] ball in which all the ladies were Sir Joshuas, Gainsboroughs, or Romneys, and all the men in uniform, court dress or evening hunt dress. (I went as – guess what! – alas, nothing smarter than the one black coat in the room.) It is a world of generals, aide-de-camps and colonels, of military colour and sentinel-mounting, which amuses for the moment and makes one reflect afresh that in England those who *have* a good time have it with a vengeance.'[34]

'Ireland was very kind to me,' he wrote to Edmund Gosse on his return to London – 'that is the sweet Wolseley's were: for my six days in the Castle were, like those of everyone else

there . . . a simply unmitigated hell. His Excellency is insane –
simply. But I will tell you all. *Pazienza*.' Henry was a Home
Ruler by political sympathy, although he did not feel so passionately on the issue as his sister Alice had done. (She had died
three years previously.) 'I don't believe much in the Irish,' he
had written when Gladstone was bringing forward his first
Home Rule Bill in 1886, 'and I believe still less in (consider
with less complacency) the disruption of the British Empire,
but I don't see how the management of their own affairs can be
kept away from them – or why it should. I can't but think that,
as they are a poor lot, with great intrinsic sources of weakness,
their power to injure and annoy England (if they were to get
their own Parliament) would be considerably less than is
assumed.'[35]

By 'the Irish', of course, Henry was thinking of the mass of
the people, nationalist in politics and Catholic in their religious
faith. He seems never to have been particularly conscious of
his own Irish or rather Ulster stock, stemming on both sides of
his family from the Protestant minority in the north, his
father's people having originally come from County Cavan and
his mother's from County Down. In the whole course of his life,
he only paid three short visits to Ireland. The first was on his
way back from his visit to America in 1882, when he disem-
barked at Cork and went on to Dublin for a few days; the
second was nine years later when he spent several weeks in the
Royal Marine Hotel in Kingstown, as Dun Laoghaire was then
called, recovering from an attack of influenza; the third was
the last occasion when he stayed in Dublin Castle and the
Royal Hospital and did not move outside the capital. Unlike
his father, he was never tempted on any of these occasions to
seek out his Irish relatives, nor, in spite of the letters he
exchanged with a great variety of correspondents, does he
ever appear to have been in touch with them. Yet in the autobiographical *Notes of a Son and Brother*, which he composed in
his old age, he recalled with relish some of the details of the
visit paid to his Irish cousins by the elder Henry James, as he
had heard them from his father's lips.

The visit had taken place in 1837, when his father was 26.

He had been accompanied by a Negro servant from his home in Albany, New York, and his presence in the small market town of Bailieborough, the son of an incredibly successful and wealthy emigrant – for the elder Henry's father William James had departed from Bailieborough, according to tradition, with ten shillings and a Latin grammar in his pocket and had died worth well over two million dollars* – must have created a considerable stir among the James cousins who were for the most part tenant farmers, shopkeepers and small merchants in Bailieborough and its neighbourhood. In talking to his son, Henry's father had evoked 'a small town in country Cavan as forming an horizon' to a circle, 'which consisted, we used to delight to hear with every contributive circumstance, of the local lawyer, the doctor and the (let us hope – for we *did* hope) principal "merchant", whose conjoined hospitality appeared, as it was again agreeable to know, to have more than graced the occasion: the main definite pictorial touches that have lingered with me being that all the doors always stood open, with the vistas mostly raking the provision of whiskey on every table. . . .' Indeed one cousin (Robert James) was medical superintendent of the Bailieborough Dispensary and another (Henry) was a draper and haberdasher with a shop in the town's main street. Their children were living in Bailieborough when Henry himself visited Ireland, but the latter's existence seems to have been unknown to him or at any rate unnoticed by him. Worthy folk as they were, and leading members of their community, they were scarcely likely to have received invitations to parties in 'the Castle'.†

---

* William James (1771–1832) arrived in America about 1789 and settled in Albany, where he amassed his fortune as a general merchant, banker, and investor in real estate, including a salt works and other property in Syracuse, N.Y. James Street in Albany was named after him. He married three times, his third wife Catherine (née Barber) being the elder Henry James's mother. Her paternal grandparents both came from Co. Longford, Ireland. See Kathleen Hastings. *William James of Albany, N.Y. and his Descendants* (1924), pp. 1–6.

† Robert and Henry James were children of William's elder brother Robert (1765–1823), who was in business in Bailieborough as an apothecary. Their sister Mary, who married John Higginbotham of Cootehill, Co. Cavan, was the present writer's great-great-grandmother. See Hyde, *The Story of Lamb House*, at p. 81.

Although he had been charmed on his previous visit by the Wicklow mountains and coastal scenery ('The very waves have a brogue as they break.'), he felt that Ireland was not the place for the long retreat he had in mind. He announced to his Boston friend Mrs Isabella Gardner that he was returning to his 'humble fireside' in De Vere Mansions and would then get away as quickly as possible into the country, 'to a cot beside a rill, the address of which no man knoweth', there to remain for the next six months. This plan was upset by the unexpected appearance of the French writer Alphonse Daudet, his wife and four children, who wished to see the English sights and enlisted Henry as their guide. Henry gallantly obliged with trips to Windsor, Box Hill (to see George Meredith) and elsewhere. At the end of two months London had become for him 'the nethermost circle of the Inferno', and he was glad to flee, not to the rural cottage of his dreams but to the commodious Osborne Hotel in Torquay. He stayed there until well into November, only returning to town for an occasional night or two. He liked it so much that he was strongly tempted to spend the winter there in spite of the inconvenience of its distance from London.

His friend Edward Warren, 'a very *distingué* architect and loyal spirit', had recently married the beautiful Margaret Morrell and Henry had become godfather to their first child Dorothy. The Warrens were spending some weeks in the 'antient town' of Rye on the borders of Sussex and Kent, and Edward wrote enthusiastically of the beauty and old-world charm of the place, begging Henry to pay them a visit. But Henry preferred to stick to 'this warm little corner', as he called Torquay, 'where the sea is still surely blue and the sound of of its waves on the beach under my windows still deliciously drawling.' However, as soon as he returned to London he hastened to look up his friends and to see 'the tender infant from whom I have so unnaturally withheld the light of my countenance.'[36] They lived in 'a pleasant old house' in Cowley Street, 'a funny little provincial purlieu of Westminster'. There in the Warrens' drawing-room Henry's eye caught a coloured sketch of a striking Georgian façade, which Edward Warren had done during his stay in Rye. Warren, who was later to make Henry a gift of the drawing, now told him that it was a garden room or garden house which formed a separate addition to Lamb House, the town's principal mansion.[37]

'I must take a house, this time – a small and cheap one,' Henry wrote to another friend from De Vere Mansions early in 1896, 'and I must (deride me not) be somewhere where I can, without disaster, bicycle. Also I must be a little nearer town than last year. I'm afraid these things rather menace Torquay. But it's soon to say – I must wait. I shall decide in April – or by mid-March – only. . . . I'm intensely – thank heaven – busy.'[38] William Heinemann, his new publisher, had commissioned two novels from him – they were to be called *The Spoils of Poynton* and *What Maisie Knew* – and he was again hard at work. Another architect, Reginald Blomfield, whom Henry may have met through the Warrens, had a cottage at Playden on the top of Point Hill, just outside Rye, and he offered it to Henry for three months beginning in May. Henry gladly accepted and brought his bicycle with him. 'I've taken to it but very recently,' he told Arthur Benson, 'but it seems to give me a glimpse of the courts of heaven. (*Absit omen.*) What a pity we can't pedal into them together!'[39]

[FIVE]

While he was staying at Point Hill, Henry had a letter from Mrs Edward Compton, who was planning a theatrical garden party in London in aid of the Actors' Orphanage. One of the side-shows was to be a flower stall, and the idea occurred to her of getting various distinguished men and women to let her know what were their favourite flowers and to write their autograph on tags which would be attached to the flowers before they were exposed for sale.

The response was tremendous, and a wide range of politicians, writers, artists and actors and actresses wrote in with their choices. But the gem, as Mrs Compton's son, Compton Mackenzie, was quick to recognize, came from Henry James.[40]

Point Hill,
Playden,
Sussex.
June 14th, 1896

Dear Mrs Compton,

I only know the names of 2 or 3 flowers: so I have to take one of them. I have decided after a sleepless night, on the *white carnation* and if it will relieve your pressure (which I deeply commiserate) to know so slight a thing I rejoice to be able to help you.

I feel, here, blissfully far from bazaars. I enclose signed the luggage-tags – with as much curiosity for your denoument (with them) as we could have ever wished all the plays I haven't written to excite.

Yours with all good wishes

HENRY JAMES

The summer of 1896 was remarkably warm and dry. Every evening throughout the whole of the three months he was there Henry was able to dine outdoors on the terrace, with its view across Romney Marsh. ('So the climate of England is, literally, not always to be sneezed at.') 'Point Hill is just the very thing for these particular weeks,' he told Warren. 'I love it tenderly and enjoy it every hour . . . The little terrace is as amiable as a *person* – as some *persons*. In short I cherish the whole thing.'[41] 'It is charmingly quiet and quaint here, and I hope to put in some work,' Henry wrote the day after he arrived at Point Hill. 'My little hill-top bungalow has a view – but naught else.'

Meanwhile Henry 'biked' away vigorously pedalling to Brede, Northiam, New Romney and Lydd among other places, with the result that he would find himself next day 'exhausted and relaxed for work.' One day, he walked down the hill into Rye so as to look at the subject of Warren's drawing and the adjacent house and, as he afterwards remarked facetiously, 'to make sheep's eyes at it (the more so that it is called Lamb House!)' He was immensely taken with 'the pleasant little old-world town angle into which its nice old red-bricked front, its high old Georgian doorway and a most delightful little old

architectural garden-house, perched alongside of it on its high
brick garden-wall – into which all these pleasant features together so happily "compose"'. Having thus lost his heart to it,
he inquired from the local ironmonger, when making some
small purchase, whether there was any chance of the place
becoming vacant. He was told that there was not, at least in
the foreseeable future, since the owner, Mr Francis Bellingham, a retired banker and former Mayor of Rye, was living
there with his wife and son, who would no doubt continue to
live there, should anything happen to 'old Mr Bellingham'. As
Henry afterwards recalled, 'there was no appearance whatever
that one could ever have it; either that its fond proprietor
would give it up or that if he did it would come at all within
one's means. So I simply sighed and renounced; tried to think
no more about it . . .' Nevertheless, some inward feeling
prompted him to leave his name and London address with 'the
good local ironmonger', who promised to let him know in the
unlikely event of there being any change in the Bellingham
family's domestic arrangements.[42]

Henry was obliged to vacate Point Hill at the end of July,
as the Blomfields wanted it for themselves. Since he did not
wish to return to stifling London, he looked round for another
place in the neighbourhood. Fortunately for him the Vicarage
in Rye happened to be available and he moved in there for the
next two months. It was 'shabby, fusty – a sad drop from
Point Hill', he told his brother, 'but close at hand to this (fifteen
minutes walk) and has much of the same picturesque view
(from a small terrace garden behind – a garden to sit in and
more or less to *eat* in) and almost the same very moderate
loyer. It has also more room, and more tumblers and saucepans,
and above all, at a moment when I am intensely busy, saves
me a wasteful research . . . The place, unfortunately, isn't quite
up to the pretty suggestion of the name. But this little corner
of the land endears itself to me – and the peace of the country
is a balm. It is all, about here, most mild and mellow and lovable. . . . I wish you were here to feel the repose of it'.[43]

While he was at the Rye Vicarage, Henry received a letter
from a young fellow writer, Ford Madox Hueffer. Hueffer, who

later changed his surname to Ford, was 26. He had published a fairy story entitled *The Brown Owl* and had just completed a critical study of his grandfather, the artist Ford Madox Brown. He wrote to Henry at the suggestion of their mutual friend the English novelist Mrs W. K. Clifford, who had heard from Henry that he had some eye trouble and had asked Hueffer to call, as she was greatly concerned for his health and peace of mind. Henry responded by inviting the young man to come at 2.30 one Monday afternoon ('I go out later (for exercise) and don't get in very early').[44] But there seems to have been some change in the arrangement as, according to Hueffer, he was asked to lunch.

In his gossipy volume of reminiscences, *Return to Yesterday*, Hueffer who was afterwards to get to know Henry well, has given a vivid account of his visit:

I certainly felt not infrequently something like awe in the presence of James. To anyone not a fool his must be a commanding figure. He had great virility, energy, persistence, dignity and an astonishing keenness of observation. And upon the whole he was the most masterful man I have ever met.

On that first occasion he was bearded, composed and magisterial. He had taken the house of the vicar furnished and had brought down his staff of servants from De Vere Gardens. At lunch he was waited on by his fantastic butler. The fellow had a rubicund face, a bulbous red nose, a considerable paunch and a cutaway. Subsequently he was to become matter for very serious perturbation to his master.

His methods of service were startling. He seemed to produce silver entrée dishes from his coat-tails, wave them circularly in the air and arrest them within an inch of your top waistcoat button. At each such presentation James would exclaim with cold distaste: 'I have told you not to do that!' and the butler would retire to stand before the considerable array of plate that decorated the sideboard. His method of service was purely automatic. If he thought hard about it he could serve you without flourishes. But if his thoughts were elsewhere the flourishes would return. He had learnt so to serve at the table of Earl Somebody – Brownlow, I think.

At any rate James seemed singularly at home where he was. He was well-off for a bachelor of those days when £400 a year was sufficient for the luxurious support of a man about town. You might have thought that he was in his ancestral home, the home itself one of some elegance in the Chippendale-Sheraton-Gainsborough fashion. He had the air of one of the bearded elder-brother statesmen of the court of Victoria, his speech was slow and deliberate, his sentences hardly at all involved. I did not then gather anything about the state of his eyes.

He was magisterial in the manner of a police-magistrate, civil but determined to receive true answers to his questions. The whole meal was one long questionnaire. He demanded particulars as to my age, means of support, establishment, occupations, tastes in books, food, music, painting, scenery, politics. He sat sideways to me across the corner of the dining table, letting drop question after question. The answers he received with no show at all of either satisfaction or reproof.[45]

After the meal, according to Hueffer, his host 'let himself go in a singularly vivid display of dislike for the persons rather than the works of my family's circle'. For his father Francis Hueffer, the German musical critic, and for his grandfather Ford Madox Brown, who 'were at least staid and sober men', Henry 'expressed perhaps a feigned deference', but for the rest of the pre-Raphaelite circle, particularly the painter D. G. Rossetti, who was Hueffer's uncle, and the poet Swinburne, he had not a good word to say. Apparently Rossetti had received him at tea-time in a long garment which Henry took to be a dressing-gown and from which he concluded that the painter was 'disgusting in his habits, never took baths, and was insupportably lecherous'. As for the poet, 'he mimicked the voice and movements of Swinburne with gusto. He let his voice soar to a real falsetto and jerked his body sideways on his chair extending his hands rigidly towards the floor below his hips. He declared that Swinburne's verse in its flood and noxiousness was only commensurate with the floods of bad chianti and gin that the poet consumed. He refused to believe that Swinburne in those days, under the surveillance of Watts-Dunton, drank no more than two half pints of beer a day. And he particularly refused to believe that Swinburne could swim. Yet Swinburne was one of the strongest salt water swimmers of his day'.

The painter's brother William, the art critic and editor, Henry found frankly a bore. W. M. Rossetti had formerly been employed in the Inland Revenue Board, then located in Somerset House, and Henry had once heard him recounting how he had seen the philosopher Herbert Spencer proposing to the novelist George Eliot on the leads of Somerset House terrace overlooking the Thames. 'You would think that a man would make something out of a story like *that*,' exclaimed Henry indignantly, 'but the way he told it was like this.' He then proceeded to imitate the thin, slightly querulous voice of the Inland Revenue official.

I have as a matter of fact frequently meditated on the motives which induced the lady's refusal of one so distinguished; and after mature consideration I have arrived at the conclusion that, although Mr Spencer with correctness went down upon one knee and grasped the lady's hand, he completely omitted the ceremony of removing his high hat, a proceeding which her sense of the occasion may have demanded.

'Is that the way to tell *that* story?' Henry concluded, contemptuously dismissing William Rossetti's lack of literary imagination.[46]

Henry would have liked to return to Rye for the following summer, but the Blomfields were enlarging Point Hill cottage into a house and the Vicarage was likewise not available. So he divided his time between hotels in Bournemouth and Torquay and the Suffolk coast, where he stayed first with an American cousin, Elly Hunter, who had taken a house at Dunwich, near Saxmundham, and then at the local inn where his cousin had bespoken rooms for him.* 'Can they give me a little *sitting-room* as well as a bed-room?' he had asked her. 'I always *need* some small literary bower other than the British bed-room – and in this case I would of course "meal" there, as that makes them always more zealous. I don't know the East Coast to speak of at all – and I can imagine no more winsome introduction to it.'[47] He seems to have enjoyed the quiet of Dunwich. 'It's a sweet little queer, quaint, surviving corner of a wonderful place, one is assured, long since devoured by the cold North Sea,' he told Warren, who had taken a house at nearby Felixstowe, '– primitive and rough, but with a very delicate and delightful charm.' On the last day of Henry's stay, Warren cycled over to meet him and amongst other things they talked of, as they 'bumped and bounced and vainly shifted sides' on their bicycles, was Rye and in particular Lamb House.[48]

Next day Henry returned to De Vere Mansions to find by a remarkable coincidence, a letter from 'the good local ironmonger' in Rye to the effect that Lamb House was suddenly and unexpectedly to let and that Henry had better move quickly if he wished to secure it. He immediately wrote to Warren whom he had already arranged to meet again a few days later. 'The place in question is none other than the mansion with the garden-house perched on the wall; and though to be fairly confronted with the possibility and so brought to the point is a little like a blow in the stomach, what I am minded to say to you is that perhaps you may have a chance to tell me, on Friday, that you will be able to take some day next week to give me the pleasure of going down there with me for a look. I feel as if I couldn't *think* on the subject at all without seeing it – the subject – again; and there would be no such seeing it as seeing it in your company.'[49]

---

* Mrs George Hunter (née Temple) was a daughter of the elder Henry James's sister Catherine. Mrs Hunter's sister Mary ('Minnie') was the novelist's intimate boyhood friend, who died young of tuberculosis. The characters of Isabel Archer in *The Portrait of a Lady* and Minnie Theale in *The Wings of the Dove* were based upon Minnie Temple.

Three ❧ Rye

A telegram Henry received from Rye on September 16th, 1897, the day after he had written to Warren, determined him to go down to Sussex immediately without waiting for his friend and ask the late Mr Bellingham's son for the first refusal of Lamb House. As soon as Henry got back to London, he begged Warren to come down with him again on the 22nd. 'I have got the refusal of the house till the p.m. of that day,' he told his friend, 'but should immensely like you, for reasons that I will tell you, to see it before I finally pronounce. All my good impression of it is confirmed and all my inclination is to take it – I feel in fact *doomed* to do so. But I shall immensely value the chance to ask you, on the spot and in its presence, two or three questions, absolutely helpless ones for myself unaided, as to condition and crudition (*sic*). There will at the best be, later on, things to do, which oh, how I shall want you to do! But the place is, to me, a teetotal charm!'[1]

The two friends accordingly journeyed down to Rye on September 22nd and met the new owner, Mr Arthur Bellingham, who explained that he did not require the house for himself, as he was emigrating to Canada to seek his fortune in the Klondyke gold rush. He offered Henry a twenty-one-year lease of the property at a rental of £70 a year, and on Warren's advice Henry immediately accepted it. The local solicitor, Mr Walter Dawes, was instructed to draw up the lease to run from that September Quarter Day; the lease was duly engrossed on parchment and dispatched to Henry for his signature. On September 25th, Henry wrote from De Vere Mansions to Arthur Benson: 'I am just drawing a long breath from having

signed – a few moments since – a most portentous parchment:
the lease of a smallish, charming, cheap old house in the
country – down at Rye – for *twenty-one* years! (One would
think I was *your* age:) But it is exactly what I want and hopelessly coveted (since knowing it) without dreaming it would
ever fall. But it *has* fallen – and has a beautiful room for you
(the "King's Room" – George II's – who slept there;* together
with every promise of yielding me an indispensable retreat
from May to October.'[2]

To his sister-in-law, Alice James, his brother William's wife,
Henry expatiated upon the 'terms, for a long lease, well within
one's means – terms quite deliciously moderate'.

The result of these is, naturally, that they will 'do'
nothing to it: but, on the other hand, it has been so well
lived in, and taken care of that the doing – off one's own bat
– is reduced mainly to sanitation and furnishing – which
latter includes the peeling off of old papers from several
roomfuls of pleasant top-to-toe wood panelling. There are
two rooms of complete old oak – one of them a delightful
little parlour, opening by one side into the little vista, church-
ward, of the small old-world street, where not one of the
half-dozen wheeled vehicles of Rye ever passes; and on the
other straight into the garden and the approach, from that
quarter to the garden-house aforesaid, which is simply the
making of a most commodious and picturesque detached
study and workroom . . .

In the meantime one must 'pick up' a sufficient quantity
of ancient mahogany-and-brass odds and ends – a task
really the more amusing, here, where the resources are great,
for having to be thriftily and cannily performed. The house
is really quite charming enough in its particular character,
and as to the stamp of its period, not to do violence to
any rash modernities; and I am developing under its influence and its inspiration, the most avid and gluttonous
eye and most infernal watching patience, in respect of

---

* It was George I (not George II) who slept in Lamb House. See below, and
for further details, Hyde. *The Story of Lamb House Rye.*

lurking 'occasions' in not too delusive Chippendale and Sheraton.

The 'King's Room' will be especially treated with a pre-occupation of the comfort and aesthetic sense of cherished sisters-in-law; King's Room so called by reason of George Second having passed a couple of nights there and so stamped it for ever. (He was forced ashore, at Rye, on a progress somewhere with some of his ships, by a tempest, and accommodated at Lamb House as at the place in the town then most consonant with his grandeur. It would, for that matter, quite correspond to this description still. Likewise the Mayors of Rye have usually lived there! Or the persons living there have usually become *mayors!* This was conspicuously the case with the late handsome old Mr Bellingham, whose son is my landlord. So you see the ineluctable dignity in store for me.)[3]

The redbrick fronted, three storeyed house, at first known as Lamb's House, was completed in 1723 by James Lamb, thirteen times Mayor of Rye and the first of the influential family to settle in the 'antient town'; it incorporated parts of a much earlier structure, notably the kitchen with its large open fireplace and the wine cellars, going back to Elizabethan times or before. It displayed the subtleties expected of an early eighteenth century building, such as shorter windows to the ground floor than the first, a three-dimensional use of brick in the vertical strips (surmounted by vases) at the ends of the elevation, and the sunk panels continuing the lines of the windows. The dormer windows in the sloping roof, belonging to the servants' quarters on the top floor, were discreetly screened by a parapet which in effect was part of the façade. Another striking architectural feature was the high canopied doorway, with its carved bracket and unusual panel proportions, which had caught Henry's attention on his first visit, also the large brass knocker on the outside of the door, which could be twisted so as to act as a latch on the inside.

A wide oak-panelled entrance hall led into a narrower staircase hall, separated by a flattened arch feature in the manner of many halls in early Georgian or Queen Anne houses. The staircase was likewise a typical example of the period with twisted balusters closely set. The drawing-room, also fully panelled in oak, was situated to the left of the entrance hall and opened into the garden. Beyond it, opposite the kitchen, was the dining-room. To the right of the hall was the little panelled 'parlour', where Henry had the telephone installed; it was also to be used as a writing-room by guests.

The first floor contained a charming sitting-room known as the Green Room from the colour of its panelling, a dressing-room (originally no doubt a powder room) and three bedrooms. The panelled King's Room, which was of course the master bedroom, looked out on one side over the garden and on the other the cobbled street leading to the parish church. The adjacent Green Room, which Henry was to use as a winter writing-room, had windows facing south and west, the former on to the garden and the latter across an attractive walled courtyard towards Winchelsea.

Henry was greatly intrigued by what he called 'the intimate relations between the House of Lamb and the House of Hanover'. Apparently Warren had seen a book in the local solicitor's office, which stated that both the first two Georges had been entertained in Lamb House. 'Two Georges!' wrote Henry to his friend excitedly. 'I thought that in the rent I was only paying for one and getting him extraordinarily cheap. But *this* is a bargain indeed; and as little gardener Gammon is also George he may count as the third, so that I seem to be on the way to have them all four. I thirst to get at the book in Dawes's office. In short I thirst for everything. . . .'[4] Henry later realized that there was some confusion as to which George had stayed in the house and that he had not been quite correctly informed. The facts were that George I had spent four nights in the house, as the Mayor James Lamb's guest in January, 1726, after his ship had been driven ashore on nearby Camber Sands, while on his way from Hanover to open Parliament at Westminster. George II was never entertained there, but thirty years later his son William Augustus Duke of Cumberland, 'the butcher of Culloden', had been accommodated for a night also by James Lamb, while on a tour of inspection of the coastal defences in view of the threatened French invasion at that time. In addition, there was a legend that one of George IV's mistresses had occupied the house when it had been let by its then owner, the parson George Augustus Lamb, and that the monarch had once been rowed ashore from a battleship in the Channel and had been received by the lady in the Garden House. [5]

As for the gardener George Gammon, the owner had said that he had a very good gardener to whom he was rather attached, and would Mr James consider taking him on? So Henry said, oh yes, of course he would be delighted to take on the gardener. Encouraged by this expression of willingness on his tenant's part, young Mr Bellingham went on, 'There's another matter. I wonder if I might mention to you a dog to which I am very much attached, whether you would take the dog as well?'

'Alas, no!' replied Henry, with his Dachshund bitch Tosca in mind. 'I myself have an elderly matron of the tribe!' [6]

The Garden House, or Garden Room, as it was later called, with its red brick façade and facings of Portland stone, and large bow fronted window dated from about twenty years after the main house. It had been built by James Lamb for formal entertaining and was known as the Banqueting Room in his time, for besides his regular terms as Mayor, Lamb had held other offices, particularly in connection with the management of the borough's parliamentary representation. (Rye was a 'rotten borough' which returned two members to the House of Commons until the Reform Act of 1832 and James Lamb had acted as manager for the great Whig borough monger, the Duke of Newcastle, who controlled Rye for the Government.) It made an ideal work room, particularly in the summer months. The entrance was from the garden by a flight of seven steps flanked by iron railings at right angles to the French window which opened on to the garden from the drawing-room of the main house. Underneath the bow window on the street side was a small door leading to a cellar which contained a handcart used for conveying guests' luggage between

LAMB HOUSE

(Above) Front entrance showing projection of the Garden Room on the left

(Below) View from the garden

'The house itself, though modest and unelaborate, is full of a charming little stamp and dignity of its period . . . without as well as within.'

From photographs by courtesy of Mr John S. R. James

The Green Room
'It had many advantages of a winter work-room . . .'

A corner of the 'little oak parlour'
From photographs by courtesy of Mr John S. R. James

the house and the railway station.* And, just as Warren had promised to do what was necessary in the way of restoration and redecoration inside, so another friend, Alfred Parsons, 'best of men as well as best of landscape-painters-and-gardeners', took charge outside and revealed to Henry 'the most charming possibilities for the treatment of the tiny out-of-door part – it amounts to about an acre of garden and lawn, all shut in by the peaceful old red wall aforesaid, on which the most flourishing old espaliers, apricots, pears, plums and figs, assiduously grow. It appears that it's a glorious little growing exposure, air, and soil – and all the things that were still flourishing out of doors (November 20th) were a joy to behold'. The garden also boasted a small orchard, a wide variety of flowering shrubs, and a fine old mulberry tree, which had been there for centuries. On the garden side of the wall dividing the garden from the courtyard at the back of the house, there was a large glass greenhouse, which contained vines and a bignonia, one of the biggest in the country. For aesthetic as well as practical reasons, Henry persuaded the landlord to remove the greenhouse, which he planned to replace with a smaller one in the corner of the garden near the gardener's cottage.

As the solution of Henry's 'long-unassuaged desire for a calm retreat', Lamb House was as near perfect as anything. 'It is the very calmest and yet cheerfullest that I could have dreamed,' he told his sister-in-law – '*in* the little old cobble-stoned, grassgrown, red-roofed town, on the summit of its mildly pyramidal hill and close to its noble old church – the chimes of which will sound sweet in my goodly old red-walled garden. The little place is so rural and tranquil, and yet discreetly animated, that its being within the town is, for convenience and immediate accessibility, purely to the good; and the house itself, though modest and unelaborate full of a

---

* On August 18th, 1940, a bomb from a German aircraft scored a direct hit on the Garden Room, completely demolishing it and most of its contents, including nearly 200 of Henry James's books, many of them presentation copies from the authors. The Garden Room was not rebuilt, but an ornamental wall and plaque, completed in 1965 by the National Trust, marks where it stood.

charming little stamp and dignity of its period . . . without as
well as within'. As he put it to Arthur Benson, 'the merit of it is
that it's such a place as I may, when pressed by the pinch of
need, retire to with a certain shrunken decency and wither
away in – in a fairly cleanly and pleasantly melancholy manner – towards the tomb. It is really good enough to be a kind of
little, becoming, high-door'd, brass-knockered *façade* to one's
life'.[7]

[TWO]

Henry had hoped to be installed in Lamb House by the following Easter, but things went slowly in Rye and there was
much to be done. Easter came and went and he was still in De
Vere Gardens, which he had to think of disposing of, since he
felt it would be too expensive to keep it going as well as the
new house. On April 20th, 1898, he wrote to his brother
William:

> I shall certainly do my best to let my flat when I am ready
> to leave town; the difficulty this year, however, will be that
> the time for 'season' letting begins now, and I can't depart
> for at least another month. Things are not ready at Rye,
> and won't be till then, with the limited local energy at work
> that I have very wisely contented myself with turning on
> there. It has been the right and much the best way in the
> long run, and for one's good little relations there; only the
> run has been a little longer. The remnant of the season here
> may be difficult to dispose of – to a sub-lessee; and my books
> – only a part of which I can house at Rye – are a complica-
> tion. However, I shall do what I can this year; and for
> subsequent absences, so long as my present lease of De Vere
> Gardens runs, I shall have the matter on a smooth, organized,
> working basis.
>
> I mean to arrange myself always to let – being, as such
> places go, distinctly lettable. And for my declining years I
> have put my name down for one of the invaluable south-
> looking, Carlton Gardens-sweeping bedrooms at the Reform
> Club, which are let by the year and are of admirable and

convenient (with all the other resources of the place at one's elbow) of *general* habitability. The only thing is they are so in demand that one has sometimes a long time to await one's turn. On the other hand there are accidents, occasions' . . .

With Lamb House but £70 a year and the Reform Club but £50, I shall, in respect to *loyer*, have taken in a great deal of pecuniary sail. This business of making Lamb House sanitary and comfortable and very modestly furnishing is of course, as it came suddenly, a considerable strain on my resources, but I shall securely outweather it – and this year and next, thank heaven, my income will have been much larger than for any year of my existence.[8]

Meanwhile his friends were generous with their help, Parsons in the garden and the Warrens with the interior alterations and redecorating, which included the installation of a bathroom with running water, an amenity which the house seems previously to have lacked, and the provision of very ample and extensive curtaining. He asked Margaret Warren to cope with the curtains and the man who came to measure for them. 'It is for *all* the windows (hall, staircase, garden-house, etc.) on the two best floors. I shan't trouble him for the 3rd storey. And most gratefully, I leave the matter – and the whole authority – in your hands. I am thinking of a stuff he showed me that is dearer than the dyed Irish linen (of *course* I am!) but so admirable for the purpose.' The oak panelling in the King's Room, which Henry intended to use as his own bedroom, had to be stripped and painted. 'The idea for a wardrobe for the clear space (I mean by you constructed) is full of charm,' he told Edward Warren. 'It seems to me indeed *the* thing to do: unless the space be good *bedspace*; which, as it's the space opposite the windows (I gather) is rather the stretch of wall I had thought of for my little couch. In that case clearly – *tapestry*!'[9]

Another friend, Miss Muir Mackenzie, who was staying at Winchelsea, reported progress from time to time. Henry wrote to thank her:

34, De Vere Gardens, W. Thursday [*May 19, 1898*]
Forgive the constant pressure which has delayed the expression of my gratitude for your charming, vivid, pictorial report of – well, of everything. It was most kind of you to paddle over to Rye to minister to my anxieties. You both assuage and encourage them – but with the right thing for each.

I am content enough about the bathroom – but hopeless about the garden, which I don't know what to do with, and shall never, *never* know, I am *densely* ignorant – only just barely know dahlias from mignonette – and shall never be able to work it in any way. So I shan't try – but remain gardenless – only go in for the lawn; which requires mere brute force – no intellect! For the rest I shall do decently, perhaps – so far as one can do for two-and-ninepence. I shall have nothing really 'good' – only the humblest old fifth-hand, 50th hand, mahogany and brass. I have collected a handful of feeble relics – but I fear the small desert will too cruelly interspace them. Well, *speriamo*.

I'm very sorry to say that getting down before Saturday has proved only the fondest of many delusions. The whole place has to be matting-ed before the ricketty mahogany can go in, and the end of that – or, for aught I know, the beginning – is not yet. I have but just received the 'estimate' for the (humblest) window-curtains (two tiers, *on* the windows, instead of blinds: white for downstairs, etc. greeny-blue for *up*, if you like details,) and the 'figure' leaves me prostrate. O, what a tangled web we weave!

. . . Of an ordinary – a normal – year, I hope always to be there in May.[10]

It was not until the second week in June that at last the house was ready and he was able to move in with his furniture, 'domestic complications of the gravest order', as he described the process. Two days later he had to dash back to town and then go down to Surrey to spend the week-end with Edwin Godkin, editor of *The Nation*, who had taken a house for the summer at Cobham. On his return to De Vere Gardens, where he seems to have been fussed by other problems connected with the move, Henry dropped a note to Warren to tell him 'without wincing or mincing how intensely delighted I was with Lamb House on Thursday and Friday last, which I spent there. I won't attempt details, but only thank you and bless you, tenderly, and reserve everything . . . till I see you on Thursday'.[11] Meanwhile his servants were working hard to get the place straight. This task was accomplished to his general satisfaction, since he was back in Rye around midsummer's day and did not stir far from his new abode for the rest of the year.

So far as the weather went, the summer was a repetition of the one he had spent two years before in Rye. He seems to have had a steady stream of visitors throughout, judging by a letter he wrote to the young H. G. Wells, who was recovering from a prolonged kidney ailment in nearby New Romney. 'I should have been over to see you before this, were it not that my little house has been stuffed with people and my attention wrenched – even from hideously belated work – to the supplying of their strikingly numerous wants.' The visitors arrived not merely to see him but because he had 'something to show' them. 'My little old house is really pretty enough for that,' he wrote several months later, 'and has given me, all this wonderful, hot, rainless summer, a peace that would pass understanding, if I had only got through the first botherations a little earlier in the season. However, I've done very well – have only not been quite the anchorite as I had planned. The bump of luggage has been frequent on my stair, and the conference with the cook proved a greater strain than, in that particular way, I have ever before had to meet. But it's doubtless my own fault. I should have sought a drearier refuge.'[12]

Guests who stayed at Lamb House that summer included Edmund Gosse, the Warrens, and Henry's nephew Harry, then an undergraduate at Harvard and on a vacation trip to Europe. The latter brought with him a set of blue china which his mother had purchased for Henry's new home. Henry had been very touched by the sympathetic notice of *Guy Domville*, which H. G. Wells had contributed to the *Pall Mall Gazette*. Learning that the young writer was quite seriously ill in New Romney, he and Gosse bicycled over the marsh to find out how he was and, although they naturally did not tell him so at the time, to inquire on the part of the Royal Literary Fund, whether he was in need of any financial help. They took tea with Wells and his wife and doctor. The Wells's found them 'very charming and friendly' and were 'greatly flattered by their visit'. 'It never dawned upon me,' wrote Wells afterwards in his autobiography, 'that they had any but sociable motives in coming over to see me.' It was fitting that Wells should record his appreciation in this way, although in the event he was never offered any assistance from the Fund and in fact did not need it.[13]

This was the first time that young Harry James had met Edmund Gosse, and years later he was to remind Gosse's son Philip of the literary conversation which he heard during this visit. 'I sat by one evening while the two elder men discussed [George] Meredith's origin at great length and very interestingly,' Harry recalled. 'They didn't arrive at any conclusion, but I was left with the conviction that they both recognized it as mysterious and interesting – probably not entirely English. It has remained in my mind as a curious commentary on Meredith and in a certain sense of my uncle and your father, for there was apparently no necessary mystery and yet they were both unusually well informed.'[14]

The Warrens came down later in the season. 'It's but a few days since that we were grilling here,' Henry wrote to Margaret Warren on September 23rd, 'and now the autumn sun in the old garden is delicious to feel, even though the autumn lawn be as a large sheet of brown paper, and very crumpled at that. The flowers are going, the best of the fruits have gone; but I am nursing along the element of a nosegay and a meagre dish. There will, however, be no sense of destruction if you bring your bicycles. I want you both, in spite of the hills, to see Tenterden if you haven't seen it. . . . I shall look for you at 6.30 and feverishly pace the platform to that end.' Then after the Warrens had left, he wrote to Edward:

I echo with all my heart your view of our two days together here as a great felicity. The felicity was singular and complete – and the sweetness of this old house comes out – or almost so – in those quiet late hours of night when the little virtuous town sleeps and the clock ticks loud in the hall.[15]

He also had the company of his *protégé,* the crippled American writer Jonathan Sturges, who beguiled Henry with social and literary gossip. He turned up in mid-October for a prolonged stay. ('He remains till over Christmas; but save as making against pure intensity of concentration, he is altogether a boon.')[16]

'These October weeks have endeared this sweet little place to me more than ever,' Henry wrote again to the Warrens at the end of that month; 'they really have been the cream of the whole period – for colour, atmosphere, tone and general (when it hasn't rained) autumnal sunning and brownness. My very interesting young friend Jonathan Sturges has been here for a fortnight (is here still), and as he is lame I've strolled and pottered and sat with him a great deal in small afternoon wanderings and pauses – and all with a new fascination and attachment. The whole thing is more charminger in summer; and more and more, in short, my exact fit.'[17]

Less demanding in some ways were those visitors who came down from London for the day. Among them were Mrs James T. Fields, widow of the Boston publisher, who came with her friend Sarah Orne Jewett, the writer of New England short stories. Mrs Fields later recorded her recollection of the visit.

We left London about 11 o'clock for Rye, to pass the day with Mr Henry James. He was waiting for us at the station with a carriage, and in five minutes we found ourselves at the top of a silent little winding street, at the green door with a brass knocker, wearing the air of impenetrable respectability which is so well known in England. Another instant and an old servant, Smith (who with his wife has been in Mr James's service for 20 years), opened the door and helped us from the carriage. It was a pretty interior – large enough for elegance and simple enough to suit the severe taste of a scholar and private gentleman.

Mr James was intent on the largest hospitality. We were

asked upstairs over a staircase with a pretty balustrade and plain green drugget on the steps; everything was of the severest plainness, but in the best taste – 'not at all austere', as he himself wrote to us ... [Downstairs] we sat in the parlour opening on a pretty garden for some time, until Mr James said he could not conceive why luncheon was not ready and he must go and inquire, which he did in a very responsible manner, and soon after Smith appeared to announce the feast. Again a pretty room and table. We enjoyed our talk sincerely at luncheon and afterwards strolled into the garden. The dominating note was dear Mr James's pleasure in having a home of his own to which he might ask us.

From the garden, of course, we could see the pretty old house still more satisfactorily. An old brick wall concealed by vines and laurels surrounds the whole irregular domain: a door from the garden leads into a paved courtyard which seemed to give Mr James particular satisfaction; returning to the garden and on the other side, at an angle with the house, is a building which he laughingly called the temple of the Muse. This is his own place *par excellence*. A good writing table and one for his secretary, a typewriter, books and a sketch by du Maurier, with a few other pictures (rather mementoes than works of art) excellent windows with clear light – such is the temple! Evidently an admirable spot for his work.

[After sight-seeing at Winchelsea] Mr James drove us to the station, where we took the train for Hastings. He had brought his small dog, an aged black-and-tan terrier, with him for a holiday. He put on the muzzle, which all dogs just now must wear, and took it off a great many times until, having left it once when he went to buy the tickets and recovered it, he again lost it and it could not be found; so as soon as he reached Hastings he took a carriage again to drive us along the esplanade, but the first thing was to buy a new muzzle. ... We began to feel like tea, so ... we went into a small shop and enjoyed more talk under new conditions. 'How many cakes have you eaten?' 'Ten,' gravely replied Mr James – at which we all laughed. 'Oh, I know,' said the girl with a wise look at the desk. 'How do you suppose they know?' said Mr James musingly as he turned away. 'They always do!' And so on again presently to the train at Hastings, where Mr McAlpine [Henry's secretary] appeared at the right instant. Mr James's train for Rye left a few moments before ours for London. He took a most friendly farewell and having left us to Mr McAlpine ran for his own carriage. In another five minutes we too were away, bearing our delightful memories of this meeting.[18]

Besides entertaining his friends, Henry worked hard all the summer and autumn at *The Awkward Age*, the first of his novels to be written at Lamb House. It appeared serially in *Harper's Weekly*, beginning in October, in fact before Henry had finished it. Mr Longdon's country place in the story was admittedly based on Lamb House.

> Mr Longdon's garden . . . full of charming features, had for its greatest wonder the extent and colour of its old brick wall, in which the pink and purple surface was the fruit of the mild ages and the protective function, for a visitor strolling, sitting, talking, reading, that of a nurse of reverie. The air of the place, in the August time, thrilled all the while with the bliss of birds, the hum of little lives unseen and the flicker of white butterflies. . . . There were sitting-places, just there, out of the full light, cushioned benches in the thick wide spread of old mulberry-boughs. . . .
>
> Mr. Longdon had not made his house, he had simply lived it, and the 'taste' of the place. . . was nothing more than the beauty of his life. Everything on every side had dropped straight from heaven, with nowhere a bargaining thumb-mark, a single sign of the shop.[19]

Henry's rush in completing the serial instalments for the printer he gave as an excuse to H. G. Wells for having 'feebly to suffer frustration in the matter of trundling over the marsh to ask for your news and wish for your continued amendment. The shortening days and the deepening mud have been at the bottom of this affair. I never get out of the house till 3 o'clock,

when night is quickly at one's heels. I would have taken a
regular day – I mean started in the a.m. – but have been so
ridden, myself, by the black care of an unfinished and *running*
(galloping, leaping and bounding), serial that parting with a
day has been parting with a pound of flesh. I am still a neck
ahead, however, and *this* week will see me through. . . .'[20]

A few days later, on December 19th, he wrote to his sister-
in-law from Lamb House:

All the good that I hoped of the place has, in fine,
profusely bloomed and flourished here. It was really about
the end of September, when the various summer super-
numeraries had quite faded away, that the special note
of Rye, the feeling of the little hilltop community, bound
together like a very modest, obscure and impecunious, but
virtuous and amiable family began most unmistakably to
come out. This is the present note of life here, and it has
floated me (excuse mixture of metaphor) very placidly along.
Nothing would induce me now *not* to be here for Christmas
and nothing will induce me not to do my best at least to be
here for the protrusion of the bulbs – the hyacinths and
tulips and crocuses – that, in return for expended shillings,
George Gammon promises me for the earliest peep of spring.
As he has broken no word with me yet, I trust him implicitly
for this. Meantime too I have trusted him, all the autumn,
for all sorts of other things as well: we have committed to the
earth together innumerable unsightly roots and sprigs that
I am instructed to depend upon as the fixed foundation of a
future herbaceous and perennial paradise.

Little by little, even with other cares, the slowly but
surely working poison of the garden-mania begins to stir in
my long-sluggish veins. Tell Harry, as an intimate instance,
that by a masterly inspiration I have at one bold stroke
swept away all the complications in the quarter on which the
studio looks down, uprooting the wilderness of shrubs,
relaying paths, extending borders, etc., and made arrangement to throw the lawn, in one lordly sweep, straight up
into that angle – a proceeding that greatly increases our
apparent extent and dignity: an improvement, in short,

quite unspeakable. But the great charm is the simply *being* here, and in particular the beginning of the day no longer with the London blackness and foulness, the curtain of fog and smoke that one has each morning muscularly to lift and fasten back; but with the pleasant, sunny garden outlook, the grass all haunted with starlings and chaffinches, and the in-and-out relation with it that in a manner gilds and refreshes the day. This indeed – with work and a few, a very few, people – is the *all*.[21]

[THREE]

'Two-and-twenty years on end of London,' Henry told Arthur Benson at this time, 'have qualified me in perfection for a small brown hilltop community islanded in a more or less drained, though much diminished and otherwise curtailed and simplified imitation of the Roman Campagna. Romney Marsh only wants a few aqueducts and ruins and tombs and temples and tourists to *strike*, really, with that resemblance.'[22] He fitted remarkably easily into the little Rye community, and the local people quickly regarded him as a good neighbour. 'He greeted everyone we met most genially', the American novelist Hamlin Garland recalled. 'He was on terms with the postman and the butcher's boy. There was nothing austere or remote in his bearing. On the contrary he had the air of a curate making the rounds of his village. . . . The people everywhere greeted him with smiling cordiality. They liked and honoured him, that was evident, and it gave me a keen sense of satisfaction to find him more and more neighbourly, taking an interest in what his fellow citizens were doing and thinking. This phase of him was as surprising as it was amusing.'[23]

The weather was so mild up to Christmas, following the scorching summer, that apart from a few brief visits to London 'in a pure picknicking way' in his flat, he planned to stay at Lamb House until the spring and then go to Italy. But the winter gales, which began immediately after Christmas, drove him back to London for several weeks. On his return to Rye, he received a letter from George Alexander, asking him if he would dramatize his short story, *Covering End*, which had just appeared along with *The Turn of the Screw* in his book *The Two Magics*, as a one-act play.

It's strange how this little renewal of contact with the vulgar theatre stirs again, in a manner, and moves me, [he noted in his journal on January 22, 1899.][24] Or rather, it isn't at all the contact with the theatre – still as ever, strangely odious: it's the contact with the DRAMA, with the divine little difficult, artistic, ingenious, architectural FORM that makes old pulses throb and old tears rise again. The blended anguish and amusement again touch me with their breath. This is a grey, gusty, lonely Sunday at Rye – the tail of a great, of an almost, in fact, *perpetual* winter gale. The wind booms in the old chimneys, wails and shrieks about the old walls. I sit, however, in the little warm white study – and many things come back to me. I've been in London for 3 weeks – came back here on the 20th; and feel the old reviving ache of desire to get back to work. Yes, I yearn for that – the divine unrest again touches me. This note of Alexander's is probably the germ of something. I mean of a little wooing of something ingenious. Ah, the one-act.' Ah, the 'short story!' It's very much the same trick!*

The gales abated, and on February 22nd, 1899, Henry wrote to his nephew Harry, who by this time had returned to Harvard:

We've had of late a good lot of wondrous, sunny, balmy days – to-day is splendid – in which I have kept saying to myself 'What a climate – dear old much-abused thing – after all!' and feeling quite balmily and baskingly southern. I've been 'sitting' all the last month in the green upstairs south-west room, whose manifest destiny is clearly to become a second-story boudoir. Whenever my books arrive in their plenitude from De Vere Gardens it will be absolutely required

---

* James, who had originally written the story in dramatic form, sent the script to Alexander, only to have it turned down. Some years later the actor-manager Sir Johnston Forbes-Robertson, asked him to rewrite it in three acts, which James did. It was eventually produced under the title *Summersoft* in Edinburgh in 1908, with some success, and later in London.

to help to house them. It has been, at any rate, constantly flooded with sun, and has opened out its view towards Winchelsea and down the valley in the most charming way.

The garden is beginning to smile and shimmer almost as if it were already May. Half the crocuses and hyacinths are up, the primrose and the jonquil abound, the tulips are daily expected, and the lawn is of a rich and vivid green that covers with shame the state in which you saw it. George Gammon proves as regular as a set of false teeth and improves each shining hour. In short the quite essential amiability of L.H. only deepens with experience. Therefore see what a house I'm keeping for you . . .

P.S. Am just up again from such a sweet sunny spacious after-luncheon stroll in the garden. You'll think it very vulgar of me, but I continue to find it ravishing.[25]

The day before he was due to leave for Italy Henry had a severe shock, which obliged him to postpone his departure. In the early hours of February 27th, a fire broke out in Lamb House which might have proved disastrous if he had not been on the spot to deal with it. He related what happened to Warren, to whom he had previously sent a telegram for help.[26]

Lamb House,
Rye.

Monday afternoon [*February 27th, 1899*]

My dear Edward,

It will be a great joy and refreshment, after somewhat of a scare and the strain of a teetotally sleepless night, to see you tomorrow if you can conveniently come. I'm *tired,* so I'll be brief.

I sat up late writing letters – in the Green Room – most unusually late by the blessing of providence, and towards 1.30 in the small hours of the morning, after an odour that had long puzzled me, found smoke coming up through the boards of the floor, near the fireplace. I roused Smith [the manservant], we got a pry, an axe, saw – *que sais-je?* and getting portions of the planks up found *fire* under and behind the hearth and 'stove'. We rushed for police and fire brigade, and they arrived with very decent promptness and operated with intelligence and tact.

They did us practically no harm with water, though they were 2 or 3 hours. The inflamed material-morsels of *beams* going *under* the 'stove', which has been nobly hot for 6 weeks – as well as other compromised or compromising elements dropped (while the men tore away fireplace, grate, tiles, hearth, brickwork and all – leaving a gaping void) down into the *pocket* beside the flue of the dining-room chimney, and there began *inside* naturally, to burn the dining-room walls. So a great square cavity had to be pick-axed from the dining-room in the portion above the mantel, through which opening the burning portion, which was not large but very active, was got at and quenched and extracted.

Voilà! The brave pumpers departed with the early dawn. But I was sickened by the little desolation and defacement – the house befouled and topsy-turvy – and couldn't sleep. I won't deny that I want awfully to see you. The Green Room, Dining Room and (for fire purposes, through contact) the oak parlour are all impossible and I am relegated to the white study and, praised be the Lord, the Garden Room, which I have again taken hold of and, with a coke fire, is once more delightful.

A quelque chose malheur est bon, à demain. I am really tired – somehow – to exhaustion and the pen drops from my nerveless grasp.

Love to all,

Ever yours,

HENRY JAMES

He fervently thanked providence that he had sat up so late writing 'many procrastinated letters'.

That saved me [he wrote to Gosse.] I sniffed the danger much sooner than if I had been with my head under the bedclothes, and could quickly summon the pumpers who arrived promptly and showed much laudable tact, sanity and competence. They pumped most subtly – and in short save for a scare and an absolutely strained and sleepless – *debout* – night – with the temporary loss of two rooms (insured completely), I am not the worse; and I am on the other hand cheaply *warned* – old houses have insidious structural traps; old recklessness and barbarity of fireplace-building – infamous juxtaposition of *beams* and chimnies.

It is all to be made better and safer and saner than it *ever* was – and I want a week longer to see the reparations started. Then I go at last away for 10 weeks.[27]

The obliging Warren agreed to carry out the architectural alterations, which this alarming outbreak involved, during Henry's absence on the Continent. Before Henry left, in the middle of March, the architect sent a revised plan of the work remaining to be carried out. 'As for your emendation plan of the dining-room fireplace – the brick piers, arch, etc., as per drawing – I rapturously and gratefully applaud and adopt it,' Henry wrote. 'It is the thing – the blessed thing; *damn* the expense! It will make both above and below perfect and retrieve a little – or rather greatly – the meanness of the actual – or late! – dining-room chimney corner in every way . . . Am I better of the fatal night? Why, my dear Edward, the "spring" of that new mantel-arch is alone worth it all.'[28]

After talking matters over with the building contractor, whom Warren sent down, Henry was inclined to have new open grates and baskets in the upstairs rooms in the interests of 'positively ideal security', but on Warren's advice he agreed that this was really only necessary in the dining-room, and that the same or similar metal registers should be left in the King's Room and the Green Room in order to regulate the passage of air, heat and smoke.

This will do excellently, it being a shame to *introduce* the shade of a possibility of upstairs smoke where it didn't exist before in *any* degree: the Green Room, for instance, smoking, through all the winter gales, *only* the night of the conflagration – and then for such good reasons. So all thanks again. King [the contractor] will have told you that he arranged with the extremely intelligent and competent young William Bourn (with the assistance he requires) to do the work, and the latter is ready to start as soon as a detailed plan comes.

> H.J. 'You require nothing but that – the detailed plan?'
> W.B. 'Lord bless you, sir, no. I've never *seen* such plans to work from as Mr Warren's!'

So Adonis waits – and understands. I dare say you will arrange that his labour be *seen* and passed upon before it's wholly finished; otherwise, I take for granted he can go on straight for some time by himself. If King can come down again – before the carpenter takes over – or if you could, better still, then bliss would be mine. I must at last depart – there's a very serious obligation on me, long shirked, in Rome, and it's getting late. Otherwise I would wait and supervise discreetly. But I've watched the man; he's thoroughly trustworthy, I feel, and has, moreover, a vast desire to please us. . . .

I wish I could see you *staying* here ever and anon in my absence. The Smiths and the Garden Room so yearn for you. The latter – not the former – becomes with the elapsing season more and more a *dream*.[29]

[FOUR]

Henry's first stop was Paris, where he put up at the Hotel Meurice. Here he learned from the servants at Lamb House that work had begun in the dining-room, 'so that all, doubtless is well.' 'If you would think it well to go down before Easter,' he again invited Warren, 'don't fail to write, or wire to Mrs Smith so that victuals may smoke before you.' As a relief from his labours, Warren replied that he might be able to join Henry a little later in Italy. 'This is excellent news,' rejoined Henry, still at the Meurice. 'I wish even we might be *here* a little, sometime or other: this extraordinary Paris, with its new – I mean and more multiplied manifestations of luxurious, and extravagant extension – grandeur and general chronic *expositionism*, is a spectacle it would be so interesting to assist at with you in some detail: awfully curious in its way. It strikes

About 1898   In the garden of Lamb House

With William James, about 1901
'. . . my protector, my backer, my authority, and my pride'

From photographs at Lamb House

THE GARDEN ROOM

'. . . a most commodious and picturesque detached study and workroom . . .'

(Above) Front view

From the drawing by Edward Warren in the Houghton Library, Harvard University

(Below) Interior

From a photograph by courtesy of Mrs Nathaniel Lloyd

The Garden Room was destroyed in a German air raid, August 18th, 1940

Rye Sept 26ᵗʰ 1895 E P Warren

me as a monstrous massive flower of national decadence, the biggest temple ever built to material joys and the lust of the eyes, drawing to it thereby all the forms of the nation as to a substitute for others' – I mean other than Parisian – achievement. It is a strange great phenomenon – with a deal of beauty still in its expansive symmetries and perspectives – and such a beauty of light.'[30]

With his usual competence the obliging Warren took charge of the insurance claim arising out of the fire as well as all the incidental repairs, and Henry was duly grateful.

Le Plantier, Costebelle, Hyères. March 29, 1899.
Your letter of the 25th is, as usual, a benediction. I am extremely obliged to you for your trouble over the insurance question and for getting £28 allowed. This is admirable and I beg of you to be tenderly thanked. Be not less so, please, over the question of the 3 new fireplaces, hearthstones, etc.; your arrangements and decision in regard to each of them I accept with the eye of criticism ecstatically closed. Let everything be exactly as you best see it. Bravo to the thick stone hearth laid flush with the flooring in the Royal Retreat.

I've been here since Saturday (with the P. Bourgets) – my impression of Paris being rather squelched and superseded by the extraordinary beauty and interest of this region. It is so long since I had seen the foreign and the Southern that it all rather rolls over me here like a wave – the harmony and loveliness and nobleness of this wondrous French Riviera, the light, the grace and style and general composition. The Bourgets have a fabulous retreat of 25 acres in an admirable position, with vegetation and views and flowers and terraces before which poor dear little Lamb House veils its face with humility and misery. Wondrous are the resources of this people but (let us bear up!) hideous – apparently, mainly – their villas as villas.

. . . do remember that if the banqueting hall makes your work the least sign or invitation for quiet concentration, a word and Mrs Smith will secure the strewing of roses for your approach to it. It chronically yearns for you.[31]

Warren's industry revealed further hidden fire dangers, which he attended to with his usual efficiency. 'I thank you from the bottom of my proprietory heart', Henry wrote from Rome on May 22nd. 'What a state of general fireplace villainy you must have discovered – and how I rejoice in every abolished and annihilated danger you have dealt with. *Bravo bravissimo!* I assent to – *que dis-je?* – I applaud with frenzy everything – and desire no money spared for any *complete and total* rectification of study and east bedroom firetraps. But I understand that you will have done everything that could be done. The servant's bedroom chimney doesn't matter for the present – it remains fireless – thanks.'[32]

A week or so later found him in the Alban Hills at Castel Gandolfo, where he was the guest of the fashionable English novelist and social worker, Mrs Humphry Ward, and her husband – 'the irrepressible Humphry Wards', Henry called them. They had taken 'this wondrous place' for several months so that the hostess 'may do an "Italian" novel', on which Henry had promised to help her with some of the characters and background. (The novel was *Eleanor*, which came out in the following year.) 'The villa, vast, rambling, bare, shabby and uncomfortable', was how Henry described it to Warren; 'but the position, circumstances, walks, drives, sensations of every aesthetic order, ravishing and inexpressible. We hang on a high hill with the windows of one side suspended over vast sea-like Campagna, and of the other side over blue, deepbosomed Alban Lake with Rocca di Papa and Monte Cavo perched opposite. In our garden, among ilexes and old statues, wondrous perspectives and cedar alleys, the huge windows and porticoes of a villa of Domitian.'[33]

On this occasion Mrs Ward was delighted with her guest. 'Never did I see Henry James in a happier light,' she wrote afterwards. 'A new light too. For here in this Italian country, and in the Eternal City, the man whom I had so far mainly known as a Londoner was far more at home than I; and I realized perhaps more fully than ever before the extraordinary range of his knowledge and sympathies. Roman history and antiquities, Italian art, Renaissance sculpture, the personalities and events of the Risorgimento, all these solid *connais-sances* and many more were to be recognized perpetually as rich elements in the general wealth of Mr James's mind. That he had read immensely, observed immensely, talked immensely, became once more gradually and delightfully clear on this new field.'

Mrs Ward remembered how her daughter Dorothy, who was in charge of the housekeeping at the villa asked Henry's opinion as to how to deal with the Neapolitan cook, who had been anything but satisfactory over her last lunch-party. Miss Ward decided to write the cook a letter, asking him to do his best next time and pointing out his recent shortcomings. Since her Italian was rudimentary, she brought the draft to Henry, who 'walked up and down the vast *salone* of the Villa, striking his forehead, correcting and improvising.' What was wanted was 'a really nice pudding', seeing that the Neapolitan genius for sweets was justly famous. After various attempts, Henry eventually hit upon the perfect phrase – *'un dolce si deve'* – which remained with the Ward family as the description of the ultimate perfection.

While staying at the Villa Barberini, Henry was taken on an expedition to Lake Nemi and the ruined walls of the Temple of Diana rising amid the nearby strawberry beds. Here, according to Mrs Ward's other daughter Janet, who later married the historian G. M. Trevelyan and wrote her mother's biography, Henry 'found the peasant youth with the glorious name, Aristodemo, and set him talking of Lord Savile's diggings,* and of the marble head that he himself had found – yes, he! – with nose and all complete, in his own garden, while the sun sank lower towards the crater-rim, and the rest of us sat spell-bound, listening to the dialogue.'

Mrs Ward has also left an account of this excursion, particularly Henry's meeting with Aristodemo.

Mr James's face lit up; and he walked over the historic ground beside the lad, Aristodemo picking up for him

---

* The second Lord Savile, who died in 1896, had been a keen amateur archaeologist when he was British Ambassador in Rome some years previously.

fragments of terracotta from the furrows through which the plough had just passed, bits of the innumerable small *figurines* that used to crowd the temple walls as ex-votos, and are now mingled with the *fragole* in the rich alluvial earth. It was a wonderful evening; with a golden sun on the lake, on the wide stretches where the temple stood and the niched wall where Lord Savile dug for treasure and found it; on the great ship-timbers also, beside the lake, wreckage from Caligula's galleys, which still lie buried in the deepest depth of the water; on the rock of Nemi, and the fortress-like Orsini villa; on the Alban Mount itself, where it cut the clear sky. I presently came up with Mr James and Aristodemo, who led us on serenely, a young Hermes in the transfiguring light. One almost looked for the winged feet and helmet of the messenger god! Mr James paused – his eyes first on the boy, then on the surrounding scene. 'Aristodemo!' he murmured smiling, and more to himself than me, his voice caressing the word – 'what a name! what a place![34]

Henry also seems to have enjoyed the experience, as in writing to thank Mrs Ward for her hospitality, he told her that of all the time he spent in Italy that summer 'the Nemi Lake, and the walk down and up (the latter perhaps most) and the strawberries and Aristodemo were the cream'.[35]

Henry's letters during this trip were full of homesick longings. 'My nostalgia for Lamb House is already such as to make me *capable de tout*,' he told his brother.[36] By the beginning of July, he anticipated that the servants, in spite of their fireless bedrooms, were 'gorged with long luxurious leisure and panting for the renewal of domestic detail,' adding that, as regards himself, 'even after a last fortnight at Venice the detail, domestic and other, of L.H. has power to solicit her jaded absentee'. He eventually reached Rye on July 9th, after an absence of nearly four months. He was delighted with everything Warren had done, and as soon as he was unpacked and 're-ensconced' he wrote with characteristic enthusiasm to the architect.

Oh, it is a joy to be once more in this refreshed and renovated refuge! How I thank you again and how you've hit everything off! The place is charming and to be, accordingly, for the I trust long future, both quaint and fireproof; that consciousness plays into me like the scented spray at Truefitt's.

Everything is perfect – the new bookcase in the drawing room perhaps the most perfect of all. I have provisionally filled it (already) with my 2nd-best (my best are in London, but as many as possible shall come down), and so, virified consecrated, it becomes really the 'making' of the little oak parlour. Even after Italian palaces (of which I saw this time perhaps more than usual) the trodden Lambkin turns – does hold up its head. The dining room monument is a gem – in its setting of Siena marble. . . .[37]

Henry had not been home for more than a few weeks when he heard from Mrs Bellingham's solicitor that her son's exertions in the Klondike gold rush had proved too much for the landlord, who had died in Canada, and that in accordance with the terms of the lease the solicitor was instructed to offer Henry the freehold, together with the studio house beyond the southern wall of the garden in Watchbell Street, which also belonged to the Bellingham family, for the sum of £2,000. Henry immediately decided to accept the offer. 'It is admirable and I am jumping at it,' he told Warren; 'but there are things of detail, two or three questions, etc. However, I'm not going to worry *you* about them (how interminable will you think Lamb House!!) and I think I see my way to treat the matter as a perfectly simple transaction'. One of the 'things of detail', on which Henry was tempted to seek Warren's advice by reason of his own 'constitutional vagueness in business matters', was the fact that the freehold of the house was subject to two mortgages amounting to £1250, taken out on the property by the late owner. However, this turned out to be a convenience for Henry, as his travels had temporarily depleted his finances, and he now had to put down only £750 besides undertaking to pay the interest on the mortgages.

His brother William, whom he also consulted, thought the purchase price asked by Mrs Bellingham was too much, since the late owner's father had only paid £1200 for the property. But Henry flatly told his brother that he regarded Lamb House as 'my *home* for the rest of my days,' and that not to have it would mean life without any joy for him. 'This achieved sense will be inestimably precious to me, will *do* more for me than anything else *can*', he told William. 'There is no solid sense of home without it, and nothing could have possibly been more mature and more accumulated than this long vision, for I nourished it all the year before I could take the house. No competent person would say that I don't get the realization of it on easy terms.'

Reassured by Warren's opinion that Henry was getting a bargain, William withdrew his opposition, and Henry wrote to his friend:

I am happy to say I have *closed* with Mrs Bellingham's offer, though it comes at a moment when I was a little depleted and unexpecting. If I had known it was so near at hand the 1st of January last, I would have arranged, as bearing on a purchase, a little differently (by which I don't in the least mean the chimney and office affairs, the being done of which is nothing but a pure blessing to me.) On the other hand, the conditions are so very reasonable and comfortable that I shall find it all convenient and manageable. I have only to sit close the next six months and attend to my business – which, heaven knows, is all I *want* to do. Meanwhile it is a great blessing to have the question at rest: it makes me love dear little L.H. more than ever.

I have arranged to get rid, at a *probably* early date, of 34 De Vere Gardens – and the only drawback to that is that the things I shall thereby have in my hands to bring down here are biggish and crowdingish for the place, besides endless prints and photos (*all* the latter valued for association) and 5,000 books! I'm afraid poor little L.H. won't look the better for them. But *à la guerre comme à la guerre*.[38]

In fact he was able to let his London flat furnished for a year, at a good rent, to Stopford Brooke the younger, son of the famous and popular preacher. Fortunately at the end of that time he found he could secure the bed-sitting-room in the extension to the Reform Club, for which he had put down his name, as a London pied-à-terre, and shortly afterwards he succeeded in disposing of the remainder of the lease in De Vere Gardens. He was glad of what he called 'my newly acquired perch (105 Pall Mall)' in London, as he had spent the whole of the previous winter in Rye, which he now found rather isolated. 'I have sat here in the rain and wind for months on end, holding on tight, but feeling I hadn't a word worth anyone's having, to communicate', he had written in the spring of 1900, depressed by the news from the Boer battle front. 'A gruesome public and private winter, and with the publicity and the privacy all mixed.'

He was at his London club when he heard that the old Queen – 'little mysterious Victoria', he called her – was dying. The prospect of her son's accession to the throne caused him no pleasure and he wrote pessimistically of the imminent change of sovereign.

Reform Club, Pall Mall, S.W. January 22, 1901 . . .
Blind, used up, utterly sickened and humiliated by the War, which she hated and deplored from the first (it's what has finished her) and by the way everything is going, she is a very pathetic old monarchical figure. She had been failing fast for days before it became public, and was far gone when the first news of her being ill came. It is a simple running down of the old used up watch – and no winding-up can keep her for more than from hour to hour. . . .

I feel as if her death will have consequences in and for this country that no man can foresee. The Prince of Wales is an arch-vulgarian (don't *repeat* this from me); the wretched little 'Yorks' are less than nothing; the Queen's magnificent duration had held things magnificently – beneficently – together and prevented all sorts of accidents. Her death, in short, will let loose incalculable forces for possible ill. I am very pessimistic. The Prince of Wales, in sight of the throne, and nearly 60, and after all he has done besides of the same sort, is 'carrying on' with Mrs George Keppel (sister-in-law of Lord Albemarle) in a manner of the worst

men for the dignity of things. His succession, in short, is
ugly and makes all for vulgarity and frivolity.[39]

That winter, which he spent much more agreeably in London
than the previous one in Rye, made Henry appreciate Lamb
House all the more on his return in the spring. 'You restored
Lamb House to good purpose, my dear Edward', he wrote to
Warren in May, 1901: 'I never felt it more than during these
last weeks of wondrous weather here, and never was so
conscious of the local fondness to which your brave touch, all
about me, ministers. It's astonishing how, within and without,
everything *wears*, and how, even now, I discover new charm in
the familiar and new assurances in the usual.'

One small but somewhat irritating incident occurred to mar
Henry's enjoyment of the spring weather at Rye. This was the
rumour which was circulating in America and had appeared in
a newspaper there that he had become engaged to marry a
rich and beautiful young red-haired heiress named Emilie
Grigsby. Miss Grigsby had recently arrived in London from
New York and in the manner of some of the American belles
in Henry's stories was making determined attempts to be
received by English 'society' with the help of lavish entertaining. There was some mystery about her origin which she would
never discuss; she was said to be the illegitimate daughter of
the American railway financier and art collector Charles
Tyron Yerkes, who presented the observatory which bears his
name to the University of Chicago and was later to figure under
a thinly disguised alias in several of Theodore Dreiser's novels.
At first she lived in the Savoy Hotel but later took a house in
Mayfair, where her cuisine and wines easily surpassed those
of any of her rivals. (Her soup had twenty-six ingredients.)
Although 'society' was always nervous of accepting her, she
never lacked guests at her dinner table, where soldiers like
Lord Kitchener, Sir John French and Colonel Repington
fought for her favours, while artists and writers of the calibre
of Rodin and Yeats were content to be patronized by her.
When he first made her acquaintance, Meredith said he had
at last met the heroine of *The Ordeal of Richard Feveral*. This

admission may have encouraged her in the belief that one of Henry's well-known characters was based upon her, which added to Henry's annoyance when he heard about it from his brother.

> There *is* a Miss Grigsby whom I barely know to speak of who has been in London [and] whom I have seen in all 5 or 6 times, in the company of a dozen people and *once* alone, for 10 minutes, when in consequence of 3 or 4 *declined* invitations I called on her at the Savoy Hotel. She is, I believe, a Catholic, a millionaire and a Kentuckian, and gives out that she is the original of 'Milly' in *The Wings of the Dove* published before I had ever heard of her apparently extremely silly existence. I have never written her so much as 5 words save 2 or 3 times at most to tell her that I couldn't come up from Rye to lunch or dine with her (I've never done it!). . . .
>
> It's appalling that such winds may be started to blow about by not so much as the ghost of a exhalation of our own. . . .

While he dismissed the rumoured engagement as 'worthy of the work and laughter of the Homeric gods', Henry resolutely refused to be drawn into his countrywoman's charmed circle. It may be added that like him Miss Grigsby never married, although her great wealth led to proposals from two impoverished dukes. Nor would Henry even consent to regard her as a patroness, disdaining to promote the sale of his works in this way. She was to survive into the nineteen-sixties, a faded Southern beauty, forgotten by most of those whom she had generously adopted in the past.[40]

[FIVE]

Henry's private worry in the first winter of the Boer War was occasioned by his brother William who was on a visit to him with his wife and young daughter Peggy. William had been obliged to take a year's leave from Harvard owing to heart trouble and he came to stay at Lamb House after taking a cure at a German spa. 'My brother, for whom this snug and secure little nook appears to have been soothing and sustaining is better than when he came, and I am proportionately less depressed', Henry wrote to Edmund Gosse on New Year's Day, 1900; 'but I still go on tiptoe and live from day to day. However, that way one does go on. They go, probably by the middle of the month, to the South of France – and a right climate, a *real* one, has presumably much to give him.'[41]

William was delighted with the 'real little *bijou* of a house and garden', as he wrote during this visit, adding that Henry 'seems absolutely adapted to his environment, and very well and contented in the leisure to write and to read which the place affords'. William further wrote at this time:

> Harry's place is a most exquisite collection of quaint little stage properties, three quarters of an acre of brick-walled English garden, little brick courts and out-houses, old-time kitchen and offices, panelled chambers and tiled fire-places, but all very simple and on a small scale. Its host, soon to become its proprietor, leads a very lonely life but seems in perfect equilibrium therewith, placing apparently his interest more and more in the operations of his fancy. His health is good, his face calm, his spirits equable, and he will doubtless remain here for many years to come, with an occasional visit to London.[42]

It was during this visit that William presented his brother with a gold watch. William's wife Alice told Henry that they were going to get two watches, one for him and one for their son Harry. According to his sister-in-law, 'Henry demurred at once; he said he should lose it, he should break it, we must on no account give him anything so valuable'. The result was that they got an excellent example of the workmanship of Vacheron & Constantin from Geneva for their son, and a less good one for Henry. When Alice brought the inferior watch to her brother-in-law, he took it in his hand and looked at it with his head on one side. 'Not as good as Harry's', he said regretfully. '*Not* as good as Harry's!'

'Give it back to me', said Alice James. She then went to her husband and told him, 'I am the most stupidly literal-minded woman in the world. When Henry said he didn't want a watch as good as Harry's, I actually believed him'.[43]

Another watch of as good a quality as Harry's was thereupon obtained and given to Henry, who used it until his death, when it was given to his friend and future editor of his *Letters*, Percy Lubbock.*

Immediately after Henry had seen off his ailing brother at Dover on his journey to the Riviera, he received a visit from his friend Arthur Benson. Benson was staying at Brighton and had suggested coming over to Rye for the day, but Henry did not consider that such a proposal was 'at this season feasible with any sort of comfort or cheer. The ugly, disconcerting truth is that I haven't the assurance to speak of it favourable to you unless you can *sleep* . . . There is in the business a vast deal of train (on the one day supposition) and of changing and waiting (Hastings, Lewes, etc.,) for a very little stay when you get here – and train, etc., now in damp and darkness and cold'.[44] The result was that Benson came for the night and stayed until after lunch on the following day. On this occasion Benson found his host most friendly and hospitable, although not looking so well as he had appeared to William, and he was greatly taken with 'the charm of the place'. Indeed the description of his visit which Benson subsequently wrote in his diary remains one of the most vivid and touching accounts, if not the best, penned by any visitor to Lamb House.[45]

Lamb House, Rye, January 17, 1900 . . . Henry James, looking somewhat cold, tired and old, met me at the station: most affectionate, patting me on the shoulder and really welcoming, with abundance of *petits soins*. . . .

We walked slowly up and came to Lamb House. It is sober red Georgian; facing you as you come up is the bow-window of the Garden House with all its white casements – used by H.J. to write in in summer. The house has a tall door, strangely fortified inside by bolts, admitting into a white

---

* The watch is now at Lamb House.

panelled hall. There are three small panelled sitting rooms, besides the dining room. The place has been carefully done up, and is very clean, trim, precise, but all old and harmonious . . .

Dined simply at 7.30 with many apologies from H.J. about the fare . . . He was full of talk, though he looked weary, often passing his hand over his eyes: but he was refined and defined, was intricate, magniloquent, rhetorical, humourous, not so much like a talker, but like a writer repeating his technical processes aloud – like a savant working out a problem. He told me a long story about —, and spoke with hatred of business and the monetary side of art. He evidently thinks that art is nearly dead among English writers – no criticism, no instinct for what is good . . .

He talked of Mrs Oliphant, Carlyle – whatever I began. 'I had not read a *line* that the poor woman had written for *years* – not for years; and when she died, Henley – do you know him, the rude, boisterous, windy, headstrong Henley? – Henley, as I say, said to me "Have you read *Kirsteen*?" I replied that as a matter of fact, no – h'm – I had not read it, Henley said. "That you should have any pretensions to interest in literature and should dare to say that you have not read *Kirsteen*!" I took my bludgeoning patiently and humbly, my dear Arthur – went back and read it, and was at once confirmed, after twenty pages, in my belief – I laboured through the book – that the poor soul had a simply *feminine* conception of literature: such slipshod, imperfect, halting, faltering, peeping, down-at-heel work – buffeting along like a ragged creature in a high wind, and just struggling to the goal, and falling in a quivering mass of faintness and fatuity. Yes, no doubt she was a gallant woman – though with no species of wisdom – but an artist, an artist! —' He held his hands up and stared woefully at me . . .

H.J. works hard; he establishes me in a little high-walled, white parlour, very comfortable, but is full of fear that I am unhappy. He comes in, pokes the fire, presses a cigarette on me, puts his hand on my shoulder, looks inquiringly at me, and hurries away. His eyes are *piercing*. To see him, when I came down to breakfast this morning, in a kind of Holbein square cap of velvet and black velvet coat, scattering bread on the frozen lawn to the birds, was delightful . . .

We lunched together with his secretary, a young Scot. H.J. ate little, rolled his eyes, waited on us, walked about, talked – finally hurried me off for a stroll before my train. All his instincts are of a kind that make me feel vulgar – his consideration, hospitality, care of arrangement, thoughtfulness . . . He seemed to know everyone to speak to – an elderly clergyman in a pony-carriage, a young man riding. Three nice-looking girls met us, two of fourteen and fifteen, and a little maid of seven or eight, who threw herself upon H.J. with cooing noises of delight and kissed him repeatedly and effusively, the dogs also bounding up to him. He introduced me with great gravity . . .

We got to the station; he said an affectionate farewell, pressing me to come again; I went away refreshed, stimulated, sobered, and journeyed under a dark and stormy sky to the dreary and loathsome town of Hastings.

Although he was to become a tenant of Lamb House after Henry's death, along with his brother E. F. Benson, with whom he shared it for some years, Arthur Benson's visits were infrequent compared with those of the American novelist Edith Wharton, who was to become one of his closest literary friends in his later years. The account which she gave of Lamb House and its owner in her autobiography, *A Backward Glance,* well matches that of Arthur Benson. Like Benson, Mrs Wharton felt that with Henry 'the pride that apes humility concerned itself (oddly enough) with material things', such as his table fare.[46]

He lived in terror of being thought rich, worldly or luxurious, and was forever contrasting his visitors' supposed opulence and self-indulgence with his own hermit-like asceticism, and apologizing for his poor food while he trembled lest it should be thought too good. I have often since wondered if he did not find our visits more of a burden than a pleasure, and if the hospitality he so conscientiously offered and we so carelessly enjoyed did not give him more sleepless nights than happy days.

I hope not; for some of my richest hours were spent under his roof. From the moment when I turned the corner of the grass-grown street mounting steeply between squat brick houses, and caught sight, at its upper end, of the wide Palladian window of the garden-room, a sense of joyous liberation bore on me. There *he* stood on the doorstep, the white-panelled hall with its old prints and crowded book-cases forming a background to his heavy loosely-clothed figure. Arms outstretched, lips and eyes twinkling, he came down to the car, uttering cries of mock amazement and mock humility at the undeserved honour of a visit. The arrival at Lamb House was an almost ritual performance, from those first ejaculations to the large hug and the two solemn kisses executed in the middle of the hall rug. Then, arm in arm, through the oak-panelled morning-room we wandered out on to the thin worn turf of the garden, with its ancient mulberry tree, its unkempt flower-borders, the gables of Watch-bell Street peeping like village gossips over the creeper-clad walls, and the scent of roses spiced with a strong smell of the sea. Up and down the lawn we strolled with many pauses, exchanging news, answering each other's questions, delivering messages from the other members of the group, inspecting the strawberries and lettuces in the tiny kitchen-garden, and the chrysanthemums 'coming along' in pots in the greenhouse; till at length the parlour-maid appeared with a tea-tray, and I was led up the rickety outside steps to the garden-room, that stately and unexpected appendage to the unadorned cube of the house.

In summer the garden-room, with its high ceiling, its triple window commanding the grass-grown declivity of West Street, and its other window looking along another ancient street to the Gothic mass of the parish church, was the centre of life at Lamb House. Here, in the morning, James dictated to his secretary, striding incessantly up and down the room, and in the afternoon and evening, when the weather was too cool for the garden, sat with outstretched legs in his deep armchair before the hearth, laughing and talking with his guests.

On the whole he was happy at Rye, and in spite of the house-keeping cares which he took so hard, the change was all to the good for a man who could never resist invitations, yet was wearied and irritated by the incessant strain of social life in London. At Rye, in summer at least, he had as many guests as his nerves could endure, and his sociable relations with his neighbours – among whom were, at one time, his beloved friends, Sir George and Lady Prothero – must have prevented his feeling lonely. He was very proud of his old house, the best of its sober and stately sort in the town, and he who thought himself so detached from material things tasted the simple joys of proprietorship when, with a deprecating air, he showed his fine Georgian panelling and his ancient brick walls to admiring visitors.

In spite of Henry's deprecatory allusions to the simple fare provided for his guests, it seems that the guests were well enough served. Gerard Hopkins, the translator and critic, once recalled a characteristic incident when as a boy in his early teens he spent a week-end at Lamb House and how 'the house was run in that beautiful American lavish manner in which nothing was too much trouble'. One of the things always done for the guests was that they had breakfast in their rooms. At least, they were supposed to have breakfast in their rooms, if they felt so inclined. 'But also there was a large breakfast laid out in the dining-room, and my father, thinking I was too young to indulge in breakfast upstairs, sacrificed his own comfort and insisted on going down to the dining-room with me. So we entered the dining-room, and there was an enormous, luxurious display of side dishes and ham and eggs and scrambled eggs and kidneys and God knows what, and suddenly I noticed at the far end James standing lost in a kind of brooding fit, heavy and portentous and looking at the table. He didn't see us come in, and as we entered we heard this remarkable sentence from him; looking at the table, he said, "Oh, what a woeful waste of wonder!" '

According to his devoted manservant Burgess Noakes, who

entered his service in 1901, Henry's favourite drink was barley
water, to which lemon and sugar were added. A jug of this
beverage always stood on the sideboard. But Henry was never a
teetotaller, although he drank sparingly of alcohol. 'When he
had company', Burgess Noakes recalled, 'there was always
plenty for his guests, anything they wanted, on the table;
and then, of course, he would take a glass of claret, you know,
with his dinner, and after dinner, why coffee – and then he'd
take a small liqueur, more out of courtesy to his guests, I mean.
But otherwise he never touched anything'. He was likewise a
moderate smoker, according to Burgess, confining himself
mainly to cigarettes. 'When he was dictating, he used to
smoke a little bit then, probably to concentrate his mind on'.[47]

Different features of Lamb House and its master impressed
different visitors. What always remained in H. G. Wells's
memory, for instance, was the table with its display of headgear, gloves and walking sticks suited to various social occasions laid out in the entrance hall. 'On the table (an excellent
piece) in his hall at Rye lay a number of caps and hats, each
with its appropriate gloves and sticks, a tweed cap and a stout
stick for the Marsh, a soft comfortable deerstalker if he were to
turn aside to the Golf Club, a iight-brown felt hat and a cane
for a morning walk down to the Harbour, a grey felt hat with a
black band and a gold-headed cane of greater importance, if
afternoon calling in the town was afoot.'[48]

The longer he lived in Lamb House, the more Henry James
came to love it. 'All the good things that I hoped of the place
have, in fact, properly bloomed and flourished here', he wrote
soon after he had settled in. A year later he could say that 'the
quiet essential amiability of Lamb House only deepens with
experience' and that he continued to find it 'ravishing'.
Whenever he went abroad, it was the goal to which he gratefully returned. '*Never* again will I leave it', he wrote from the
south of France on the occasion of his first separation, and
years later in America he was prepared to give 'the whole
bristling State of Connecticut' for 'the old battered purple
wall' of the 'poor dear little Lamb House garden'. To Edward
Warren, he wrote: 'I have been to the South, the far end of

Florida, etc. – but I prefer the far end of Sussex! In the heart
of the orange-groves I yearned for the shade of the old L.H.
mulberry tree. So you see I am loyal. . . .'[49] Even when failing
health and the solitude and confinement of the Rye winters
drove him to spend more and more of his time in London, he
continued to cherish 'the blessed, the invaluable, little old
refuge-quality of dear L.H.'[49]

[SIX]

Rye society in those days consisted of perhaps a score of
households besides the local shopkeepers and tradesmen. There
were one or two writers and artists, but the majority of the
residents were retired folk, soldiers, sailors and civil servants,
besides whom there was the usual run of professional people to
be met with in any English country town, such as lawyers
and doctors, not to mention various old ladies. The principal
industry, indeed the only one, was fishing. Henry mixed
freely with everyone in the 'antient town' and seems to have
been generally liked, although he was not always understood.
For his part, he appreciated his neighbours, who treated him
with profound respect. But one lady thought it was a great
pity that he did not play bridge. 'For he really has a very good
clear mind,' she said. Another neighbour, to whom he took a
fancy, was the travel writer and sportsman, Arthur Bradley,
who later recorded his recollections of him at this time.

He attended Rye tea-parties freely, had beautiful manners and no aversion to local gossip, which was of course in
his favour. His talk over the tea table was generally quite
light and human, but always whimsical. He had no trace of
American accent. Indeed his diction was ultra-fastidious, like
that of the older University dons. There was more than a
touch of his books in his talk, when he would raise his hand
and half close his eyes in quest of exactly the right word,
which, when found, not seldom brought a twinkle into his
eyes as he met yours. For the gesture had a half-conscious
touch of humour in it.

He was always very nice to me, partly because I had written a good many books, though they were not the sort he read – when he read anything – and also because I was the only person in the locality who knew America as a former resident and understood his personal and local allusions. Not that he was partial to his countrymen in general. The tone in which he pronounced the words 'Middle West' was worth hearing.[50]

Bradley found Henry 'a stout, cheerful, humourous and altogether delightful person with a noble head and twinkling eye, which did not, however, detract from an abiding sense of dignity'. They went for walks together along Camber Sands, and on the return to Rye would often drop in for tea at the Golf Club, to which Henry belonged, although 'he would have been the first to make merry at the idea of swinging a club'. Indeed he was much intrigued by the local passion for this pastime. Once, when he was coming back from Camber to Rye by the tram, a golfer buttonholed Henry and told him a long and boring story about how many strokes he had gone round in. Finally, Henry seized him by the lapel of his jacket and said: 'My dear fellow, what a princely expenditure of time!' To E. F. Benson, also a keen golfer, he once described the game as 'some beflagged jam pots, I understand, my dear Fred, let into the soil at long but varying distances – a swoop, a swing, a flourish of steel, a dormy'. He liked to tell the story of a certain prosperous neighbour in Rye who was taken by his wife to Rome for the first time and asked what he thought of it. 'Nothing at all' was the reply. 'It has the worst golf course in Europe!' This gave Henry huge delight, according to Bradley. 'It was not the mere absorption in amusements that puzzled him, but the self-complacency which so often accompanied it.'[51]

'He talked to the people in Rye, the fishmonger and the greengrocer's wife exactly the way he'd talk to me or you', one visitor to Lamb House recalled. 'He didn't talk down to them at all, and they all loved him.'[52] Although he liked children – his goddaughter Dorothy Warren adored him in return –

occasionally he seems to have been too much for the Rye youngsters. Hugh Walpole remembered once walking with him in the fields beyond the town, when two small, very grubby children opened the gate for them.

He smiled beneficently, felt in his deep pocket for coppers, found some and then began an elaborate explanation of what the children were to buy. They were to go to a certain sweet shop because there the sweets were better than at any other; they were to see that they were not deceived and offered an inferior brand, for those particular sweets had a peculiar taste of nuts and honey with, he fancied, an especial flavour that was *almost* the molasses of his own country. If the children took care to visit the right shop and insisted that they should have only that particular sweet called, he fancied, 'Honey-nut' – or was it something with 'delight' in it? 'Rye's Delight' or 'Honey Delights' or – But at this moment the children, who had been listening open-mouthed, their eyes fixed on the pennies, of a sudden took fright and turned, running and roaring with terror across the field.

He stood, bewildered, the pennies in his hand. What had he done? What had he said? He had meant nothing but kindness. Why had they run from him crying and screaming? He was greatly distressed, going over every possible corner of it in his mind. He alluded to it for days afterwards.[53]

'He had a great reputation as a talker and people enjoyed quoting some of his strange and complicated sayings, but he didn't want to talk about his own work, except perhaps to a few very special friends', his secretary Theodora Bosanquet recalled. 'So on fine afternoons he could be seen perambulating about the old town or along the road over Romney Marsh. Anyone watching the progress might be sure that from time to time Henry James would stop still and stand facing his companion putting all the force of his mental energy into finding and uttering the right words for the thing he was trying to convey.'[54] Once, when attending the funeral of some local civic dignitary, he found himself about the middle of a long

column, marching two and two up Point Hill to the cemetery.
The procession reached one of the spots where he was accus-
tomed to halt on his daily walks, often for a chat with a
friend, and on this solemn occasion, he was seized by a fit of
absent-mindedness. 'He stopped as usual, and, turning round
to his companion, began an oration. Some dozen or more
couples behind him, being thus brought to a standstill, were
impatiently marking time, while the foremost half of the
column were marching on up the hill. His friend, not a little
embarrassed, managed to hook the great man by the arm and
gently slip out of the procession to take the last place in the
rear, which did not catch up with the main body till the
cemetery was nearly reached.'[55]

He had a profound respect for the Corporation of Rye,
whose history went back to the thirteenth century, although
he never himself aspired to membership of this body which was
chosen by popular election. Indeed it is doubtful whether
he could have been a member on account of his United States
nationality. Once, when by an oversight his name was included
in the voters' list for Rye, he was considerably perturbed in
mind, since he felt that this jeopardized his citizenship. One of
the councillors, who later became mayor, was a local stationer,
whose name was Joseph Adams, and who numbered Henry
among his best customers. It was to Mr Adams that he protested at his inclusion among the Rye voters at elections and
impressed upon him that he was an American citizen. One
year Adams was a member of a municipal delegation from the
town to its namesake in New York, and in the course of their
visit the delegation went to the White House, where they were
received by President Theodore Roosevelt. When Adams told
the President that Henry James was one of the most esteemed
residents in Rye, England, the President was delighted. 'Henry
James', he exclaimed. 'I know him well. He has been my guest
on two or three occasions. When you return home, will you
convey to him my very kindest regards?'[56]

Henry was greatly touched when this message was duly
delivered to him one morning towards the end of 1907. He
even interrupted his dictating to receive the stationer in Lamb

House. 'Really Americans *are* kind', he told his secretary when
he had seen Mr Adams. 'He really had the time of his life, and
he's just been up to say that the President of the United
States has sent me his special remembrances. Fancy a message
from President Roosevelt sent to me – through Adams!'

Many of what his secretary called his strange and complicated sayings, as well as the circumstances which gave rise
to them, have been collected by Simon Nowell-Smith in his
engaging anthology, *The Legend of the Master*. According to
E. F. Benson, Henry once described a call he paid on some
neighbours at Rye, how he rang the bell and nothing happened,
how he waited and waited, and how at last steps along the
passage and the door was slowly opened, and 'from the dusky
entry there emerged something black, something canine'.[57]
On the whole he liked animals, except cats, and owned a
succession of dogs, although he was once heard at one of his
own tea parties on the lawn at Lamb House to refer to a
neighbour's albino Pekingese as 'a positive emetic'. On
another occasion, when Henry received some visitors and the
conversation flagged, for they were a little shy, one of them
praised the canary, which at that time he kept in a cage in the
drawing-room. 'Yes, yes,' said the Master, 'the little creature
sings his song of adoration each morning with – er – the
slightest modicum of encouragement from me'.[58] But he
hated cats and would always chase them out of the garden
whenever he saw them. He once described to some friends how
'under the extreme provocation of its obscene caterwauling' he
had killed one on his lawn. 'The act was followed by nausea
and collapse'.[59]

When three actresses who were staying at Winchelsea
expressed a desire to come over to Rye and call upon him,
they were invited to tea. 'Were they pretty?' asked Edmund
Gosse, when Henry told him about their visit. 'Pretty!'
Henry exclaimed. 'Good heavens!' Then, with the air of
one who would be scrupulously just, as Gosse put it, he
added: 'One of the poor wantons had a certain cadaverous
grace'.[60]

Henry himself usually presided at the Lamb House tea

parties, pouring the tea and passing round the cups. Once, when Joseph Conrad and Ford Madox Hueffer and their wives were invited, Henry inadvertently passed the first cup to Mrs Hueffer. This provoked the latter to remark with an absence of tact to Mrs Conrad afterwards: 'Did he give me my tea first because he thinks I'm older than you!' 'I don't know', replied Jessie Conrad, controlling her inclination to laugh – she was in fact Mrs Hueffer's senior – 'Anyhow you can hardly expect me to make a scene and insist on having mine first on that account, can you?'[61]

It was not often that the Master was at a loss for a word or a phrase however long in time the *mots justes* took to evolve. Arthur Bradley recalled one such occasion when he was sitting in the garden at Lamb House with William Meredith, the great George's son, who was a director of the publishing house of Constable. Henry's long sustained efforts to send a suitable greeting to his fellow novelist gave the visitors some amusement. 'William, tell your dear father' – there would be a pause, followed by a slap on the head. Then, after another pause, 'Tell your father, William —' Another slap and a longer pause followed, whilst a suitably composed message was struggling for birth. Finally, after two or three more bangs on the head, it finished in anticlimax. 'William, give your father my love', was all William Meredith eventually had to convey to his father.

Americans used to disturb him during his working hours, often without introductions and in search of autographs. 'My devastating countrymen' he called them, but on the whole he bore their intrusions remarkably well. Others, notably amateur artists and art schools, would often crowd round his doorstep with their easels and sketch books, since the vista seen from the front door of Lamb House up the street, taking in the church and the old house with the crooked chimney where Queen Elizabeth had stayed on her visit to the town in 1573, was a favourite subject for the artist's brush and crayon. According to his friend Bradley, Henry used to declare that he often could not get out of Lamb House without 'taking a flying leap over the heads of art and industry'.

Another diverting scene which Bradley recalled occurred at a musical afternoon in a large house near Rye. Bradley was sitting exactly opposite Henry who was perched on a cushioned window-seat with a lady beside him. An orchestral piece was in progress, and Henry who was not particularly musical, was wrapped in thought, his eyes fixed on the floor and a concentrated frown on his face. The lady, on the other hand, was obviously a musical enthusiast, since she was swaying her head from side to side in time with the music. She was wearing a hat with a feather which had a drooping tip to it. Each time she swayed in her abstracted neighbour's direction the feather's tip touched and tickled his broad bald head. 'At every contact, mistaking it for a fly, and without moving a muscle of his solemn abstracted face, he shot his arm up and slapped his crown in impatience at the persistency of the supposed insect. This little scene went on till the conclusion of the piece roused him from his reverie and the swaying lady had settled down, to ask him, no doubt, what he thought of the performance'.[62]

It was a close-knit little society in Rye during those vintage years. But Henry was not impervious to the changing face of the town as time went on, particularly when some of the fine old half-timbered houses were pulled down by the speculative builder to make room for shops and banks. 'Rye meanwhile is going to the dogs', he wrote to Mrs Ford Hueffer in 1908, 'with increase of population, villas, horrible cheap suburbs, defacements, general ruinations.'[63] But these changes had no affect upon the cloistered seclusion of Lamb House and its lovely old walled garden. 'I hope you won't undervalue the possession of a house in the country', he told his friend Gosse, who was thinking of securing a similar retreat for himself. 'Cling to it, believe in it; don't sacrifice or surrender it. It is *everything* to have one – a refuge out of London. . . . *You won't get another,* and I find this asylum has been of unspeakable worth to me.'[64]

[SEVEN]

Towards the end of 1907, a young man named Sydney Waterlow came to live at Rye. An old Etonian and classical scholar
of Cambridge, Waterlow had been in the Diplomatic Service,
but he had suffered a serious illness with much loss of weight,
which obliged him to resign after only five years in the service.
In the hopes of regaining his health, he settled in Rye, where
he occupied himself in translating Greek plays and mixing with
the local society. He was widely read in English literature as
well as the ancient classics, and Henry whose acquaintance he
made soon after his arrival was attracted by his obvious
intellectual qualities. During the next three years they saw a
good deal of each other, particularly on walks, and from time to
time Waterlow would record his impressions of Henry and his
talk in the diary he kept at this time. Some revealing extracts
follow from this diary, hitherto unpublished except for one or
two short passages.[65]

November 9, 1907. . . . H.J. said the presence of the work
house was a drawback to the sites of Rye Hill. Figures of woe
on the roads. We fell to discussing the problem of the tramps
who come out of the casual ward and ask for bread and
cheese. Should one give it them, and so turn one's establishment into an adjunct of the Union, incidentally defeating
the ends of the Poor Law? He said that no doubt the organi-
zation of a supply of bread and cheese would tend to make
this particular Union fashionable in picturesque – in
Bohemian circles. But there was no problem for him: the
supply *must* be arranged, in spite of the disagreeableness of
having your maids spending their time distributing suste-
nance to possibly truculent tramps. As for the economic
bugbear which is constantly poking its nose into these
questions, he would like to kick its bottom.

December 2, 1907. . . . We talked about Mrs Wharton. He
said that Lily in *The House of Mirth* was simply Madame
Bovary transplanted; both were romantic, sentimental
creatures, in love with luxury.
At tea he abounded in gossip about Rye people.

December 7, 1907. In the afternoon a longish walk with H. James. He talked of [George] Meredith in terms of the most generous admiration – of the heroism of his life, his struggle against adverse circumstances and poverty, the high and gallant spirit with which he sat and watched bodily decrepitude creep on (it seems his legs began to fail some time ago) with never a syllable of complaint. He described his conversation: always a monologue with no opportunity for interchange of ideas: a piling up of one fantastic brilliant idea on another (as in his tirades against the English whom he always speaks of as They, with a glance at his own Celtic stock) until he caps the structure with some final absurdity and it all comes down like a house of cards, himself laughing at the crash more heartily than anyone else.

We had begun by talking about G.M.'s Italian novels: he had lately been re-reading *Sandra Belloni* and had been amazed to find in how many ways it was extraordinarily bad. The apparent vagueness of idea and plan, so that you never knew where you were or what it was all about, astonishes him; and yet there are those scenes and passages of exquisite beauty, with the breath of greatness blowing through it all, good and bad alike. *Vittoria,* he said, was like the opening of a series of windows on history. He gives you glimpses, but is never doing things really from the inside. G.M. had gone out as a newspaper correspondent and had only a very hurried and perfunctory contact with scenes and events, having arrived too late for the fighting. Not indeed that that mattered. You give these men of genius an inch and they take an ell (here repeating a phrase he used in *Partial Portraits*): with them a hint or a glimpse is a key to unlock vast treasure-houses. But H.J. is always beset by a sense of the immense difficulty of being really inside things; the Italian events, for instance, had been of his own time, and he evidently feels it impossible that any writer should adequately reproduce their real proportions and complexities.

This train of thought was started by my mentioning G. M. Trevelyan and his *Garibaldi*. Here particularly, H.J. remarked, how hopeless to expect anything like an inside view from a mind of such narrow, rigid, Macaulay-cum-Arnold simplicity! George Meredith, of course, is a genius, and not in the same boat; but yet how far from the realities of life he is! Think, for instance, of his enthusiasm for French things and his fancied immersion in the French character; and all the time how profoundly, how extravagantly misinformed! Then again what are we to make of the England which he draws; an England of fabulous 'great' people, of coaching and prize-fighting and yachting, flavoured with the Regency, yet incapable of precise mention anywhere in space or time. . . .

H.J. has an extraordinary faculty of creating vivid pictures of persons in words. He adds, quite slowly, always taking his time about getting precisely the right epithet, one touch after another, until the whole portrait stands out clearly.

January 8, 1908. . . . After lunch met **H.J.** in the street and brought him back to tea. He is adventuring himself on the stage again and talked of this at great length. Forbes-Robertson is going to produce the little play which he wrote years ago for Ellen Terry, and which owing to the flightiness of that lady and 'the abysmal perfidy of the stage' never saw the light as a play and was printed by him as a story called *Covering End.* He has worked over this with excitement and interest – the interest of the absorbing dramatic form – and has turned it into a 3-act piece, the curtain merely to fall between the acts with no intervals.

Then, feeling that as he had taken the plunge he might as well take it thoroughly while he was about it, he had cast about among his old stories to see whether there was any that could be dressed up as a short play, and had ascertained from Forbes-Robertson that he would gladly put on a short piece, if he could produce one in that way, before the longer one. At last it had struck him that a certain story (he would not tell me which) would do, if only he could overcome one supreme difficulty in it. He set himself to get over this, and worked feverishly at the thing – a gloomy, sinister little thing, he said, admirably suited for Forbes-Robertson to act, and also for her – faced the difficulties, compressed it into the right form, and sent it off to F.R. But, strangely, he had heard nothing from F.R. though he had telegraphed his anxiety as to the fate of the piece. Why did F. make no sign? What could he be doing? He might so easily have telegraphed, at least, that he was interested, was considering it.*

And so he rambled on, speculating as to F's possible attitude and motives. I thought the whole conversation rather pathetic as bringing out his constant preoccupation with drama. The stage still fascinates him, and he can't get away from the idea that he really does know how to handle the dramatic form. Thus he is always saying that that form, in spite of its many faults, has the one great compensating merit – the merit of intensity. Yet it is impossible not to feel that this second assault on the stage will be a failure.

January 16, 1908. In the afternoon A[lice Dew] and I called for H. James, and we all went over a new fishing smack which has just been turned out from the little ship building yard on the south side of Rye. He came back with us to tea, and described at considerable length and in a very dramatic way the agonies which he had endured at the hands of a Boston dentist during six months when his mouth was being entirely renovated the last time he was in America.

January 31, 1908 . . . H.J. began talking about politics, the immense waste of talk and energy and solemnity that Parliament is. He often wondered how so complex and cumbersome a thing as the British Empire managed to go on at all; there must be some mysterious tough element in it; perhaps it was simply easier for it to go on than to stop.

He said that the older he grew the more acutely and passionately did he feel the huge absurdity and grotesqueness

---

* This play was *The Saloon* which had been adapted from *Owen Wingrave*. Forbes-Robertson turned it down, as did the Stage Society. It was eventually produced as a 'curtain raiser' at the Little Theatre in London in 1911.

of things, the monstrous perversity of evil. He also said his taste grew more and more delicate and sensitive. I said I found I attached less and less importance to taste. A foolish remark; but it drew the reply: 'Attach importance! That isn't what one does or ever did to it. Why it attaches importance to me!' He felt tempted to call himself a rabid Socialist, so often does a great wind carry him off his feet and set him down somewhere far beyond and ahead of the present world. He couldn't make up his mind about Protection v. Free Trade: the question was too enormous. Yet he felt, deep down, that the things he respected were ranged on the side of Free Trade, and *vice versa*. He thought the Women Suffragists probably had about them all the signs of the beginning of a great movement in spite of the ease of ridiculing them for desiring martyrdom on such cheap terms, 'for the terms *are* cheap.'

. . . He suggested a good subject for a dissertation, the vulgarity of modern French literature. . . . The vulgarity he defined as consisting, not in the absence, but in the badness of their moral standards. They are vitiated through and through, blind to all distinction between good and evil: hence that emptiness and thinness in their work which is what we mean by vulgarity. And it is just as real, he insisted, in France as in England, though masked in France by perfection of form. In England there is constant vulgarity of form in addition to other vulgarities.

I remarked that a good illustration of his point was the contrast between Tourgenieff and the literary circle in which he lived in Paris. He agreed, and said that once you got the Teutonic element you escaped the peculiar French vulgarity: the French genius was limited in spite of its definite and amazing good qualities. He told how Daudet had conceived an entirely false idea of what T. thought of him – an idea based solely on casual friendly intercourse; when something was published showing that T. regarded him with mild liking mixed with amusement at his antics – T. described him as a *'faux bon enfant'* – D. raised the cry of *'trahison'*.

Flaubert (H.J. said), for whom he always had a warm corner in his heart, was head and shoulders above the rest of them. His letters to his niece, indiscreetly published, are a wonderful picture. They show him *en pantoufles,* with trousers loose, unbuttoned, sitting on his W.C., scribbling away to her. He was a gentleman, though sometimes not without a touch of cabotinage. None of the others were gentlemen. De Goncourt was only a '*gentilhomme.*'

On another occasion, when Waterlow had been reviewing a posthumous volume of Lord Acton's essays, he talked to Henry about the historian, mentioning his views in the domain of political theory; for example, that Austria was nearly the ideal state, his condemnation of the North in the American Civil War, and his hatred of the modern theory of nationality. Henry agreed with Waterlow that this was 'all verbal juggling.'

'How unreal,' he said, 'how remote it all is from the realities of practical life! Acton was an intellectual dilletante, wallowing in curious intellectual luxury. An interesting figure, of course, from his social station and his cosmopolitanism: it's rare one finds anyone at once so distinguished and so cosmopolitan. But he must have been stupid at bottom. There must have been a great fund of stupidity in anyone who could write such long letters to Mary Gladstone. He never got his nose down to the grindstone of facts.'

This was only a vague personal impression, based on casual meetings, Henry was careful to point out: he had never read anything of Acton's. Nevertheless, Waterlow thought it 'singularly clear sighted and correct'.[66]

Another literary contemporary on whom Henry held forth to Waterlow was the Norwegian dramatist Henrik Ibsen.

He couldn't believe that Ibsen's highly evolved dramatic art sprang as it were out of nothing. He must, he thought, have been largely indebted to the French, though he professed to be hardly able to read French, and said he loathed Dumas. This may have been a lie. Or he may, in his early time at Rome, have gone often to the play. The Italian theatre was then fed and inspired by French plays.

What a bare, poor, miserable existence he had! What absence of contacts! That horrible café life, for instance:

when he would sit day after day on the red plush benches, buttoned up in his black frock coat, glowering at everyone and drinking – champagne of all things, and more of it than was good for him. What a way of establishing contact with life![67]

August 10, 1908. Went for a walk in the afternoon with William James, to the sea by Camber Castle. Very pleasant. He is much easier to get on with than Henry, mainly because he is simpler and full of enthusiasms and freshness, whereas Henry is jaded and reticent.

The last entry about Henry James, in Sydney Waterlow's diary for November 29th, 1911, described a dinner party in London at which Henry explained why he no longer spent the winter in Rye.

Rather a gathering of celebrities, very ill-assorted, and all more or less uncomfortable. There was H. James, H. G. Wells, Lady Mond, the Frederick Macmillans, Herbert Trench, Gertrude Kingston and various smaller fry. I thought them all vulgar frauds except H.J. and H.G.W. These two, I fancy, had not met since H.G.W. became disreputable, and it was amusing to see them, moving round one another suspiciously, like cat and dog. . . .

I hadn't seen H.J. since William James died, and I was overcome by emotion at meeting him again. He was kind and elaborate as ever. An amusing incident occurred before dinner. He was standing with his hand affectionately on my shoulder, orating to me in circumvolutions, explaining that he couldn't live at Rye in the winter. 'Little Rye – poor little Rye – I find life there intolerable – yes, Rye has had to be deserted – no, not *permanently* deserted, heaven forbid – but I have had to make a nest – a perch – for myself in London, which involves the desertion of Rye for the winter – only temporarily, *hibernatially* speaking.'

In the middle of this 'Mr Galsworthy' was announced, and our hostess brought up to us a dapper little man with turned up moustaches and brass-buttoned white waistcoat, and interrupted H.J. with 'Mr James, I don't think you know Mr Galsworthy'. Whereupon H.J. breaks off and turns to look at the intruder. A puzzled look comes over his face, followed by amazement, almost horror and disgust; then, after a few moments, 'Surely – surely you are not Mr *John* Galsworthy'. By this time the little man is dreadfully embarrassed, and can only stammer out 'No . . . no . . . I am his cousin'. Then H.J. with 'Oh, ah, hem' and a chuckle, turns back to me, saying. 'Now I can continue my statement!'

But Rye always remained very near to his heart. Even amid the winter rains and storms he found that Rye 'dared to be cheerful', while, from the opposite hill, Winchelsea merely had 'the courage of its desolation.'[68]

Four ❧ The Lamb Household

It was characteristic of Ford Madox Hueffer that he should have credited Henry James with the employment of seven servants at Lamb House – housekeeper, butler, upper house-maid, lower housemaid, 'tweeny' maid, knife-boy and gar-dener. This exaggeration may be partly due to Hueffer's having seen different servants performing their duties at different times, although he was given to romancing in his various volumes of reminiscences, and his stories about his friends and acquaintances certainly lost nothing in the telling. The truth was that Henry kept an indoor staff of four, namely manservant, cook, parlour-maid and house-maid, who all 'lived in'. Besides these, there was George Gammon, the gardener, whose cottage was conveniently situated in a corner of the garden. His wages were twenty-two shillings a week.

As a bachelor, Henry was well enough served, although he had his occasional domestic trials. On September 19th, 1901, he wrote: 'I have seen, as it were, my two guests, and my tardy servants, to bed. ... It has been a more convivial 24 hours than my general scheme of life often permits. ... But I hate the care of even a tiny and twopenny house and wish I could farm out the same. If someone would only undertake it – and the back garden – at so much a year, I would close with the offer and ask no questions'. His momentarily despairing mood was caused by the conduct of his manservant Smith. The latter and his wife, who had come as butler-valet and cook when Henry moved to De Vere Mansions and had once been described by him as 'the mainstay of my existence', had continued in his service at Lamb House. Unfortunately Mr Smith's fondness for liquor became such a nuisance that, after enduring it for nearly four years, the Master decided that he must get rid of him. He wrote again on the subject a fortnight later.

I'm just emerging from a domestic cyclone that has, in one way and another cost me so much time, that, pressed as I am with a woefully backward book, I can only for the present hug my writing-table with convulsive knees.* The figure doesn't fit – but the postponement of all joy, alas, does.

My two old man-and-wife servants (who had been with me sixteen years) were, a few days ago, shot into space (thank heaven at last!) by a whirlwind of but 48 hours duration; and though the absolute rupture came and went in that time, the horrid accompaniments and upheaved neighbourhoods have represented a woeful interruption. But it's over, and I have plunged again (and am living, blissfully, for the present, with a house-maid and a charwoman, and immensely enjoying my simplified state and my relief from what I see now was a long nightmare).[1]

'I sit amid the ruins of a once happy household, clutching a charwoman with one hand, and a knife-boy – from Lilliput – in the other', Henry wrote a little later to Miss Muir Mackenzie, who had helped him with gardening advice and whom he had nicknamed 'the Grand Governess'. 'I've picknicked (for very relief) ever since – making futile attempts at reconstruction for which I have had no time, and yet which have consumed so much of it that none has been left, as I began by hinting, for correspondence. I've been up to London over it, and haunted Hastings, and wired to friends, and almost appealed to the Grand Governess – only deterred by the fear of hearing from her that it isn't her province. Yet I did wonder whether I couldn't lawfully work it in under kitchen-garden. No matter; my fate closes round me again, and the first thing I think of now when I wake up in the morning is that a "cook-house-keeper" in a Gorringe costume is to arrive next week. I tremble at her.'[2]

---

* The book, which he was writing at this time, was *The Wings of the Dove*. It was finished in the following May and published in August, 1902.

The Lilliputian 'knife-boy' – although he did not stand much over five feet in height, he was a future bantam weight champion of Sussex – had been engaged shortly before the Smiths left. His name was Burgess Noakes and his mother had recently been left a widow, so that it was necessary for him to go out to work at fourteen. Indeed, in order to get the job, his mother, who accompanied him for the interview with his future employer, pretended that he was two years older than he actually was. 'I can see Mr James in the chair now, in the drawing room', Burgess Noakes was able to recall after a lapse of sixty-five years. 'He had a beard in those days. He said I was rather small for my age, but I could come along and he would give me so much, and if I suited, he would raise my wages.'[3] And so young Noakes was taken on as house-boy at the modest wage of four shillings a week with all his meals, although for the time being he continued to lodge with his mother round the corner in Watchbell Street. He was destined to graduate from house-boy to butler-valet and to serve his master with touching devotion until Henry's death.

The cook-housekeeper, whose appearance on the domestic front seems to have been so much dreaded by Henry, turned out to be a great success, whether or not she bought her clothes at the fashionable Gorringe's stores. Although her expression was somewhat forbidding, she always treated her master with the greatest respect and would even curtsy to him on entering his presence. But he did not think so well of the housemaid's clothes, at least when she was off duty. Once, when he was dictating to his secretary in the Garden Room, he interrupted himself on catching sight, out of the window, of the said housemaid, to give vent to his feelings on the subject of the 'incongruous, incoherent shoddiness' of the dress of the English lower class woman, as contrasted with French women – 'a rather pet grievance of his', according to his secretary.

A propos of the housemaid, Henry once asked Ford Madox Hueffer in the course of a walk, 'Are you acquainted with the terrible, the devastating words, if I may call them so, the fiat of

Doom: "I don't know if you know, sir"? As when the housemaid comes into your bedroom in the morning and says: "I don't know if you know, sir, that the bath has fallen through the kitchen ceiling!" '[4]

However, when he was about to let Lamb House just before he revisited America some years later, Henry wrote enthusiastically about the housekeeper-cook and the rest of the Lamb House establishment to his future tenants Mrs Louise Boit and her sister Miss Horstmann.

Lamb House, Rye, Sussex. August 12, 1904. . . .
I make the house over to you, practically, just as I have been living in it, and you will find it, I make bold to say, in very good and tidy condition. I leave all the Servants, who amount to five in number, including the Gardener and the Houseboy. The latter has his meals in the house, but doesn't sleep, and the Gardener of course does neither, having his cottage close by the garden gate. You will find this functionary, George Gammon, an excellent, quiet, trustworthy fellow in all respects – a very good carpenter into the bargain and thoroughly handy at mending anything that gets broken in the house. I have endowed him with a small hand-cart, which is kept in the vault beneath the Garden-room highly convenient to the House door, and which I find quite sufficient for the conveyance of my luggage, or that of visitors, to and from the Station for all comings and goings. The distance is so short that it means, save in some extra-ordinary rain, the complete suppression of flies – which is a great simplification.

The Cook-Housekeeper, Mrs Paddington, is really, to my sense, a pearl of price; being an extremely good cook, an absolutely brilliant economist, a person of the greatest order, method and respectability, and a very nice woman generally. If you will, when you let her see you each morning, in the dining-room after breakfast, just also suffer her to take you into the confidence, a little, of her triumphs of thrift and her master-strokes of management, you will get on with her beautifully – all the more that she gets on beautifully with her fellow-servants, a thing that all 'good' cooks don't do.

133

She puts before me each week, with the Tradesmen's books, her own weekly book, by the existence of which the others are distinctly, I think, kept down. But these are matters that you will of course know all about.

The Parlour-maid, Alice Skinner, has lived with me for six years – that is with an interval of no great length, and is a thoroughly respectable, well-disposed and duly competent young woman. And the Housemaid is very pretty and gentle – and not a very, *very* bad one. The House-Boy, Burgess Noakes, isn't very pretty, but is on the other hand very gentle, punctual and desirous to please – and has been with me three years. He helps the Parlour-maid, cleans shoes, knives, doorsteps, windows, etc. and makes himself generally useful. Also takes letters to the Post-Office and does any errands. Naturally he brushes clothes and 'calls' in the morning those of his own sex who may repose beneath the roof. Lastly, though of such diminutive stature he is, I believe, nineteen years old.*

The servants were expected to look after Henry's pet dog, particularly during their master's absences. Tosca, who will be remembered at De Vere Mansions, died at Lamb House in 1899 and was buried in a corner of the garden – 'my domestic mortuary', he called it. She was followed by Tim and then by Peter, 'my admirable little Peter', ('He passed away . . . at St Leonard's, fondly attended by the local "canine specialist" – after three days of dreadful "little dysentery".') And after that by Nick, a terrier, who died in 1902. Nick's place in his master's affections was taken by Max, a 'very beautiful and valuable little Dachshund pup of the "red" species, who has been promising to be the joy of my life up to a few hours since', so he wrote to his brother on May 24th, 1903, 'when he began to develop a mysterious and increasing tumification of one side of his face, about which I must immediately have advice. The things my dogs have, and the worries I have in consequence! I already see this one settled beneath monumental alabaster in the little cemetery in the angle of my garden,

---

* Actually 17. See above p. 132.

where he will make the fifth.'* However, thanks to the
attentions of the 'canine specialist' in St Leonards, Max survived, to become, as Henry told Mrs Boit and her sister 'the
best and gentlest and most reasonable and well-mannered as
well as most beautiful small animal of his kind to be easily
come across – so that I think you will speedily find yourselves
loving him for his own sweet sake'.

The Servants, who are very fond of him and good to him,
know what he 'has', and when he has it; and I shall take it
kindly if he be not too often gratified with tid-bits between
meals. Of course what he most intensively dreams of is being
taken out on walks, and the more you are able so to indulge
him the more he will adore you and the more all the latent
beauty of his nature will come out. He is, I am happy to say,
and has been from the first (he is about a year and half old)
in very good, plain, straightforward health, and if he is
not overfed and is sufficiently exercised, and adequately
brushed (his brush being always in one of the bowls on the
hall-table – a convenient little currycomb) and Burgess is
allowed occasionally to wash him, I have no doubt he will
remain very fit. In the event, however, of his having anything at all troublesome the matter with him, kindly remember that there is an excellent 'Vet' a dozen miles away, who
already knows him, and would come by to see him, for a
moderate fee on any sign made. This person is 'Mr Percy
Woodroffe Hill,' Canine Specialist, St Leonard's-on-Sea – a
telegram would promptly reach him.

Indeed Henry felt the parting from Max as keenly as he did
from the house itself. 'I left L.H. yesterday looking so dreadfully sorry to part with me', he wrote a week later, 'and so
easy and pleasant to stay in withal, that I took refuge in bury-
ing my nose in Max's little gold-coloured back and wetting it
(the back) with my tears'. Four months later, he was writing

---

* Tosca, Tim, Peter and Nick, were buried in the south-west corner of the
garden beneath small stone slabs fixed to the wall, on which their names and
dates of death were carefully recorded. They are still there.

to Mrs Boit from his brother's home in Cambridge, Mass., and thanking his tenants for their kindness to the dog. 'Yes, I am homesick and I even yearn at times a little for curtsying Mrs P[addington] – no one curtseys to me here! But the heartbreak is nearest when I think of poor sweet-pawing little Max, for all of your patience with whom I effusively thank you. I hope he isn't too constant a burden.'[5]

[TWO]

It is interesting to compare Henry's opinion of his domestic servants with their opinion of their master and also incidentally of each other. Fortunately Burgess Noakes was still alive at the time these pages were written and the many talks their author was able to have with him yielded some noteworthy details of life at Lamb House in the Master's time. Burgess and George Gammon, the gardener, had a nickname for him. 'We used to call him "the old toff",' Burgess recalled. 'I always thought it was a very appropriate name – old toff he was, in his looks and in his manner'. Burgess also remembered his kindness. 'Oh, yes, he was very generous,' he said: 'he did a lot of good in Rye. On two or three occasions he asked me – he said he had a letter from So-and-So– did I know him, and what sort of man he was – and that sort of thing; and of course they always got help. I don't remember anyone he ever turned away from his door. And he never gave you anything less than half-a-crown. When I was a boy, and the butler was there, well, sometimes he couldn't take his afternoon walk, and of course I used to take the dog for a walk. There was always half-a-crown – yes – and if I washed the dog, I got another half-crown'.

Burgess Noakes also gave a characteristic account of his master's daily routine:

I used to call him every morning regular at eight o'clock. After that he'd have his breakfast. He'd come down about nine o'clock, and about ten o'clock would start and work with his secretary. He was very regular in his habits, and he'd work on till about one o'clock; in the summer, of course, he'd work in the Garden Room. He'd have his lunch, and after lunch, he'd take his walk. He was a stout, heavily built man, but he was very active, right to the last, too. Off he'd go with his little dog, and many a time I watched him out of the door. Before he got half way up the street towards the church, you'd see him stop, the stick would go down – there he'd stand, with his head slightly bent and his finger in his watch-chain, like that, and all of a sudden off he'd go again. But he had a habit – if he wanted to remember anything or remind himself of anything – he had a habit of tying a knot in his watch-chain, sometimes two.

'Poor little Burgess', as his employer used to refer to him, was 'so diminutive that he takes up little room, but also so athletic that he yearns to make himself generally useful; in short an intensely modest pearl.' He waited on his master at all hours. Henry objected to the use of coal gas except in the kitchen, and always used oil lamps to illuminate the living rooms. It was one of Burgess's jobs to trim them, but the lamps frequently smoked and the Master would often fall asleep late at night in his chair in his study, after he had finished his letters, which he habitually wrote after dinner, only to be awakened by the faithful Noakes, his face covered in lamp black.[6]

Nor, in spite of appearances, did Burgess Noakes have to follow the late butler's mental gymnastics when he received an order from Henry. According to Edith Wharton, 'Burgess soon learned to dispense with them, and without any outward appearance of having understood what his master was saying carried out his instructions with stolid exactitude. Stolidity was his most marked characteristic. He seldom gave any sign of comprehension when spoken to, and I remember once saying to my Alsatian maid, who was always as quick as a flash at the uptake:"Do you know, I think Burgess must be very stupid. When I speak to him I'm never even sure that he's heard what I've said." My maid looked at me gravely. "Oh, no, Madam: Burgess is remarkably intelligent. *He always understands what*

Mr James's says." And that argument was certainly con-
clusive.'

Burgess Noakes had other memories of his master which he
was able to record:

> He was very careful with his books. No one was allowed
> to touch them – only himself and I. We used to dust them
> together and never with anything but a silk handkerchief.
> There were bookcases in every room, and he knew exactly
> where every volume was placed – could go to it straight
> away.*
>
> I wasn't very talkative then. I remember particularly one
> day when he was dressing to go out to lunch; probably he
> was in the mood for talking, and I didn't say anything
> much, I suppose. So he said: 'Burgess', he said, 'why are
> you so damnably dumb?'
>
> He had beautiful clothes from the best tailors, jackets
> made in London, the trousers in Rye – those were the days
> when the two didn't match – and the trousers were held up
> by an old belt from the American Civil War. His cuff-links
> were miniature cannons. He liked to see other people well
> dressed too.
>
> He liked good food and always had the best. Sometimes
> especial delicacies were ordered from London, but always
> through the local shops. I remember when Mr Fletcher,
> the diet man, came to luncheon, with his 'Fletcherising'
> diet, he and Mr James sat munching each bit of beef sixty
> times.

'You must chew', he would tell his neighbours in Rye,
insisting that every disorder could be cured by chewing, and he
would give them copies of Mr Fletcher's book *The New Glutton
and Epicure,* which he would inscribe, begging them 'to try the
same cure'.

On the whole, Henry's regimen was one of plain living and
high thinking, and Burgess Noakes may well have exaggerated
the attractions of the table fare. According to another witness,

---

* See Appendix below for an account of the library.

Edith Wharton, 'at Lamb House an anxious frugality was combined with the wish that the usually solitary guest (there were never at most more than two at a time) should not suffer too greatly from the contrast between his or her supposed habits of luxury, and the privations imposed by the host's conviction that he was on the brink of ruin. If anyone in pecuniary difficulty appealed to James for help, he gave it without counting, but in his daily life he was haunted by the spectre of impoverishment and the dreary pudding or pie of which a quarter or half had been consumed at dinner reappeared on the table next day with its ravages unrepaired'.[7]

The parlour-maid, Alice Skinner, also lived to recall in retirement her recollections of her master:

I was always very happy with Mr James. . . . He was very particular about his appearance and about having the house 'just right.' He had some lovely furniture and it was kept beautifully. I didn't read what he wrote. He liked fish best, particularly soles. Sometimes at lunch, when he had no guests, he would walk about the house eating as if he didn't want to sit down. When he was working, he became absent-minded. One day a friend of his called at lunch time and I knew that Mr James hadn't ordered luncheon for two. I went to Mr James and told him. 'Oh, Alice', he cried out, 'oh dear, oh dear, what have I got to do?' You had to help him out a bit, and we soon got luncheon for two.

The cook told me that one day in the High Street she made a bee-line for him to tell him that she'd had the rest of the lamb made into rissoles, but she could tell as she went towards him that he hadn't the faintest idea who she was, and that he was obviously racking his brain to place her; and that only after she had spoken to him did recognition appear.

He was, what shall I say, he was quite all right, but at times – well, when he was on a book, you'd hardly dare speak to him. He was normally very pleasant, but he got irritable when people worried him and he wanted to write; when you lived in the same house with him you got used to it; his work was the one thing he lived for. Sometimes people called when he was like this, and I didn't dare tell him, and I sent them away. When interrupted during his work he would shout.

We had a lot of visitors, Americans whom he did not know coming to get his autograph. And then other authors used to come for criticism of their books. H. G. Wells was one. After dinner they'd read out loud to him. They say he was a very good critic.

All of us who stayed with him for any length of time felt we belonged. I know the housekeeper Mrs Paddington felt this – she wasn't quite as severe as she looked, though she gave that impression. Once when some people called and Mr James was away, I heard her saying to them: 'I've sent him away for my spring cleaning, and I'll not have him back till it's done!'[8]

People would also send him copies of his books to be signed and returned. He did not mind this when he was at Lamb House, but when he was away from home and the books were sent on to him he objected strongly. 'I am the happy possessor of a priceless parlour-maid, who loves doing up books, and other parcels, and does them up beautifully,' he wrote in anticipation of such a despatch. 'But if the volume comes to me here, to be inscribed, I shall have to do it up myself, an act for which I have absolutely no skill and which I dread and loathe and tumble it forth clumsily and insecurely!'

More than once Henry issued luncheon invitations and then forgot about them until the guests made an unexpected appearance. On one occasion, when he was in the Garden Room dictating to his secretary, Theodora Bosanquet, shortly before one o'clock, a knock on the front door was heard. Henry tiptoed to the window and looked out cautiously. 'I don't know who they are', he said. 'Motor people – two of them – done up in goggles.'

A few moments later, Burgess Noakes came in, and the following dialogue took place between him and his master:

BURGESS: A lady and gentleman to see you, sir.
H.J: But what are their names? Always say their names.

BURGESS: Mr and Mrs Clark, sir.

H.J: Clark?

BURGESS *(uncompromisingly):* Clark.

H.J: What are they like: Are they young or old or blue or green?

BURGESS: Middle-aged, sir.

H.J. *(with a horrid memory vaguely dawning)* The gentleman – is he a little, elderly man, short?

BURGESS: Yes, sir. They seem to think you're expecting them, sir.

H.J. *(groans and falls back in his chair, covering his face with his hands)* Oh, good Lord! *(Pause)* They've come to lunch. I asked them. I'd forgotten all about it. I must *(rising)* go and see Mrs Paddington at once. Oh *(going out), why* can't people keep away?

He came back after a few minutes and explained that the visitors were honeymooning in Brighton. 'You see', he said, 'I ought to have known. They wrote to tell me. I put the letter in a conspicuous place. I put the date in my book – but I absolutely forgot.'

His secretary expressed the hope that Mrs Paddington had risen to the occasion.

'Oh, yes, she did,' he said. 'She drew out of the oven a fillet of beef which she had been cooking for herself. "Give that to me!" I cried. But what an infernal nuisance it all is! Motor cars are the curse of the age. Before their day no one would have dreamt of coming over from Brighton or Worthing or where-ever to lunch at Rye.'[9]

The incident reminded him that he had to entertain another luncheon guest on the following day, his former publisher, William Heinemann ('as if he hadn't done me enough bad turns'), and the prospect was anything but congenial. Incidentally Heinemann came to lunch and added salt to whatever wounds he had previously inflicted by comparing the modest sales of Henry's novels with those of the popular Manx novelist Hall Caine, who, he said, had an income from writing of £30,000 a year, had 'engineered' *Queen Alexandra's Christmas Book* of her

141

photographs, and was to be made a baronet. 'What an age!' was Henry's despairing comment.*

Then there was the gardener George Gammon, by whom Henry was generally content to be guided in horticultural matters, together with the advice and plans he received from time to time from 'the Grand Governess', Miss Muir Mackenzie. Theodora Bosanquet has recalled: 'Like most Americans he left gardens entirely to professional hands – he never attempted to cultivate intimate acquaintance with his plants – he liked eating the good fruit and vegetables, he admired the flowers but he couldn't bear cut flowers. Never had them inside the house for decoration. He faithfully visited the Rye flower shows, out of respect for the gardener whose competitive entries were often rewarded by large cards stating that Henry James, Esq., had won a prize. Very good English flavour in those prize takings. Nothing like that could have happened to him in his native land.'[10]

Two letters which Henry wrote to the 'Grand Governess' in 1901 show how he had taken her advice to heart and how grateful he was to her for the results.

Lamb House, Rye, June 15, 1901. ... we cherish and inscribe on our precious records every word that drops from you, and we have begun by taking up your delightful tobacco-leaves with pious and reverent hands and consigning them to the lap of earth (in the big vague blank unimaginative border with the lupines [*sic*] etc.,) exactly in the manner you prescribe; where they have already done wonders toward peopling its desolation. It is really most kind and beneficent of you to have taken this charming trouble for us.

We acted, further, instantaneously on your hint in respect to the poor formal fuchsias – sitting up in their hot stuffy drawing-room with never so much as a curtain to draw over their windows. We haled them forth on the spot, everyone, and we clapped them (in thoughtful clusters) straight into the same capacious refuge or omnium gatherum. Then,

---

* Hall Caine was knighted in 1918 for his war propaganda work in the United States, but he never got a baronetcy.

while the fury and frenzy were upon us, we did the same by the senseless stores of geranium (my poor little 22/-a-week gardener's *idée fixe!* – we enriched the boundless receptacle with *them* as well – in consequence of which it looks quite sociable and civilized. Your touch is magical, in short, and your influence infinite. . . .

Your real place is *here* – where I would instantly ask your leave to farm myself out to you. I want to *be* farmed; I am utterly unfit to farm myself; and I do it, all round for (seeing, alas, what it is) not nearly little enough money.

Lamb House, Rye, October 17, 1901. . . . I want you in particular to know what a joy and pride your great proud and pink tobacco-present has proved. It has overlorded the confused and miscellaneous border in which your masterly eye recognised its imperative – not to say imperial – place, and it has reduced by its mere personal success all the incoherence around it to comparative insignificance. What a bliss, what a daily excitement, all summer, to see it grow by leaps and bounds and to feel it happy and hearty – as much as it could be in its strange exile and inferior company. It has all prospered – though some a little smothered by more vulgar neighbours; and the tallest of the brotherhood are still as handsome as ever, with a particular shade of watered wine-colour in the flower that I much delight in. And yet, – ninny that I am! – I don't know what to do with them for next year. My gardener opines that we leave them, as your perennial monument, just as they are. But I have vague glimmerings of conviction that we cut them down to a mere small protrusion above ground – and we probably both are fully wrong. Or do we extract precious seed and plant afresh?

Forgive my feeble (I repeat) flounderings. I feel as the dunce of an infant school trying to babble Greek to Professor Jebb (or suchlike). I am none the less hoping that the garden will be less dreadful and casual next year. We've ordered 105 roses – also divers lilies – and made other vague dashes. Oh, you should be in controlling permanence! Actually we are painfully preparing to become bulbous and parti-coloured. One *must* occupy the gardener. The grapes have been bad (bless their preposterous little pretensions!) but the figs unprecedentedly numerous. And so on, and so on.[11]

One year he won as many as thirteen prizes at 'our annual little horticultural show', mostly firsts. 'It always seems to point, more than anything else, the moral, for me, of my long expatriation and to put its "advantages" into a nutshell,' he wrote to Grace Norton after this signal triumph. 'In what corner of our native immensity could I have fallen – and practically without effort, helpless ignoramus though I be – into the uncanny flourish of a swell at local flower shows? Here it has come of itself – and it crowns my career. How I wish you weren't so far away for me to send you a box of my victorious carnations and my triumphant sweet peas! However, I remember your telling me with emphasis long years ago that you hated "cut flowers", and I have treasured your brave heresy (the memory of it) so ineffaceably as to find support in it always, and fine precedent, for a very lukewarm adhesion to them myself, except for a slight inconsistency in the matter of roses and sweet peas (both supremely lovable, I think, in their kind,) which increase and multiply and bless one in proportion as one tears them from the stem.'[12]

George Gammon, his 'good little gardener', Henry regarded as 'a real pearl of price in the way of a serving-man.' Unfortunately the gardener's charming old gabled cottage did not go with the house. With the next-door cottage it belonged to a neighbour of Henry's who at one period threatened to evict George and demolish it to make way for a modern monstrosity – 'a horrid inhuman stab at the very heart of old Rye,' as Henry described his plan. As usual in his domestic problems, Henry appealed to Edward Warren to help him disperse the 'black cloud' which had so suddenly descended and disconcerted him.[13]

Lamb House, Rye, May 24, 1903. . . . The little black cloud is that the pitiless, the almost infamous Whiteman, my opposite neighbour and proprietor of the two little old-world whitey-grey cottages at the end of my garden wall, threatens them with imminent and remorseless destruction unless the horror can be very quickly averted. I am trying, with feeblest resources, and another person or two is trying, to avert it if possible; but so far as I myself am concerned, I should derive no end of moral support, by such brief communion with you on the spot (and face to face with the threatened treasure) as would morally (I speak only of *moral* aid) back me up.

You remember well of course the small quaint structures I mean – to the right of the little eternally-sketched vista stretching from my front doorstep toward the church: of which the one nearest me has the pretty little small-paned, squarecornered bay window resting its short pedestal on the cobblestones. Both have their little old gables, colour, character, almost silvery surface, and have always been the making – the very *making* of the hundred or so watercolour sketches of the vista annually perpetrated from in front of my door. It would *go*, without them – vista, character, colour, subject, composition, everything: above all the very tradition of the little old bit of street itself, and the long-descended pleasant legend of its sketchability.

What Whiteman proposes is to put two raw, cheap, sordid workingmen's cottages and let them at 8 shillings a week apiece. My gardener has for the last year occupied the hither one (the position is of course perfect for him, and for me). I have tried to intervene and supplicate, and with the effect of the *possibility* either of purchase (not by *me* – his terms are of course colossal) or of a lease, on conditions scarcely less exhorbitant, in which I *should* have, rageingly, to play my part. The latter would be a 'repairing' lease – and it is on *that* matter that I pine for some kindly light from you: as to what it would cost me, currently, to meet the repairing obligation.

The only thing is that time rather sickeningly presses. Whiteman is shaky, and his devilish little builder, Ellis, who has completed the horrible new plans for him, is, I fear, unremittingly and intensely poisoning his mind. I am trying to get him to give me (and the other person) to the end of the week to turn round. If you can't come for a night could you, possibly, for a few hours of the day? – though I fear that my importunity makes, at the best, ducks and drakes, for you, of golden minutes, each with its beauty and its sanctity.

Happily the threatened destruction of the old cottages was averted, exactly how is not clear, but probably through Henry assuming responsibility for the repairing lease. At all events, the gardener continued to occupy his cottage for as long as his master lived at Lamb House and indeed for many years afterwards.*

[THREE]

It was not until he took Lamb House that Henry first employed a regular secretary, or amanuensis, a term which he felt more accurately described the duties of his literary assistant. Previously he used to write his books and articles in longhand and then give them to a secretarial agency to be typed. But about 1897, he began to dictate to an amanuensis, who took down his words straight on to the typewriter, and he continued this habit for the rest of his life; he would also occasionally employ the amanuensis for his correspondence, although he still used to write most of his letters in his own hand. So far as his books were concerned, the amanuensis would type his dictated words with wide-spaced lines so that Henry could make the many revisions he found necessary. The resultant script was then re-typed and sent to the printer

---

* Gammon was still living in the cottage in the summer of 1939, when E. F. Benson, the then tenant of Lamb House, wrote in his autobiography, *Final Edition*: 'He is over eighty years old, long, lean and upright with a pepper and salt beard stained with nicotine, full nine inches long from the extremity of his chin. He is not up to doing much work, and in cold weather he keeps indoors for he suffers from "me bronchitis". He has had an attack of it lately, and found great consolation in a glass of port with his dinner. Now that the weather has turned so hot he has come out to look after the garden again, busying himself with small jobs like planting out seedlings from the summer-garden and getting "his young man", a youth of about sixty, to do the heavier work. He disapproves of any change being made in the garden, which, like all proper gardeners, he considers his own, without his consent, but he allows me the produce, and is open to suggestions about flower-beds.'

after which there would be a further agonizing struggle with the proofs, which usually involved more alterations.

Henry's first amanuensis was a young Scot named Macalpine who lived in rooms beside the Hope Anchor Hotel in Watchbell Street. He worked with Henry in the mornings and in the afternoons he would often accompany him on his cycling expeditions. 'This young man is just the person to help Mr James', wrote an American visitor. 'He has a bump of reverence and appreciates his position and opportunity.' On the other hand, the quality of what Henry dictated seems to have made singularly little impact upon the Scot, judging by Henry's remarks about *The Turn of the Screw,* which seems to have been the first entire work which he dictated. 'Do you know', he said to a friend some years later, 'I wrote that story with the intention of terrifying every reader, and in the course of its composition, I thought it would be a total failure. I dictated every word of it to a Scot, who never from the first to last betrayed the slightest emotion, nor did he ever make any comment. I might have been dictating statistics. I would dictate some phrase that I thought was blood-curdling; he would quietly take this down, look up at me and in a dry voice, say "What next?" '

'My pressing want,' Henry noted at this time, 'is some sound, sane, irreproachable young type-writing and bicycling "secretary companion," the expense of which would be practically a 100-fold made up by increased facilitation of paying work. But though I consider the post enviable, it is difficult to fill. The young typists are mainly barbarians, and the civilized here are not typists.'

Macalpine ('my excellent Scotch amanuensis') left after three years to take up a better paid job, which the ever obliging Edward Warren had obtained for him at Henry's instigation. On May 12th, 1901, Henry wrote to Warren: 'A propos of the Scot, your mention of his prosperity renews my sense of gratitude, for him, to you; and also for myself. You never did a kinder stroke. It's everything to me to feel him placed. His "lady-successor" here, in Mermaid Street, is an improvement on him! And an economy!'[14]

William and his wife happened to be staying with Henry at this time, and it was Mrs Alice James who suggested that her brother-in-law should have a lady secretary, a thing hitherto unheard of in Rye. The result was that he got in touch with Miss Petherbridge's Secretarial Bureau in London and explained his requirements. Miss Mary Weld, who had been trained there, seemed to Miss Petherbridge to be most suited for the job; she was the daughter of a British judge in India and had been educated at Cheltenham Ladies College, the most stylish academy of its kind, and had been 'finished' in Berlin. When Henry's request arrived, she was having a holiday, and Miss Petherbridge wrote off to her immediately (March 27th, 1901).

I am sorry to have to ask you to cut short your holiday, but Mr Henry James wants me to send him a secretary directly after Easter, and I should like you to take the work. You ought to have some days dictation on the typewriter to prepare you for it.

When can you come back?

The work is to be done in the country and you will have to live at Rye in Sussex. It is only for a short time to begin with I believe, but he will want you later for varying periods of time. He is disposed to be extremely friendly and I think you ought to have a very pleasant time . . .

P.S. Your bicycle would be very nice there . . .

A week or so later, after she had put in some practice at the bureau, Miss Weld went down to Rye. Her future employer met her at the station and together they walked along the cobbled streets to Lamb House. Their first interview took place in the Garden Room, and Miss Weld always remembered that both of them were so nervous that they both did nothing but shake. In explaining that he liked to eliminate shorthand by dictating straight on to the typewriter, Henry said that if he paused, as he frequently did, he did not wish to feel that he was keeping her waiting. Her predecessor, he said, had smoked during these pauses. The question now arose what she was to do, as well-bred young ladies did not smoke at that time. Miss Weld demurely suggested that she might crochet or knit – and this was agreed upon.

At luncheon, where they were joined by William James and his wife, another question arose. What should the amanuensis wear for work? The secretarial college had suggested that the most appropriate clothes were a dark coat and skirt and a sailor hat, and these were decided on as satisfactory. After the meal, Mrs Alice James went with the new amanuensis in search of rooms, and suitable accommodation was eventually found in Mermaid Street, Henry later took Miss Weld round the local boat-yard, where she noted how he seemed to like talking to the boat-builders and asking how the wood was seasoned and so on. 'He was so delightful' that Miss Weld 'felt that she could have done anything for him,' and it was with this feeling that she returned to London, after it had been agreed that she should start work in a fortnight's time.

Afterwards she would recall how considerate Henry was; how during the first day's work he noticed her need for a foot-stool and got her one; how he discovered her liking for flowers and each morning would put a small bunch which he had picked beside her typewriter. She was particularly intrigued by one incident. 'I had not been working for him long when one of the Rye ladies called', she said. 'When she left Mr James thanked her for coming to see him and then she replied, "Not at all, we just wanted to make sure that Miss Weld was respectable".'

Henry wrote to the Secretarial Bureau to say how pleased he was with his new amanuensis, and Miss Petherbridge sent her the letter for her to see, asking her to return it immediately. 'I knew you would suit him', she wrote, 'but still I am sure it will hearten you to hear that he quite agrees with me.' There was only one small point which remained to be cleared up. Apparently Henry expected Miss Weld to do some Sunday work, and this was not covered by Miss Petherbridge's arrangement. 'I have written to Mr James suggesting that he shall pay you a small fee whenever you work for him on Sunday, and saying that he must settle with you personally about it. It will be rather nice for you to make a little extra money like that.'[15]

During the next three-and-a-half years, Miss Weld 'took down' four full length novels, besides numerous articles and short stories and the biography of the American poet and sculptor William Wetmore Story, which Henry James also wrote at this time. Her employer told her that of the four novels *The Wings of the Dove* 'came easiest', and he gave her a signed copy of this novel inscribed 'from her collaborator'.*

By this time he had left Heinemann, whom he once described as 'the most swindling of publishers', for the house of Methuen. The change appears to have been suggested by Mr Pinker, the literary agent, whom he now employed. At all events from 1900 onwards, with one exception, Methuen were to be the English publishers of all the remaining novels to come out in his lifetime.†

James B. Pinker was described by Ford Hueffer as 'the remarkable literary agent on whose lips hung half the young writers of that day' and by Violet Hunt as 'prince of agents, kindest friend to his clients and a great rider to hounds.' A bespectacled Scot of small stature, Pinker had at one time been editor of *Pearson's Weekly*, which he had left shortly before the turn of the century to establish his literary agency in an office in Arundel Street, off the Strand. He used to hunt twice a week, which could be done cheaply enough in those days. While older established competitors in the field tended to concentrate on the big earners, Pinker went for young authors whom he spotted as promising. His first clients included H. G. Wells, George Gissing, Joseph Conrad, Stephen Crane, besides Ford Madox Hueffer and Violet Hunt. The latter remembered sitting with him in his office and noticing the back of his head 'green with some nasty fall he had had' out hunting. It

---

* According to Miss Weld's diary, *The Wings of the Dove* was begun on July 9th, 1901, and completed on May 21st, 1902, the work involving 194 days of dictation.

† *The Soft Side, The Sacred Fount, The Better Sort, The Ambassadors, The Golden Bowl, The Finer Grain,* and *The Outcry.* The exception was *The Wings of the Dove,* which was published by Constable.

was probably one of them who advised Henry, who had previously been for a short time with A. P. Watt, to try Pinker. The arrangement seems to have worked well, although Henry was no money spinner. Still Pinker succeeded in getting more for his magazine and serial rights than he had had since the days of *Daisy Miller*.

A letter which Henry wrote to Pinker, when he was in the finishing stages of *The Golden Bowl* throws a revealing light on his technique of literary composition, and explains incidentally why Miss Weld had to work on Sundays.[16]

Lamb House, Rye, May 20, 1904. . . . I have been working on the book with unremitting intensity the whole of every blessed morning since I began it, some thirteen months ago, and I am at present within but some twelve or fifteen thousand words of Finis. But I can work only in my own way – a deucedly good one, by the same token! – and am producing the best book, I seem to conceive, that I have ever done. I have really done it fast, for what it is, and for the way I do it – *the* way I seem condemned to; which is to *overtreat* my subject by developments and amplifications that have, in large part, eventually to be greatly compressed, but to the prior operation of which the thing afterwards owes what is most durable of its quality.

I have written, in perfection, 200,000 words of the G.B. – with the rarest perfection! – and you can imagine how much of that, which has taken time, has had to come out. It is not assuredly, an economical way of work in the short run, but it is, for me, in the long; and at any rate one can proceed but in one's own manner. My manner however is, at present, to be making every day – it is now a question of a very moderate number of days – a straight step nearer my last page, comparatively close at hand. You shall have it, I repeat with the very minimum further delay of which I am capable.

I do not seem to know, by the way, *when* it is Methuen's desire that the volume shall appear – I mean after the postponements we have had. The best time for me, I think, especially in America, will be about next October, and I promise you the thing in distinct time for that. But you will say that I am 'over-treating' this subject too!

One evening at this time Henry happened to be dining in the Athenaeum Club, where he encountered Arthur Benson. After dinner Benson took Henry to a secluded seat in the smoking room for a quiet talk. Benson subsequently recorded the subject of their conversation in his diary (April 29th, 1904):

> I questioned him about his ways of work. He admitted that he worked *every* day, dictated every morning, and began a new book the instant the old one was finished. He said it was his only chance because he worked so slowly, and excised so much. I asked him when the inception and design of a *new* book was formed; and he gave no satisfactory answer to this except to roll his eyes, to wave his hand about, to pat my knee and to say, 'It's all *about*, it's about – it's in the air – it, so to speak, follows me and dogs me.'

Miss Weld also recorded other impressions of Henry at work. 'He dictated beautifully. He had a melodious voice and in some way he seemed to be able to tell if I was falling behind. Typewriting for him was exactly like accompanying a singer on the piano'. She admitted that she greatly enjoyed taking down his long leisurely sentences. 'They seemed to spread out across the page like a beautiful and rambling architecture of this medieval town, to give his work a lonely individuality and a particular place in literature.'

One morning, when Edmund Gosse was staying with him, Miss Weld recalled, Henry stopped dictating, put his head out of the window and asked his guest, who was in the garden whether he was all right and happy and had all the books he wanted. Gosse replied in the affirmative, adding, 'Go back to your sibyl!'*

Another occasion when his dictation was interrupted occurred one morning in 1903. He was in the middle of a somewhat

---

* The following entry appears in Miss Weld's diary for September 14th, 1902: 'Edmund Gosse at Lamb House but work as usual.'

involved sentence and there was a knock on the door. 'Dash it, come in!' he shouted angrily. Burgess Noakes came in, holding a telegram and, as Miss Weld remembered, fairly shaking with alarm. 'Sorry, sir, telegram, sir. Mrs Paddington thought you ought to see it.' Henry took the telegram and after he had read it, turned to his amanuensis and said, 'Lady Maud Warrender asks if I can give her luncheon. She thinks of buying Leasam. What a good thing that would be for Rye! I must see Mrs Paddington at once. Miss Weld, will you see to the flowers?' So work was set aside for that day in preparation for the entertainment of the thirty-three-year-old Edwardian beauty. Lady Maud, who was a daughter of the Earl of Shaftesbury, and her husband Admiral Sir George Warrender, Bart., were prominent in the court circle and on terms of close friendship with the King. The result of her visit to Rye was that she was conquered by the charm of the place 'with its muddle of red roofs, and became one its matrons', after she had bought the nearby manor of Leasam, near Point Hill, with its attractive lawns and terraces. As Henry's most aristocratic neighbour, she certainly lent tone to 'the antient town'. Her range of friendships was wide, which prompted him to refer to her jocularly as 'the smart Bohemian'. She was the only visitor for whom he would willingly interrupt his morning work, when she arrived with several others from Leasam to call on him and see Lamb House. 'Lady Maud is such a handsome good-natured creature,' he would say, 'one has to forgive her everything!'

After she had been at Leasam for some years, Lady Maud Warrender received an amusing letter from another neighbour, the eccentric Moreton Frewen, illustrating her ebullient personality.[17]

Brede Place, Sussex, August 21, 1912. Coming away from lunching with you I met dear old Henry James, with a most attractive nephew, the son of his brother William – the Pragmatist! And they motored back and had tea with me and have just parted, happy for the break. Won't you get the dear old fellow to luncheon?

The nephew interests me very much. He is in charge of

the Rockefeller endowment to destroy 'Hookworms', which worms account for the anaemia of the tropics.*

Henry the Sage and I canvassed our friends as to who, all unbeknown, would have the hookworm, and you will be interested to know we dismissed yourself as *hopelessly* undeserving the Rockefeller millions!

'Amazonian'! he said, and again 'I say Amazonian!'

Once, when Mary Weld turned up as usual for work at nine-thirty, Henry was in bed and felt too ill to dictate. He asked her to come back at eleven to see if he would be well enough by then; when she did and he was not, he asked her to return at frequent intervals during the day in case he should recover quickly and be able to dictate. 'He was always tortured by his work', she said afterwards. 'I fancy he was sort of amazed that his talent was not more recognized. I think he was disappointed his books were not best sellers, though *Daisy Miller* nearly was.' Miss Weld also recalled his daily routine.

After working all morning, he would read in the afternoon, then after tea go for a walk, and then in the evenings he'd make notes on the next day's work, planning an outline. In the summer we worked in the Garden Room, which was long, oblong and light; in the winter we worked in the warmer, small panelled room upstairs [the Green Room]; and in winters the walks were in the afternoon. He liked company on his walks. His favourite walk was the road to Winchelsea, but unfortunately his literary flatterer Ford Madox Hueffer who lived at Winchelsea used to waylay him, and this annoyed Mr James. Once we actually jumped a dike to avoid meeting Hueffer who was looking out for us.

Mary Weld had taken Miss Petherbridge's advice and brought her bicycle to Rye. During her first year there she used

---

* Henry James, Jr (1879–1948) who inherited Lamb House under his uncle's will, was manager of the Rockefeller Institute for Medical Research in New York City from 1912 to 1918. After his death, the house was by his express wish presented by his widow in his name to the National Trust of Great Britain 'to be preserved as an enduring symbol of the ties that unite the British and American people.'

to go out on rides with her employer in the afternoons; but he seems to have abandoned this form of exercise towards the end of 1901, since the last reference to it occurs in an entry in her diary on November 2nd of that year. ('Cycled to Brede with Mr James, exquisite day with less wind'.) Thenceforward their afternoon outings were confined to walks.

On one occasion, while walking together down the steep hill of Mermaid Street, they passed a short-haired girl wearing a stiff collar and tie, which gave her a decidely masculine appearance. 'That young girl is the epitome of everything a woman should not look like', exclaimed Henry. 'Glory in your femininity, Miss Weld!' Poor Miss Weld was painfully conscious that her sailor hat was rather like the one the girl was wearing. As soon as they parted, she went off and bought a new hat with mignonette on it. She wore it next day, and although Henry did not say a word, she noticed that he looked at it approvingly. According to her, Henry James always treated women with reverence, and nothing distressed him more than a woman trying to look like a man. Once, when his niece Peggy arrived to stay, bringing some hockey sticks with her, Henry professed to be horrified. 'Miss Weld', he said, 'take her out this afternoon and teach her something feminine!' One craft which he considered suitable for women was bookbinding. Miss Weld had a friend, Marion Lane, who had been a pupil of Sangorski and Sutcliffe, and he gladly lent Miss Lane the studio in Watchbell Street so that she could instruct his amanuensis in the art. 'We bound several books for him,' Miss Weld recalled, 'and he used proudly to bring his friends to see us work.'

Mary Weld was not of such a literary turn of mind as her successor Theodora Bosanquet, nor was her critical appreciation of her employer's work as developed as was Miss Bosanquet's. In fact, when she began to work at Lamb House, Miss Weld confessed that the only work of his that she had read was *What Maisie Knew*, and she never could discover exactly what it was that Maisie knew.

Nevertheless Miss Weld was happy in her work, and she only gave it up in order to get married, which she did in 1905, when Henry was in America. Two years were to elapse before he again acquired an amanuensis who satisfied him. She was to remain with him for the rest of his working life.

[FOUR]

One morning in August, 1907, a well educated young woman in her middle twenties was at work in the top floor office of the same Secretarial Bureau where Mary Weld had been trained. Her name was Theodora Bosanquet, and she was engaged in the unexciting task of compiling a very full index to the Report of the Royal Commission on Coast Erosion. Suddenly her ears were struck by the astonishing sound of passages from a novel being dictated to another young typist in training. Miss Bosanquet, who had been to Cheltenham Ladies College like Miss Weld, and was a graduate of University College, London, immediately recognized the work of fiction as *The Ambassadors* by Henry James. On inquiring the reason for this exercise, she was informed that Mr James was on the point of returning from a holiday in Italy, that he had asked to be provided with an amanuensis, and that the lady at the typewriter was making acquaintance with his style.

Without any hopeful design of supplanting her, Miss Bosanquet lodged an immediate petition that she might be allowed the next opportunity of filling the post, supposing the young typist should ever abandon it. She was told, to her amazement, that she need not wait, and that if she set about practising on a Remington at once, she could be interviewed by Mr James as soon as he arrived in London. It appeared that the candidate who had been ear-marked for the job was far from enthusiastic about the project and indeed was only too glad to be relieved of it. Within an hour Theodora had got rid of her dreary Blue Book and begun work to dictation on the typewriter. By the time the author was ready to interview her, a fortnight later, she was able to tap out passages from *The Ambassadors* at quite a fair speed.

On the day of their meeting, which took place in Miss Petherbridge's Secretarial Bureau, Theodora wore a white shirt and green skirt, belt and tie, a business-like and what she hoped was also a becoming costume. When she was 'sent for' after waiting half an hour, she was 'fearfully cold with nervousness', but Henry immediately put her at her ease. Apparently he took it for granted that she was coming to work for him, since he asked her no question about her typing speed or for that matter about anything else. On the other hand, he explained at some length that he was preparing the New York collected edition of his *Novels and Tales* which involved the composition of a separate preface to each story as well as considerable revisions of the text. It was for this work that he primarily needed the services of an amanuensis. He went on to emphasize, as he had done with Miss Weld, that he was often very slow in dictating and that she could have knitting or a book to amuse herself with while he was 'evolving sentences'.

They sat in armchairs on either side of a fireless grate while they observed each other. He reminded her, in figure, of Coleridge, and she felt that he ought to be wearing a flowered waistcoat, very expansive, 'unrestrained' in the lower part. In fact, he wore green trousers and a blue waistcoat with a yellow check and a black coat, a combination which surprised her, as she had imagined him as always correctly dressed in London. His grey eyes were exactly what she expected, but the rest of his face she thought was too fat. Nor had he the self-possession she expected, but she was 'very gratefully aware of benign curves and ample reassurances radiating from his presence.'

In *Henry James at Work*, the extended essay which she wrote some years after her future employer's death, Theodora Bosanquet summarized her impressions of this first meeting.

I suppose he found me harmless and I know that I found him overwhelming. He was much more massive than I had expected, much broader and stouter and stronger. I remembered that someone had told me he used to be taken for a sea-captain when he wore a beard, but it was clear that now, with the beard shaved away, he would hardly have passed for, say, an admiral, in spite of the keen grey eyes set in a face burned to a colourable sea-faring brown by the Italian sun. No successful naval officer could have afforded to keep that sensitive mobile mouth . . .

If the interview was overwhelming, it had none of the usual awkwardness of such curious conversations. Instead of critical angles and disconcerting silences, there were only benign curves and ample reassurances. There was encouraging gaiety in an expanse of bright check waistcoat. He invited me to ask any questions I liked, but I had none to ask. I wanted nothing but to be allowed to go to Rye and work his typewriter. He was prepared, however, with his statements and, once I was seated opposite him, the strong, slow stream of his deliberate speech played over me without ceasing. He had it on his mind to tell me the conditions of life and labour at Rye, and he unburdened himself fully, with numberless amplifications and qualifications but without any real break. It would be a dull business, he warned me, and I should probably find Rye a dull place. He told me of rooms in Mermaid Street, 'very simple, rustic and antique – but that is the case for everything near my house, and this particular little old house is very near mine, and I know the good woman for kind and worthy and a convenient cook and in short —.' It was settled at once that I should take the rooms, that I should begin my duties in October.[18]

Theodora Bosanquet arrived in Rye a few days after her twenty-seventh birthday. Henry met her at the railway station and a grimy looking man, apparently Gammon the gardener, took charge of her luggage which he put into his handcart. Henry began by apologizing for the man's appearance. 'He oughtn't to have shown himself like that', he said, as they walked together to Marigold Cottage, the lodgings which he had secured for her in Mermaid Street. This time she found his talk slightly constrained. He spoke of the days when he used to go to see 'dear old Burne-Jones' the painter in his house in North End Road, Hammersmith, where the English novelist Samuel Richardson had once lived.* After she had

---

* The reference was to Sir Edward Burne-Jones, who had died nine years previously. His son, Sir Philip Burne-Jones, was also a friend of Henry's and painted the portrait of him reproduced in this volume.

unpacked, she went along to Lamb House where Henry introduced her to the typewriter ('a brand new Remington and very complicated, or so it seemed to me'), which stood on a desk in his writing room.

Since winter was approaching, Henry James had begun to use a panelled, green-painted room on the upper floor of Lamb House for his work. It was known simply as the Green Room. It had many advantages as a winter work-room, for it was small enough to be easily warmed and a wide south window caught all the morning sunshine. The window overhung the smooth green lawn, shaded in summer by a mulberry tree, surrounded by roses and enclosed behind a tall brick wall. It never failed to give the owner pleasure to look out of this convenient window at his English garden where he could watch his English gardener digging the flower-beds or mowing the lawn or sweeping up fallen leaves. There was another window for the afternoon sun, looking towards Winchelsea and doubly glazed against the force of the westerly gales. Three high bookcases, two big writing desks and an easy chair filled most of the space in the green room, but left enough clear floor for a restricted amount of the pacing exercise that was indispensable to literary composition.[19]

Before beginning work on her first day, Henry showed her his books in the large rose-wood case in the entrance hall, and told her that she was free to borrow any she liked, an offer she gladly accepted. They then settled down together in the Green Room and Henry began to dictate the preface to the revised edition of *The Tragic Muse*. She noted at the time that he did this considerately, slowly and very clearly, giving all the punctuation and also spelling out any words which he felt might be difficult or obscure. Indeed he went to such lengths in this respect that he told his amanuensis, whom she felt he considered to be completely ignorant of any literary knowledge, that *The Newcomes* was in one word, and that it was by Thackeray! At the same time she found him very kind, even complimentary, considering how 'abominably slow and clumsy, she was, though he admitted that he hoped she would soon go a little faster. 'At first there were difficulties, even stoppages', she said, recalling the vagaries of the new typewriter, 'Henry James watched my struggles with great patience and sympathy, but he couldn't offer any advice. He never claimed to know or understand anything whatever about the way any kind of machine worked. He just stood and waited.' He sat in a chair at first, she remembered, then paced about smoking. They finished the first day's work soon after half-past one.

On her second day, Theodora noted how the preface to *The Tragic Muse* grew even more interesting now that its author was dealing with the interrelations of the characters. She mentioned that she had read this novel. 'Oh, my rubbish!' he murmured deprecatingly. But on the whole he seemed pleased, she thought, and he remarked that his former amanuensis had 'never at all fathomed' what he wrote and had made many 'fantastic mistakes.' It was only a few weeks since she had read the story of Nick Dormer, Miriam Rooth and Peter Sheringham. 'Their names would have come safely to my fingers – even if their creator hadn't spelt them out, but he did.'

A week after her arrival, Henry was writing enthusiastically about his 'new and excellent amanuensis . . . a young, boyish Miss Bosanquet, who is worth all the others (females) that I have had put together, and who confirms me in the perception, for most kinds of diligence and production, the agent is to my perverse constitution, an intense aid and a true economy. There is no comparison!'

At first they worked only in the mornings. But soon Theodora was coming back in the evenings. These evening sessions with the Remington began immediately after dinner. To stimulate his amanuensis Henry would produce several bars of chocolate and lay them beside her machine after peeling off the silver paper. This was followed by pots of tea. 'I found myself getting so very sleepy last night,' he told her, 'and that's not favourable to the inspiration of genius!'

As we have seen, Henry began the practice of dictating his stories about ten years previously, and by this time it was a confirmed habit from which he never departed. Its effects were easily recognizable in his style, which seemed to Theodora Bosanquet to become more and more like free, involved, unanswered talk. 'I know,' he once said to her, 'that I'm too diffuse when I'm dictating.' At the same time, he felt that the gain in expression through the use of what he laughingly called 'Remingtonese' more than compensated for any loss of concision. Indeed, at the time Theodora started her work for him, he had reached a stage at which, as she put it, the click of a Remington acted as a positive spur. According to her, he found it more difficult to compose to the music of any other make. 'During a fortnight when the Remington was out of order he dictated to an Oliver typewriter with evident discomfort, and he found it almost impossibly disconcerting to speak to something which made no responsive sound at all.' Once or twice when he was ill and in bed, Theodora would take down a note or two in shorthand, but as a rule he insisted on the Remington being moved into his bedroom even for the shortest letters.[20]

On summer days, as we have seen, Henry preferred to work in the Garden Room, which had its own separate entrance, its railings twined with wisteria. The Garden Room also had its separate heating arrangements through a coke boiler which heated the adjacent greenhouse as well. The interior consisted of an octagonal chamber, with large bookcases lining the walls. The large bow-fronted window commanded the full length of the steeply sloping cobbled street which wound its way past the tall canopied front door with its twisted brass knocker. 'He liked to be able to relieve the tension of a difficult sentence by a glance down the street', Miss Bosanquet later recalled; 'he enjoyed hailing a passing friend or watching a motor-car pant up the sharp little slope. The sight of one of these vehicles could be counted on to draw from him a vigorous outburst of amazement, admiration, or horror for the complications of an age that produced such efficient monsters for gobbling up protective distance'. But Theodora did not like this room as much as the other as a workroom. 'It's too stuffy, with the hot water pipes and no open windows.'[21]

Thirty years later, the novelist E. F. Benson, who was then

living in Lamb House, remembered hearing Henry's voice coming from the Garden Room as he was dicatating.

It boomed out through the open window between the tassels of wisteria, now louder, now softer, as he paced up and down the length of the room, and the metallic click of the typewriter made response. From breakfast until the stroke of the gong for lunch he was thus invisible though not inaudible: then there came a day when, though the morning was still only half-spent, he emerged from the inviolable precinct, and taking me by the arm he walked me about the lawn, and involved himself in a noble harangue. To me, he said, fresh from the roar and reverberation of London with its multifarious movements and intensive interests, the news he was about to impart might reasonably seem to be of little moment, but to him in his quiet and red-walled *angulus terrae,* this little plot in Rye, that which had in fact happened this morning, and which was the cause of his indulging himself now with a mulberry at this unusual hour. . . .

On and on went the magnificent architectural period, and then, I suppose, not having the typist to read it out to him and thus give him a clue through the labyrinth, he confessed himself lost, and added, 'In fact, my dear Fred Benson, I have finished my book. . . .'[22]

[FIVE]

For a year or more Henry worked hard on the textual revisions and prefaces to the collected *Novels and Tales,* spending his mornings on the prefaces and most of his evenings reading over the work of former years and, in his secretary's words, treating the printed pages like so many proof-sheets of extremely corrupt text. 'The revision was a task he had seen in advance as formidable,' noted Theodora Bosanquet. 'He had cultivated the habit of forgetting past achievements almost to the pitch of sincere conviction that nothing he had written before about 1890 could come with any shred of credit through the ordeal of critical inspection.' Once, when he was considering what to select for one of the volumes of short stories, he confessed to Theodora that the difficulty of selection was mainly the difficulty of reading them all. 'They seem so bad until I *have* read them', he said, 'that I can't force myself to go through them except with a pen in my hand, altering as I go the crudities and ineptitudes that to my sense deform each page'. After the first few volumes had appeared, he wrote to the novelist Violet Hunt:

> I am ridden – and have been for months and months – by the fearful nightmare of an Edition Definitive, or rather pursued there by a pack of hell-hounds; the hell-hounds being the volumes already out, revised, rewritten, copiously prefaced and seen through the Press, and crowding close on my heels as I pant and strain over the preparation of the awful bloated remainder. It has really been a colossal task, and has made me inhuman and remorseless toward everything else, all the more that the end is not yet.

An American named Robert Herrick, who stayed at Lamb House in the summer of 1907, when Henry was working on the revisions to the first three novels to appear in the 'definitive' edition, ventured to remonstrate with the Master on the wisdom of his 're-touching' these early works. But Henry brushed aside such doubts.

> The re-touching with any insistence will *in fact* bear but on one book (*The American* – on *Roderick Hudson* and *The Portrait of a Lady* very much less), but in essence I shouldn't have planned the edition at all unless I had felt close revision – wherever seeming called for – to be an indispensable part of it. I do justice to your contention, but don't think me reckless or purblind if I say that I hold myself really right and you really wrong. The *raison d'être* (the edition's) is in its being selective as well as collective, and by the mere fact of leaving out certain things (I have tried to read over *Washington Square* and I *can't,* and I fear it must go!) I exercise a control, a discrimination, I treat certain portions of my work as unhappy accidents (Many portions of many – of all – men's work are.)[23]

163

The first two volumes of this Collected or so-called New York Edition – *Roderick Hudson* and *The American* – were published by Scribner's in December, 1907, and the remaining twenty-two appeared two at a time under the same publisher's imprint over the next eighteen months.* For them Henry wrote eighteen prefaces in all, one to each of the novels and one to each collection of tales. Each volume, which sold for two dollars in cloth to subscribers only – even at this price the sales were disappointingly poor – contained a frontispiece photogravure by Alvin Langdon Coburn, a young photographer from Boston whose acquaintance Henry had made at this time. Coburn had come to England where, among others, he photographed Bernard Shaw, George Meredith, H. G. Wells and G. K. Chesterton. His brilliant photographic portraiture began to attract attention and led to a commission from an American magazine to do a series of portraits of American authors, including Henry James. Coburn went down to Rye and the result of his work so delighted Henry that not only did he decide to use it as the frontispiece to the first volume of the forthcoming collected edition of his works, but he asked the young photographer to make photographs for use in the other volumes.

The two men were instantly drawn to each other. 'There are some people you cannot help liking the moment you see them', Coburn said afterwards, 'and Henry James was, for me, such a person'. For his part, Henry enthused over Coburn's 'beautiful photographs', and proposed that together they should hunt for 'a series of reproducible subjects . . . of images always confessing themselves mere optical symbols or echoes, expressions of no particular thing in the text, but only of the type or idea of this or that thing . . . at the most pictures of our "set" stage with the actors left out. . . .' So after Coburn had begun by photographing Lamb House for the frontispiece to *The Awkward Age* ('Mr Longdon's'), Henry sent him off first to Paris and then to Venice and Rome in search of more 'reproducible

---

* In 1918, two posthumous volumes, *The Ivory Tower* and *The Sense of Past,* were issued uniform with the original edition. An English issue, consisting of sheets of the New York Edition, was published by Macmillan.

subjects'. Henry's instructions were quite thorough; in particular, Coburn was amazed by his detailed knowledge of the Paris streets. 'Once you get the type into your head,' he told his young collaborator, 'you will easily recognize specimens by walking in the *old* residential and "noble" parts of the city. . . . Tell a cabman that you want to drive through every street of it, and, having got the notion, go back and walk and stare at your ease'. Together they then explored London, 'a field yielding a ripe harvest of treasure', as Henry wrote in the preface to *The Golden Bowl*, 'from the moment I held up to it, in my fellow artist's company, the light of our fond idea – the idea, that is, of the aspect of things or the combination of objects that might, by a latent virtue in it, speak for its connexion with something in the book, and yet at the same time speak enough for its odd or interesting self.' Their confidence that, 'as London ends by giving absolutely everything one asks, so it awaited us somewhere', was fully justified by the results as reflected by the lens of Coburn's camera.[24]

One of the photographer's best efforts was the picture of Portland Place used for the second Volume of *The Golden Bowl*, which concluded the whole edition.*

> The thing was to induce the vision of Portland Place *to* generalise itself. This is, precisely, however, the fashion after which the prodigious city, as I have called it, does on occasion meet halfway those forms of intelligence of it that *it* recognises. All of which meant that at a given moment the great featureless Philistine vista would itself perform a miracle, would become interesting, for a splendid atmospheric hour, as only London knows how; and that our business would be then to understand.[25]

In October 1908, by which date well over half the collected edition had appeared, Henry received a most discouraging letter from his New York publisher with an account of the sales to date. This was the first news he had received of how the

---

* It is regrettable that the recent reprint of the New York edition omits these magnificent illustrations.

edition was going. It was a great shock, considering how he had been counting on some profit, 'at the end of a very invaded and hospitable summer' as he told Pinker, his literary agent ('I think it would ease off my nerves not a little to see you'), considering 'the measure, known only to myself, of the treasures of ingenuity and labour I have lavished on the ameliorations of every page of the thing', and that the result was that financially he was 'rather high and dry'. However, the situation on reflection did not appear as bad as it had on first sight.

I have recovered the perspective and proportion of things [he wrote to Pinker.] I have committed, thank God, no anticipatory *follies* (the worst is having made out my income-tax return at a distinctly higher than at all warranted figure! – whereby I shall have early in 1909 to pay – as I even did last year – on parts of an income I have never received!) – and, above all, am aching in every bone to get back to out-and-out 'creative' work, the long interruption of that has fairly sickened and poisoned me. (*That* is the real hitch!)

I am afraid that moreover in my stupidity before those unexplained – though so grim-looking! – figure-lists of Scribner's I even seemed to make out that a certain $211 (a phrase in his letter seeming also to point to that interpretation) *is*, all the same, owing me. But as you say nothing about this I see that I am probably again deluded and that the mystic screed meant it is still owing *them!* Which is all that is wanted, verily, to my sad rectification! However, I am now, as it were, prepared for the worst, and as soon as I can get my desk *absolutely* clear (for, like the convolutions of a vast smothering boa-constrictor, such voluminosities of Proof – of the Edition – to be carefully read – still keep rolling in,) that mere fact will by itself considerably relieve me. And I have *such* visions and arrears of inspiration – !

The edition had been a weary grind ('such mass of obscure and unmeasurable labour'), he told Gosse who had written to congratulate him, 'but I feel all you say as the most delightful consequence of it. So I am tenderly grateful for your brave and generous words. .... I am not otherwise hardened or stricken than my great age and vast bulk render natural and even becoming'.[27]

Eight years later, within a few months of his death, he was again to write to Gosse, summing up the commercial fate of the Collected Edition:

That Edition has been, from the point of view of profit either to the publishers or to myself practically a complete failure; vaguely speaking, it doesn't sell – that is, my annual report of what it does – the whole 24 vols. – in this country amounts to about £25 from the Macmillan's; and the ditto from the Scribner's in the U.S. to very little more. I am past all praying for anywhere; I remain at my age (which you know,) and after my long career, utterly, insurmountably, unsaleable. And the original preparation of that collective and selective series involved really the extremity of labour – all my 'earlier' things – of which *The Bostonians* would have been, if included, one – were so intimately and interestingly revised.

The edition is from that point of view really a monument (like Ozymandias) which has never had the least intelligent critical justice done it – or any sort of critical attention at all paid it – and the artistic problem involved in my scheme was a deep and exquisite one, and moreover was, as I held, very effectively solved. Only it took such time – *and* such taste – in other words such aesthetic light. No more commercially thankless job of the literary order was (Prefaces and all – *they* of a thanklessness!) accordingly ever achieved.

Nor was the news from the English publishers of his current novels any more encouraging. Methuen, who treated him more generously in the matter of advances on account of royalties than either Macmillan or Heinemann had done, lost more than £670 over the seven novels they published during this period.[28] The financial details are as follows:

	Advance			Amount unearned		
	£	s.	d.	£	s.	d.
The Soft Side (1900)	150	0	0	25	3	9
The Sacred Fount (1901)	250	0	0	153	12	0
The Better Sort (1903)	150	0	0	43	6	7
The Ambassadors (1903)	300	0	0	159	1	6
The Golden Bowl (1905)	300	0	0	103	11	3
The Finer Grain (1910)	150	0	0	31	6	10
The Outcry (1911)	300	0	0	156	7	3
Totals	£1,600	0	0	£672	9	2

Thus it will be seen that in all the sum of only £927 10s. 10d. was earned from the total advances, by no means a negligible loss for the publishers.[28]*

Earnings from his other publishers were likewise pitifully small. For the year 1910, royalties from the six works published by Heinemann and still in print *(Embarrassments, Terminations, What Maisie Knew, A Little Tour in France,* and *Italian Hours)* only amounted to £17 8s. 9d. By 1914, these had dropped to £5 4s. 1d. At the time of his death, *The American Scene,* the volume of impressions of his visit to the United States in 1904–05, showed £126 16s. 7d. as unearned in England and $1234.69 as unearned in America. For probate purposes Macmillan's only valued the works published by their firm, including the two autobiographical volumes, at £75.

It is said that his friend Edith Wharton, who was also published in America by Scribner's, but with considerable success unlike Henry, on one occasion handed back her royalties with the request that they should be secretly applied to Henry's account. This was accordingly done, and Henry never knew anything about it.

Theodora Bosanquet sustained the greater part of the burden of the Collected Edition, recording on her Remington the prefaces to all the volumes of tales and all the novels, except

---

* The loss was eventually reduced by £200 through the recent post-war reprinting from the old stereo plates of *The Golden Bowl.*

those contained in the first six volumes (*Roderick Hudson, The American, The Portrait of a Lady,* and *Princess Casamassima*). She thus transcribed the last of the prefaces and the most important, that to *The Golden Bowl,* since in it the problems of the whole edition were discussed, including Coburn's admirable photographic contributions. This experience gave her the remarkable insight into Henry's works and the method of their composition and revision, which she was to embody, all too briefly, in her critical essay *Henry James at Work.*

As he got to know her better, Henry would confide some interesting revelations, for instance, when he was dictating the preface to Volume XII, which contained *The Turn of the Screw.* The idea for this macabre little tale had come to him, 'one winter afternoon, round the hall-fire of a grave old country house where (for all the world as if to resolve itself promptly and obligingly into convertible, into "literary" stuff) the talk turned, on I forget what homely pretext, to apparitions and night-fears, to the marked and sad drop in the general supply, and still more in the general quality of such commodities'.

Thus it was, I remember, that amid our lament for a beautiful lost form, our distinguished host expressed the wish that he might but have recovered for us one of the scantest fragments of this form at its best. He had never forgotten the impression made on him as a young man by the withheld glimpse, as it were, of a dreadful matter that had been reported years before, and with as few particulars, to a lady with whom he had youthfully talked. The story would have been thrilling could she but have found herself in better possession of it, dealing as it did with a couple of small children in an out-of-the-way place, to whom the spirits of certain 'bad' servants, dead in the employ of the house, were believed to have appeared with the object of 'getting hold' of them. . . .

I was to remember the haunted children and the prowling servile spirits as a 'value' of the disquieting sort, in all conscience sufficient; to that when, after an interval, I was asked for something seasonable by the promoters of a periodical dealing in the time-honoured Christmas-tide toy,

I bethought myself at once of the vividest little note of sinister romance that I had ever jotted down.*

He now told his secretary that he had heard the story, widely regarded as 'so very dreadful' from the lips of the Archbishop of Canterbury, on one occasion when he was staying with the Archbishop's son Arthur Benson, at that time a master at Eton. 'It could hardly as he said, have had a more proper source!'

Theodora also assisted in the composition of the plays which Henry wrote at this time. The success of the repertory movement, largely stimulated by the pioneering work of Miss A. E. Horniman in Dublin and Manchester, prompted actor-managers to ask for 'non-commercial' plays, and Henry, undeterred by his experience of a dozen years earlier, responded quickly and wrote four plays inside two years, and would have written more had not serious illness put an end for ever to his dramatic ambitions. Only two of these plays were produced in his lifetime, and both were adapted from short stories – *The High Bid* from *Covering End,* and *The Saloon* from *Owen Wingrave* – and, although they did not meet with anything like the humiliating disaster which befell *Guy Domville* their reception at the hands both of critics and public in London was fairly tepid. 'Do people ever say such things and in such a manner?' asked J. T. Grain in the *Sunday Times.* The answer was supplied by Miss Bosanquet. 'The men and women of Henry James could talk only in the manner of their creator', she wrote. 'His own speech, assisted by the practice of dictating, had by that time become so inveterately characteristic that his questions to a railway clerk about a ticket or to a fishmonger about a lobster, might easily be recognized as coined in the same mint as his addresses to the Academic Committee of the Royal Society of Literature. . . . It is not very difficult to believe that if Henry James had been encouraged twenty years earlier to go on writing plays he might have made a name as a dramatist, but the faithful may be forgiven for

---

* *The Turn of the Screw* (1898) first appeared in *Collier's Weekly.*

rejoicing that the playwright was sacrificed to the novelist and critic'.[29]

Theodora Bosanquet was an observant person, as well as something of a blue-stocking, and she noted a number of revealing sidelights on her employer's character. Besides the plays, he wrote several short stories at this period, one of which, *The Jolly Corner,* appeared in the first number of *The English Review,* a monthly literary magazine started by Ford Madox Hueffer towards the end of 1908. But shortly after finishing the story, in the summer of that year, Henry had mislaid the manuscript, thereby causing 'great tribulation' at Lamb House. 'I really don't see what he gains by his tidy habits', reflected Theodora. 'He is always losing MSS from having put them away too carefully!' As a Christmas present, Henry gave his secretary a glue-box, somewhat to her annoyance. She thought he might have chosen a little more carefully, or given her a book. 'The glue-box is the sort of thing one would give an illiterate housekeeper', she complained. 'However, he meant it kindly, I've no doubt'.

One of the first letters which Henry dictated to his new secretary was addressed to his brother William, which she found 'thrillingly interesting' in her rather naïve fashion. 'I *am* in luck's way', she confided in a friend. 'Fancy me being in a sense the *medium* between Henry James and William!' One communication from William to Henry, which she probably did not see, was written a few months before she arrived to take up her job. As a fraternal criticism of Henry's third fiction period, it remains unsurpassed, and indeed unanswerable, for Henry never replied to it.

You know how opposed your whole 'third manner' of execution is to the literary ideals which animate my crude and Orson-like breast, mine being to say a thing in one sentence as straight and explicit as it can be made, and then to drop it forever; yours being to avoid naming it straight, but by dint of breathing and sighing all round and round it, to arouse in the reader who may have had a similar perception already (Heaven help him if he hasn't!) the illusion of a solid object, made (like the 'ghost' at the Polytechnic) wholly out of impalpable materials, air, and the prismatic inferences of light, ingeniously focussed by mirrors upon empty space. But you do it, that's the queerness! . . .

But it's the rummest method for one to employ systematically as you do nowadays; and you employ it at your peril. In this crowded and hurried reading age, pages that require such close attention remain unread and neglected. You can't skip a word if you are to get the effect, and 19 out of 20 worthy readers grow intolerant. The method seems perverse: 'Say it *out,* for God's sake,' they cry, 'and have done with it'. And so I say now, give us *one* thing in your older directer manner, just to show that in spite of your paradoxical success in this unheard-of method, you *can* still write according to accepted canons. Give us that interlude; and then continue like the 'curiosity of literature' which you have become.[30]

William, who had been invited to deliver a course of lectures at Oxford, spent most of the summer of 1908 at Lamb House with his wife and daughter Peggy, and he made a particular impression on Theodora. ('He *is* a charming man – there's something so simple and fresh about him somehow.') He told Theodora how very fond he had got of England 'with its soft harmonious colouring' and how sorry he was to be going away.

On November 2nd, 1908, Henry wrote from Lamb House to Ellen Emmet, his American 'paintress-cousin':

. . . he [William] and Alice and Peggy will have much to tell you about their quite long summer here, lately brought to a close, and about poor little old Lamb House and its corpulent slowly-circulating and slowly-masticating master. It was an infinite interest to have them here for a good many weeks – they are such endlessly interesting people, and Alice such a heroine of devotion and of everything. We have had a wondrous season – a real golden one, for weeks and weeks – and still it goes on, bland and breathless and changeless – the rarest autumn (and summer, from June on) known for years: a proof of what this much-abused climate is capable of for benignity and convenience. Dear little old Lamb House and garden have really become very pleasant and developed through being much (and virtuously) lived in. . . .[31]

It was the last summer which found him free from physical ailment. In the following year, the first symptoms of heart trouble began to show themselves, to which were added prolonged fits of nervous depression, possibly brought on by disappointment at the failure of the New York edition of his collected *Novels and Tales*. His literary output was seriously interrupted; he despaired at times whether he could carry on and even contemplated suicide. The handsome testimonial which he wrote for Miss Bosanquet at this time suggested that she might soon be looking for other work.[32]

> *Lamb House,*
> *Rye, Sussex.*
> *May 10th, 1909*

I have the greatest pleasure in testifying to my sense of the great ability and high value of Miss Theodora Bosanquet, acquired during two years of her constant, punctual and in every way faithful service with me as literary secretary. I have the highest opinion of her intelligence and competence, alertness and discretion – her whole general accomplishment and character; to all of which I hope again frequently to resort for assistance. I have done highly important work – to myself – with her valuable aid, and I cordially congratulate those who may enjoy it.

HENRY JAMES

Theodora Bosanquet treasured this document most carefully; it was found among her papers at her death more than fifty years later. Meanwhile she continued to work intermittently for 'the Master' during the remainder of 1909, when his health allowed. In December, he experienced what he called 'the rather deadly oppression of the English Christmastide – which I have spent at home for the first time for four years – a lone and lorn and stranded friend or two being with me.' Beside Theodora and her companion Nellie Bradley, with whom she now shared lodgings in Rye, the other friends invited to eat Christmas dinner at Lamb House was Thomas Bailey Saunders, a fellow writer, who came over from Eastbourne.

The two ladies thought their host 'delightfully genial and nice', although they each found glue-boxes on their plates. ('This seems to be his one idea of gifts for ladies!)' There were crackers on the table, which added to the fun, since they contained paper masks which everyone put on – pleasant, benevolent sort of masks only down to the mouth and with a hole for the nose. The host's most successful one showed a fat old lady with side curls. This made the party so hilarious that Henry had to send for a shaving mirror to see himself in. 'Why don't we all wear masks', he asked, 'and change them as we do our clothes?'[33]

A few days later, while seeing off his friend Bailey Saunders at Rye Station, Henry felt seriously unwell. What began on 'that sad and sinister morning' as 'a digestive crisis making food loathsome and nutrition impossible' soon developed into 'sick inanition and weakness and depression permanent', in other words, a heart condition aggravated by nervous melancholia, which kept him in bed for the next four months and deprived him of all power to work. 'My conditions (of circumstance, house and care, etc.) have on the other hand been excellent,' he told a friend when he was convalescing, 'my servants angels of affection and devotion. (I have indeed been *all* in Doctor's and Nurse's hands.)[34] 'One learns strange lessons in so long an illness,' he confessed to Gosse, 'and there comes a day when one feels that all the mistakes have been at last made, and that, as there are none left to make, the straight and safe course rather stares one in the face.'[35] No doubt his attendants found him a trying patient. To another inquiring friend, he wrote:

Lamb House, Rye, April 19, 1910. . . . I have had a perfect hell of a time – since just after Christmas – nearly 15 long weeks of dismal, dreary, interminable illness (with occasional slight pickings-up followed by black relapses.) But the tide, thank the Powers, has at last definitely turned and I am on the way to getting not only better, but, as I believe, creepily and abjectly well. I sent my Nurse (my second) flying the other day, after ten deadly weeks of her, and her predecessor's, aggressive presence and policy, and the mere relief from that overdone discipline has done wonders for me. I must have patience, much, yet – but my face is toward the light, which shows, beautifully, that I look ten years older, with my bonny tresses ten degrees whiter (like Marie Antoinette's in the Conciergerie). However if I've lost all my beauty and (by my expenses) most of my money, I rejoice I've kept my friends.[36]

Meanwhile his brother and sister-in-law, who were greatly alarmed by the news of his illness, hurried across the Atlantic, preceded by their son Harry, so as to be near him. They all went off to complete his convalescence in Bad Nauheim, but the gloomy German spa did little to help. 'He has had a bad attack of nervous prostration with days of great dejection of spirits when writing, or even reading, are out of the question', William wrote to Gosse. 'He is getting out of trouble . . . but no one knows how long these nervous breakdowns will last. I think we shall probably take him back to New England with us before September.'[37] William himself only just lasted out the voyage, and died a few days after they reached his country home in New Hampshire. For Henry the loss was immeasurable, 'for from far back in dimmest childhood he had been my ideal Elder Brother, and I still, through all the years, saw in him, even as a small timorous boy yet, my protector, my backer, my authority and my pride. His extinction changes the face of life for me – besides the mere missing of his inexhaustible company and personality, originality, the whole unspeakably vivid and beautiful presence of him. And his noble intellectual vitality was still but at its climax. . . .'

To Edith Wharton's friend Walter Berry, he wrote:

Chocorua, N.H. September 3, 1910. . . . My relation to my beloved brother was such that my admiration for him and need of him were things that took the very first place in my life and understanding, and the extinction of his beautiful presence and powers (of these last at their very highest tide I'm convinced) cuts deeper than I can say.

... from the moment we embarked he went rapidly down (in spite of the most wonderful and beautiful voyage) and died here a week after his arrival. He suffered so that it was horrible, helplessly, to see it, and only yearned to go; so that there is an added pang in the sense that he consciously renounced and silently forfeited. Yet he had a very full and rich and splendid life. . . .[38]

Henry stayed on in America to comfort the family in Cambridge and to visit old friends. To attend to his physical needs, he had brought 'my devoted if diminutive Burgess' with him. Burgess Noakes later recalled what was for him the unforgettable experience of his first visit to the United States. 'We were out there a year; he went to various places, and of course he stayed with Mrs Edith Wharton – and a lady in New York, Mrs Cadwalader Jones [Edith Wharton's sister-in-law], we were there some time. . . . He was a wonderful man really, seeing that you had every comfort. Of course I had to take care of the luggage and things like that, but I wasn't shoved in with the luggage. I used to have a pullman seat next to him in the pullman car.'[39]

Henry prolonged his visit beyond what he had originally intended so as to receive the Honorary Degree which Harvard conferred upon him, thus obliging him to postpone a similar honour from Oxford to the following year. He was back at Lamb House by the middle of August, 1911, feeling much recovered in health and eager to get back to work. His brother's death had given him the idea of writing an account of his family and early years in autobiographical form. To achieve this, with Theodora Bosanquet's help, he tried what he called 'the questionable experiment' of spending the succeeding winter at Lamb House. But the experiment quickly broke down. Although he had pined for the old house and garden when he was in America, now he was home again he felt he could not face the whole winter in 'that contracted corner.' As he told his secretary, he found the place 'unmistakeably too dreary and unpropitious again (during these months) and must never more attempt to hibernate here. I dream of a small flat or such like [in London]'.

'I go back to London presently,' he wrote from Lamb House to another correspondent at this time. 'I find that since my illness, long and dismal of 1910, I can't stand lonely hibernations here, where for several years I have had too much of it. Miles of pavement and lamp light are good for me; but for 4 or 5 or even 6 months of the year (I shall be willing to compound for 6,) my little old house here is as dear to me as ever.'[40]

Meanwhile he established himself in his old bedroom quarters in the Reform Club. The drawback there was that the club rules forbade the admission of women to members' bedrooms, even for the purpose of dictation. So he appealed to Theodora to help him to find some accommodation not subject to this restriction.

For you see, by this bolting in horror and loathing (but don't *repeat* those expressions!) from Rye for the winter, my situation suddenly becomes special and difficult; and largely through this, that having got back to work and to a very particular job, the need of expressing myself, of pushing it on, on the old Remingtonese terms, grows daily stronger within me. But I haven't a seat and temple for the Remington and its priestess – *can't* have here at this club. . . .

I want a small very cheap and very clean *furnished* flat or trio of rooms etc. . . . that I could hire for 2 or 3 – 3 or 4 – months to drive ahead my job in – the Remington priestess and I converging and meeting there morning by morning – and it being preferably nearer to her than to me; though near tubes and things for both of us!

I must keep on *this* place for food and bed etc. – I have it by the year – till I really *have* something else by the year – for winter purposes – to supersede it (Lamb House abides for long summers.)

Your researches can have only been for the *un*furnished – but look, *think, invent!* Two or three little tabled and chaired and lighted rooms would do.[41]

At this time Theodora Bosanquet was sharing a flat at 10, Lawrence Street, a side-street in Chelsea, with a friend, and fortunately they had two rooms which they did not need, stretching out into a quiet yard at the back. 'He came to see those rooms; he took them,' Theodora recalled afterwards. 'He added some felt to pace on and a large chair, and one or two other things. He brought the Remington along one morning in a taxi, and afterwards he came in a taxi every morning, and started dictating *A Small Boy and Others*'.

'I apply myself to my effort every morning at a little *repaire* in the depths of Chelsea', he wrote to Edith Wharton from the Reform Club in November 1911, 'a couple of little rooms that I have secured for quiet and concentration – to which our blest taxi whirls me from hence very morning at 10 o'clock, and where I meet my amanuensis (of the days of the composition of the *G[olden]* *B[owl]* to whom I *gueuler* to the best of my power. In said *repaire* I propose to crouch and *me blottir* (in the English shade of the word, for so intensely revising an animal as well) for many many weeks. . . .'[42]

Theodora described how her employer eventually found a permanent place in the neighbourhood.

> Chelsea began to make its appeal to him before long. He walked about and made little purchases in the shops. He liked talking to the people; he liked the kind of village atmosphere that he found there. And in the spring, when he heard that the flat above ours was to be let, he rushed out to find the porter who had the key, and we all went up to inspect it, but it was a bit too small for the entire Rye household. And then he found a charming flat around the corner at Carlyle Mansions, with a delightful room to pace in and to dictate in, and watching the boats on the river.[43]

In 21, Carlyle Mansions, which formed part of Cheyne Walk, Henry James was to find his ultimate English home.

Five ❦ Visitors and Visiting

For more than a dozen years, until illness curtailed the Master's hospitality, there was a constant flow of visitors to Lamb House. Fellow writers and literary critics were particularly welcome. Besides Edmund Gosse, H. G. Wells, Ford Madox Ford, Edith Wharton and the two Benson brothers, already mentioned, they included, among others, Stephen Crane, George Gissing, G. K. Chesterton, Joseph Conrad, Rudyard Kipling, Max Beerbohm and Violet Hunt. Then, among the younger and rising literary generation there were Percy Lubbock, Logan Pearsall Smith, Hugh Walpole, Clare Sheridan and Rupert Brooke. Visitors, even from comparatively short distances, were invited to spend the night or longer, as they felt inclined.

Of all his literary cronies, perhaps Gosse was the favourite among the men, just as Edith Wharton was among the women. Certainly Henry enjoyed his conversation greatly. '*No* dress clothes,' he wrote to him banteringly on the occasion of one of his visits, 'a simple tunic and loose girdle, with a few flowers in the hair or bosom. . . . It's a long way to bring people for Spartan broth and all the rest. . . . You must stay as long as possible and come again as soon, and must also feel yourself an object of the tenderest and happiest preoccupation to yours very contentedly.'[1]

Gosse wrote of these visits after Henry's death:

> His practice in regard to such a visitor was always to descend to the railway station below the town to welcome the guest, who would instantly recognize his remarkable

figure hurrying along the platform. Under the large soft hat would be visible the large pale face, anxiously scanning the carriage-windows and breaking into smiles of sunshine when the new-comer was discovered. Welcome was signified by both hands waved aloft, lifting the skirts of the customary cloak, like wings. Then, luggage attended to, and the arm of the guest securely seized, as though even now there might be an attempt at escape, a slow ascent on foot would begin up the steep streets, the last and steepest of all leading to a discreet door which admitted directly to the broad hall of Lamb House.

The ascent of arrival from the railway grew to be more and more interesting as time went on, and as the novelist became more and more a familiar and respected citizen, it was much interrupted at last by bows from ladies and salaams from shop-keepers; many little boys and girls, the latter having often curtsied, had to be greeted and sometimes patted on the head. These social movements used to inspire in me the inquiry: 'Well, how soon are you to be the Mayor-Elect of Rye?' a pleasantry which was always well received. So obviously did Henry James, in the process of years, become the leading inhabitant that it grew to seem no impossibility. [2]

Gosse appreciated his friend's peculiarly complex manner with its remarkable mixture of deep reserve and expanding exuberance. Sometimes though rarely Gosse penetrated beneath the mask which concealed Henry's innermost thoughts and feelings and memories.

So discreet was he, and so like a fountain sealed, that many of those who were well acquainted with him have supposed that he was mainly a creature of observation and fancy, and that life stirred his intellect while leaving his senses untouched. But every now and then he disclosed to a friend, or rather admitted such a friend to a flash or glimpse of deeper things. The glimpse was never prolonged or illuminated, it was like peering down for a moment through some chasm in the rocks dimmed by the vapour of a clash of waves. One such flash will always leave my memory dazzled.

I was staying alone with Henry James at Rye one summer, and as twilight deepened we walked together in the garden. I forget by what meanders we approached the subject, but I suddenly found that in profuse and enigmatic language he was recounting to me an experience, something that had happened, not something repeated or imagined. He spoke of standing on the pavement of a city, in the dusk, and of gazing upwards across the misty street, watching, watching for the lighting of a lamp in a window on the third storey. And the lamp blazed out, and through bursting tears he strained to see what was behind it, the unapproachable face. And for hours he stood there, wet with the rain, brushed by the phantom hurrying figures of the scene, and never from behind the lamp was for one moment visible the face. The mysterious and poignant revelation closed, and one could make no comment, ask no question, being throttled oneself by an overpowering emotion. And for a long time Henry James shuffled beside me in the darkness, shaking the dew off the laurels, and still there was no sound at all in the garden but what our heels made crunching the gravel, nor was the silence broken when suddenly we entered the house and he disappeared for an hour.[3]

Henry seems to have taken Gosse more into his confidence than anyone else save his brother William. Outwardly he pretended not to be affected by what the critics thought of his work, but Gosse was an exception, particularly when he wrote kindly as he almost invariably did.

Gosse was with him shortly after he had begun the revisions of his novels and tales for the New York Edition.

This involved a labour which some of his friends ventured to disapprove of, since it included a re-writing into his latest style of the early stories which possessed a charm in their unaffected immaturity. Henry James was conscious, I think, of the arguments which might be brought against this reckless revision, but he rejected them with violence. I was spending a day or two with him at Lamb House when *Roderick Hudson* was undergoing, or rather had just undergone, the terrible trial; so the revised copy, darkened and swelled with MS. alterations, was put into my hands. I thought – I dare say I was quite mistaken – that the whole perspective of Henry James's work, the evidence of his development and evolution, his historical growth, were confused and belied by this wholesale tampering with the original text. Accordingly I exclaimed against such dribbling of new wine into the old bottles. This was after dinner, as we sat alone in the garden-room. All that Henry James – though I confess, with a darkened countenance – said at the time was, 'The only alternative would have been to put the vile thing' – that is to say the graceful tale of *Roderick Hudson* – 'behind the fire and have done with it!' Then we passed to other subjects and at length we parted for the night in unruffled cheerfulness. But what was my dismay, on reaching the breakfast-table next morning, to see my host sombre and taciturn, with gloom thrown across his frowning features like a veil. I inquired rather anxiously whether he had slept well. 'Slept!' he answered with dreary emphasis. 'Was I likely to sleep when my brain was tortured with all the cruel and – to put it plainly to you – monstrous insinuations which you had brought forward against my proper, my necessary, my absolutely inevitable corrections of the disgraceful and disreputable style of *Roderick Hudson*?' I withered, like a guilty thing ashamed, before the eyes that glared at me over the coffee-pot, and I only resolved that not one word of question should ever escape my lips on this subject again'[4]

However, Gosse made amends a few months later by a review he wrote of Henry's account of his recent visit to America.

I gave myself this morning to the beatific perusal of your beautiful notice of *The American Scene* in the *Daily Mail,* [Henry wrote to Gosse early in 1907]. 'It has given me extraordinary pleasure – more, I can emphatically say, than any appreciation of any book of mine has *ever* given me. Therefore my eyes really fill with tears as I very devoutly thank you.'[5]

One fellow American who disapproved of Henry and his circle was Harold Frederic, the London correspondent of the *New York Times*, who wrote novels in his spare time. 'Henry James is an effeminate old donkey who lives with a herd of other donkeys around him and insists on being treated as if he were the Pope', the *Times* man had written shortly after Henry had settled in Rye. 'He has licked dust from the floor of every third-rate hostess in England.' Frederic added that they had met in the house of a mutual acquaintance, probably Ford Madox Hueffer, and Henry had recommended Stephen Crane's new story *The Open Boat* which had deterred Frederic from reading it for some days.[6] On the other hand, Crane, who had recently come to live near Rye, spoke up for his compatriot. 'I agree with you that Mr James has ridiculous traits,' he wrote at this time, 'and lately I have seen him make a holy show of himself in a situation that – on my honour – would have been simple to an ordinary man. But it seems impossible to dislike him. He is so kind to everybody.'[7]

Henry's kindnesses extended to Frederic's children when they were orphaned after Frederic had died in scandalous circumstances in a house where he had been living with his mistress. (Conrad afterwards described Frederic to Hugh Walpole as 'a gross man who lived grossly and died abominably'.) Crane and his wife took in the Frederic children and when Henry heard this he immediately sent some money for their upkeep.[8]

The brilliant, lovable and eccentric Stephen Crane had come to London in 1896, having scored an international success in the previous year with his short novel of the American Civil War, *The Red Badge of Courage*. At this time he was only 25 and he was to die of tuberculosis before he was 30. Shortly after his arrival in London, he met Henry at a studio party where he rescued the Master's silk hat when an overbold young woman had poured champagne into it. In due course, Crane was joined by Cora Taylor, a twice-married lady, who was reputed to have kept a 'sporting house' in Jacksonville, Florida, where she first met Crane, and who might be described in England as a 'tart'. However, Crane boldly set up house with her and she passed as his wife, although they never seem to have been married, at least in the legal sense. Early in 1899, they took Brede Place, a few miles from Rye, at a rent of £40 a year, and kept open house to a host of friends and acquaintances on a generous scale, although Crane was already in failing health and in financial straits, judging by Cora's regular appeals to Pinker, his literary agent, for money. Brede, one of the finest examples of medieval domestic architecture in the south of England, belonged to another eccentric, More-ton Frewen, whose American wife was one of the celebrated Jerome sisters and an aunt of Winston Churchill; for the next eighteen months that Stephen and Cora were its tenants the place was the scene of some remarkable Bohemian entertainments.

Crane was usually dressed in riding breeches, leggings, spurs and a cowboy shirt. He rode about the countryside on one of two coach horses he possessed, named Hengist and Horsa, and 'on their rawboned carcasses his frail figure looked infinitely tiny and forlorn.' At times he would rein up outside Lamb House, and would alternately shock and amuse the polite company the Master happened to have at the moment, which on one occasion included the strait-laced Mrs Humphry Ward, who was presiding over the tea urn. 'My young compatriot of genius', Henry would explain with an apologetic cough after the rumbustious Stevie had departed. 'It's as if . . . oh, dear lady, it's as if you should find in a staid drawing-room on Beacon Hill or Washington Square or at an intimate reception at Washington a Cockney – oh, I admit of the greatest genius – but a Cockney still, costermonger from Whitechapel. And, oh heavens, received, surrounded and adulated . . . by, ah, the choicest, the loveliest, the most sympathetic and, ah, the most ornamental. . . .'

Henry, who had a soft corner in his heart for Crane, took his teasing in good part, although he found some of his friends and hangers-on difficult to bear. Ford Madox Hueffer wrote of them at this time:

I never heard James say anything intimately damaging

of Crane, and I do not believe he ever said anything of that sort to other people. But what made the situation really excruciating to James was the raids made by Crane's parasites on Lamb House. No doors could keep them out, nor no butler. They made hideous the still levels of the garden with their cachinations, they poked the Old Man in the ribs before his servants, caricatured his speeches before his guests and extracted from him loans that were almost never refused. There were times when he would hang about in the country outside Rye Walls rather than make such an encounter.[9]

There was a mixed club for men and women, the Mermaid Club, which had a large half-timbered room as its headquarters in the old Mermaid Inn in Rye. At Cora's request Henry sponsored her admission and also Crane's since they were both anxious to join. 'The subscriptions are very small, and the big room we saw *will* be a part of the fun,' Henry assured Cora early in August, 1899. 'I have again, today, to go up to town, on torrid and horrid business – but I shall come over to Brede again at an early date.'[10] Cora responded by sending him Harold Frederic's last novel, *The Market Place,* which she had received from the late correspondent's mistress. He read it, as he afterwards told her, 'with a lively sense of what H. F. might have done if he had lived – and above all lived (and therefore worked) differently!'[11]

Henry would bicycle over to Brede several times a week. Once, when he missed Crane and his 'wife', he left a visiting card on the back of which he scribbled a note to Cora that he 'had a dark foreboding that it was you I passed quarter of an hour ago in a populous wagonette' and that he 'will try you soon again'. Later that summer he attended a village fête in the gardens of Brede Rectory in aid of the parochial fund and the District Nursing Association. George Lynch, an old newspaper friend of Crane's, had his camera and 'snapped' Henry and Cora together, also Henry eating one of Cora's doughnuts which he had bought from her stall. Cora afterwards sent him the photographs, and in a note thanking her for the 'strange images', he added lightheartedly: 'But no, surely, it can't be

any doughnut of yours that is making me make such a gruesome grimace. I look as if I had swallowed a wasp or a penny
toy. And I tried to look so beautiful. I tried too hard, doubtless. But don't show it to anybody as H.J. trying.'[12]

Brede was reputed to be haunted and this tradition gave
Crane the idea for a play to be performed at Christmas in the
local village hall with his guests participating. He wrote most
of *The Ghost* himself, but according to the programme there
were nine literary collaborators, 'distinguished rabble', Crane
called them, in explaining the reason to one of them, H. B.
Marriott-Watson.

> *Brede Place. November 15, 1899.* We of Brede Place are
> giving free play to the villagers at Christmas time in the
> school-house and I have written some awful rubbish which
> our friends will on that night speak out to the parish.
>
> But to make the thing historic, I have hit upon a plan of
> making the programmes choice by printing thereon a terrible
> list of authors of the comedy and to that end I have asked
> Henry James, Robert Barr, Joseph Conrad, A. E. W. Mason,
> H. G. Wells, Edwin Pugh, George Gissing, Rider Haggard
> and yourself to write a mere word – any word 'it', 'they',
> 'you' – any word and thus identify themselves with this
> crime...[13]

The play, judging by the few pages of the original MS which
have survived, seems to have qualified for the principal
author's description of it. The action centres round 'the main
Brede ghost', a giant who was supposed to have been sawn in
half, and his encounters with some tourists in an 'empty room
in Brede Place' in the year 1950. One of the characters called
Peter Quint Prodmore Moreau appears to have been an amal-
gam derived from Henry's *The Turn of the Screw* and Conrad's
Nigger of the 'Narcissus'. Crane paid for the whole cost of the
production, including the printing of tickets and programmes
and the enlarging of the stage in the school hall.

The Ghost had its first and only public performance on
December 28th, 1899, in the Brede School House. A. E. W.
Mason took the part of the ghost, while the special musical

accompaniment was rendered by Mrs H. G. Wells. 'It amused its authors and caste vastly,' wrote Wells afterwards. 'What the Brede people made of it is not on record.'[14] Henry was among the eight out of ten of the play's 'collaborators' present on this historic occasion, as evidenced by his autograph on the back of one of the programmes.[15]

The following night there was a great ball at Brede. Henry, who had his ailing brother William and the latter's wife and daughter staying with him in Rye, did not go over for this, but it is on record that he was standing at the garden gate of Lamb House in the late afternoon when he saw A. E. W. Mason driving past on his way there in a dog cart and called after him facetiously that 'he might find one or two actresses in the crowd at Brede Place and had better look out – he might get caught!'[16]

Alas for 'poor Stevie', the night ended in tragedy. The exertions of the house party and the play proved too much for him, he suffered a severe lung haemorrhage, which he had tried to conceal from Cora. She woke up Wells and begged him to go for help. 'There was a bicycle in the place,' wrote Wells later, 'and my last clear memory of that fantastic Brede house party is riding out of the cold skirts of a wintry night into a drizzling dawn to call up a doctor in Rye.'[17]

It was the beginning of the end for Crane. Henry, who was genuinely fond of him, was greatly upset when he heard the news, and rushed up to London to seek the help of an eminent American doctor whom he heard had arrived from New York. 'He suffered infinitely for that dying boy,' Ford Hueffer was to recall. 'I would walk with him for hours over the Marsh trying to divert his thoughts. But he would talk on and on. He was for ever considering devices for Crane's comfort. Once he telegraphed to Wanamaker's for a whole collection of New England delicacies from pumpkin pie to apple butter and sausage meat and clams and soft shell crabs and mince meat and . . . everything unthinkable, so that the poor lad should know once more and finally those fierce joys.'[18]

For an invalid such as Crane, Brede Place with its sparse furnishings, primitive plumbing and absence of proper heating, was highly unsuitable. In a last effort to save him – by now it was too late – Cora took him off to the Black Forest towards the end of the following May. A few days after they had left, Henry brought some friends to Brede 'to show them the face of the old house', so he wrote to Cora; 'but the melancholy of it was quite heartbreaking. So will it, I fear, always be to me.' On June 5th, 1900, he sent Cora a cheque for £50, begging her to view the money as 'a convenience . . . and dedicate it to whatever service it may best render my stricken young friend. It meagrely represents my tender benediction to him'.[19]

Crane died before Henry's letter arrived, and the money helped to pay for his costly funeral. 'What a brutal needless extinction!' Henry wrote to Cora on learning the 'miserable news' from the papers. 'What an unmitigated unredeemed catastrophe! I think of him with such a sense of possibilities and powers.'[20]

[TWO]

George Gissing was another invalid writer, who was befriended alike by Henry and H. G. Wells. In June, 1901, Gissing was staying with Wells at Sandgate, and Wells suggested bringing him over to Rye. A 'strange tragic figure, a figure of internal tragedy', as Wells described him, Gissing had made two disastrous marriages, one to a Manchester prostitute and the other to a servant girl whom he picked up in the street in London; at this time he was living in Paris with a mistress who styled herself Madame Gissing, and her parsimonious mother in dreary and comfortless surroundings. By the time he arrived in Sandgate Gissing was in a starving condition, and Mrs Wells had to feed him up, 'weighing him carefully at intervals – with marvellous results'.[21]

'Please express to him that it will give me very great pleasure to see him,' Henry wrote to Wells, 'and that if he only *will* let you convey him over I will surround him with every solicitude in my power. But don't think of doing anything so arduous as to come for a couple of hours so dreadful a way. Come over in time for luncheon, of course, but stay and sleep.

... I can put you both up for the night easily – and it's a far better business than the other system of – what shall I say? – all cry and no wool. Let us at least have as much wool as possible.'[22]

Gissing was greatly taken with his host's 'lovely old Georgian house, superbly furnished'. The three men talked long into the night, Henry regaling his guests with his reminiscences of Turgeniev in Paris, which Gissing found a particularly 'interesting story'. Alas that there was no Boswell to record this talk. All Henry did was to insert a laconic note in his copy of Gissing's *New Grub Street*, the pathetic and largely autobiographical story of the ruin of an author's powers of imagination by money worries and overwork. ('George Gissing at Lamb House with H. G. Wells.')* It was Henry's first and also his last meeting with the unfortunate Gissing, who shortly afterwards returned to his French mistress after a spell in an English sanatorium and never again came home to England. 'Poor Gissing,' he remarked afterwards, 'struck me as quite particularly marked out for what is called in his and my profession an unhappy ending.'

Sydney Waterlow has recalled Henry speaking of Gissing:

> The impression made by Gissing was a peculiarly painful one. Nature had been unkind to him. The front face was not bad; he had a fine forehead and clustering hair: but when he turned his face you saw one side disfigured by a large expanse of purple birth-mark: and mouth and chin were ugly and feeble. His whole an extraordinarily ungainly, common ill-shaped figure; almost knock-kneed, bearing the unmistakeable stamp of Wakefield, his birthplace. He talked of his amazing relations with women, and said (what I didn't know) that he left his second wife and his children to live with a French woman, who passed as Mrs Gissing: even wedding cards were sent out. This woman was with him when he died. One of Gissing's queernesses was that he spoke French well, with a precise affectation that made it almost too well.

He thinks *New Grub Street* much his best book. Gissing's

---

* This copy is now in the Lamb House library.

style, he said, is horribly ugly, though it is clear and clothes his matter quite easily. It is not merely colourless: it has the colour and surface of some vulgar, mechanical gloss. His great merit is that he really describes the lower-middle-class circles which he knows, whereas most people who know these circles prefer to describe something else – either quite low life or lords.[24]

'I had a saddish letter from Gissing,' Henry wrote again to Wells in January 1902, 'but rumours of better things (I mean of reviving powers) have come to me, I don't quite know how, since.' The rumours proved unfounded, as Gissing died in the following year, Wells making the journey to the Pyrenees to be with him during his last days, 'that admirable effort for poor Gissing *in extremis*', as Henry described his action. 'And *now* I can't write of Gissing with any pertinence,' he told Wells when it was all over, 'for I am concerned only with the prospect, some day, not too long hence, of asking you, face to face, for the story of your surely most dismal, as it was a most generous pilgrimage.'[25]

Another of Wells's friends whom Henry saw something of in Rye was G. K. Chesterton, who spent some weeks in the summer of 1908 at the Mermaid Inn, round the corner from Lamb House. Henry was impressed by the way Chesterton used to retire into the corner of a room and just sat and wrote. It was wonderful to be able to do that, he told Theodora Bosanquet; he could not quite do it himself. On the other hand, Chesterton's physical appearance disconcerted him. Once, when he was dictating to his secretary in the Garden Room, he made her go and peep through the curtains to see 'the unspeakable Chesterton', as he called him, pass by the house, 'a sort of elephant with a crimson face and oily curls'. Henry told Theodora that he had been to see Chesterton at the Mermaid on the previous day and that he had 'an enormous little slavey' of a wife with him. It was very tragic, Henry remarked, that such a mind should be imprisoned in such a body.

William James happened to be on a visit to Lamb House at this time, and Wells was to recall in his autobiography how the

nearby presence of Chesterton provoked some heated ex-
changes between the two brothers.

> He [Henry] had lost his calm; he was terribly unnerved. He
> appealed to me, of all people, to adjudicate on what was and
> what was not permissible in England. William was arguing
> about it in an indisputably American accent, with an in-
> decently naked reasonableness. I had come to Rye with a
> car to fetch William James and his daughter to my home in
> Sandgate. William had none of Henry's passionate regard
> for the polish upon the surfaces of life and he was immensely
> excited by the fact that in the little Rye inn, which had its
> garden just over the high brick wall of the garden of Lamb
> House, G. K. Chesterton was staying. William James had
> corresponded with our vast contemporary and he sorely
> wanted to see him. So with a scandalous directness he had
> put the gardener's ladder against that ripe red wall and
> clambered up and peeped over!
> Henry had caught him at it.
> It was the sort of thing that isn't done. It was most
> emphatically the sort of thing that isn't done. . . . Henry
> had instructed the gardener to put away the ladder and
> William was looking thoroughly naughty about it.[26]

Another picturesque literary character seen about the neighbourhood of Rye at this time was the Polish master mariner
and naturalized English novelist Teodor Josef Konrad Kor-
zeniowski, who had wisely dropped his surname and was content to be known to his English readers as Joseph Conrad.
He had a rat-infested farmhouse near H. G. Wells in Kent but
spent much of his time, in literary collaboration, with Ford
Madox Hueffer at the latter's bungalow in Winchelsea. 'Conrad
haunts Winchelsea,' Henry told Wells, 'and Winchelsea (in
discretion) haunts Rye.' Neither expatriate liked the other
much personally, but each had a healthy respect for the other's
literary achievements, although neither was a financially successful writer. (Conrad only became so towards the end of his
life – Henry never did.) Mrs Conrad, on the other hand, liked
both Henry and his writing. 'I was very fond of this dear man,

who was so essentially a gentleman in every sense of the word,' she wrote of him, 'I could read his work, too, with very real pleasure, in spite of his wordy and often terribly involved style.'[27]

While he and his wife were living at Pent Farm, Conrad got into serious financial difficulties through the failure of a bank which had advanced him money. When he heard about this trouble, Edmund Gosse, who sat on the Committee of the Royal Literary Fund, asked Henry for a letter supporting a grant from the Fund to their indigent fellow author, since Gosse always strictly applied the test of literary merit as the basis for relief. Henry immediately sent Gosse a felicitously worded testimonial. 'I lose not an hour in responding to your request about Conrad, whom I had not in the least known to be in the state you mention,' he wrote in a covering note. 'It horrifies me more than I can say, and I applaud to the echo your attempt to do something for him. Do let me know what may result from it. *May* my letter, enclosed, and which I've endeavoured to make warm yet discreet, weigh in the scale! It is at least wholly sincere. May Heaven speed your good work! And what a drama; altogether the circumjacent crash of things!'

Lamb House,
Rye.

June 26th, 1902.

My dear Gosse,

I have the highest opinion of the title Joseph Conrad would have, on literary grounds, to become one of your beneficiaries: all the more that in spite of his admirable work he is not so known to a wide and promiscuous public that his claims may speak wholly for themselves. He has been to me, the last few years, one of the most interesting and striking of the novelists of the new generation.

His production (you know what it consists of) has all been fine, rare and valid, of the sort greeted more by the expert and the critic than (as people say) by the man in the street. His successive books have been real literature, of a distinguished sort, the record of his experience, in navigating years, of eastern seas, strange climes and far countries, all presented in a form far more artistic than has been given to any 'Tales of the Sea', among English writers and that approximates more than anything we have to the truth and beauty of the French Pierre Loti. The *Nigger of the Narcissus* is in my opinion the very finest and strongest picture of the sea and sea-life that our language possesses, the masterpiece in a whole great class; and *Lord Jim* runs it very close.

When I think moreover that such completeness, such intensity of expression has been arrived at by a man not born to our speech, but who took it up with singular courage, from necessity and sympathy, and has laboured at it heroically and devotedly, I am equally impressed with the fine persistence and intrinsic success. Born a Pole and cast upon the waters, he has worked out an English style that is more than correct, that has *quality* and ingenuity.

The case seems to me unique and peculiarly worthy of recognition. Unhappily, to be very serious and subtle isn't one of the paths to fortune. Therefore I greatly hope that the Royal Literary Fund may be able to do something for him. *Do* let me recommend him to you in the name of his charming, conscientious, uncommon work. It has truly a kind of disinterested independent nobleness.

Believe me yours always,
Henry James.

As a result of this letter, Conrad was given an immediate grant by the Fund of £300, subsequently increased by a further £200.[28]

Henry, who habitually conversed with Conrad in French – using an admirably pronounced, correct and rather stilted idiom such as prevailed in the Paris of the 'seventies, so Ford Madox Ford tells us – always addressed the Pole as '*Mon cher confrère*', while to the latter Henry was invariably '*Très cher Maître*'. According to Henry, Conrad spoke English with so marked a foreign accent that it was 'hard to believe he is the same man who writes the books'. They would regularly send each other copies of their new books as they appeared. 'I read you as I listen to rare music,' Henry wrote in thanking Conrad for one of his, 'with deepest depths of surrender, and out of those depths I emerge slowly and reluctantly again to acknowledge that I return to life . . . No one has *known* – for intellectual use – the things you know, and you have, as the artist of the whole matter, an authority that no one has approached. . . . I pat you, my dear Conrad, very affectionately and complacently on the head and am yours very constantly.'

As a Christmas present in 1908, Henry sent Conrad the first six volumes of the New York edition of his *Novels and Tales*, which included *The American*, with its new preface. Conrad, who had read this novel nearly twenty years previously 'could not resist the temptation of reading the beautiful and touching last ten pages of the story again. There is in them a perfection of tone which calmed me, and I sat for a long while with the closed volume in my hand going over the preface in my mind and thinking – that is how it began, and that's how it was done!' Or, as he put it to his friend Hueffer: 'I don't know how the Old Man does it. There's nothing he does not know; there's nothing he can't do. That's what it is when you have been privileged to go about with Turgeniev.'[28]

In 1907, Conrad moved with his wife and son Borys from Kent to Bedfordshire, taking a house at Luton called Someries, less than forty minutes in the train from London. He begged Henry to visit him there, if only for his son's sake. 'When you come up for your London period, you must extend it periodically as far as the Someries – any day when the conjunction of the planets and your inclination point favourably to my request. *N'est-ce pas?* You would not deprive the boy of boasting to his descendants that he has seen Henry James under his father's roof. It would be downright cruelty, considering what a scanty store of glamour I am likely to leave him otherwise.'[29]

By far the most successful of Henry's literary acquaintances who frequented the neighbourhood was Rudyard Kipling. On October 2nd, 1902, Henry wrote to Edmund Gosse from Lamb House:

at the Brede Rec-
tory Garden Fête,
August, 1899.
'I shall come over
to Brede again at
an early date.'

'But no surely, it
can't be any dough-
nut of yours that is
making me make
such a gruesome
grimace.'

*From photographs in
Columbia University
Library*

STEPHEN CRANE
at Brede Place

'I think of him with such a sense of possibilities and powers.'

From a photograph by courtesy of Mr Roger Frewen

(Below) Autographed programme of *The Ghost*

From the original in Columbia University Library

THE GHOST.

Written by

MR. HENRY JAMES, MR. ROBERT BARR,
MR. GEORGE GISSING, MR. RIDER HAGGARD,
MR. JOSEPH CONRAD, MR. H. B. MARRIOTT-
WATSON, MR. H. G. WELLS, MR. EDWIN PUGH,
MR. A. E. W. MASON AND
MR. STEPHEN CRANE.

BREDE SCHOOL HOUSE,

DECEMBER 28TH, 1899.

7 45 P.M

DEACON, PRINTER, RYE.

I walked this p.m., alone and purely self-supported, over to Winchelsea, to have tea with some bullying people, and in my absence the 2 Rudyards puffed up to my door in their motor, *proprio moter,* from Burwash where they have gone to live (an obscure locality in Sussex), leaving for me, on my return, but a black plume as a token – or rather a blackened card. Otherwise I might have more history, not to say poetry, for you. But we miss our precious opportunities. However I am greatly hoping this one will be renewed.[30]

The opportunity was renewed one day shortly afterwards, when Hueffer and Conrad went over from Winchelsea to Rye to see about hiring a motor-car. Hueffer left Conrad to inspect the vehicle in a local garage, while he made his way to Lamb House. As he was going up the cobbled street, he passed Rudyard Kipling and his wife hurrying down. The account which Hueffer subsequently wrote in his autobiographical *Return to Yesterday* of his meeting with Henry and of how Henry explained why the Kiplings looked so worried is worth quoting, even if it is somewhat overdrawn.

When I was admitted into his presence by the astonishingly ornate man-servant he said:
'A writer who unites – if I may use the phrase – in his own person an enviable popularity to – as I am told – considerable literary gifts and whom I may say I like because he treats me' – and here Mr James laid his hand over his heart, made the slightest of bows and, rather cruelly rolling his dark and liquid eyes and moving his lower jaw as if were rolling in his mouth a piquant tit-bit, Mr James continued, 'because he treats me – if again I may say any such thing – with proper respect' – and there would be an immense humorous gasp before the word 'respect' – ... 'I refer of course to Mr Kipling ... has just been to see me. And – such are the rewards of an enviable popularity! – a popularity such as I – or indeed you my young friend if you have any ambitions which I sometimes doubt – could dream of far less imagine to ourselves – such are the rewards of an enviable

popularity that Mr Kipling is in the possession of a magnificent one thousand two hundred guinea motor-car. And, in the course of conversation as to characteristics of motor-cars in general and those of the particular one thousand two hundred guinea motor-car in the possession of our friend . . . But what do I say? . . . Of our cynosure! Mr Kipling uttered words which have for himself no doubt a particular significance but which to me at least convey almost literally nothing beyond their immediate sound . . . Mr Kipling said that the motor-car was calculated to make the Englishman . . .' – and again came the humorous gasp and the roll of the eyes – 'was calculated to make the Englishman . . . think'. And Mr James abandoned himself for part of a second to low chuckling.

'And,' he continued, 'the conversation dissolved itself, after digressions on the advantages attendant on the possession of such a vehicle, into what I believe are styled golden dreams – such as how the magnificent one thousand two hundred guinea motor-car after having this evening conveyed its master and mistress to Batemans Burwash of which the proper pronunciation is Burridge would to-morrow devotedly return here and reaching here at twelve would convey me and my nephew Billiam to Burridge in time to lunch and having partaken of that repast to return here in time to give tea to my friend Lady Maud Warrender who is honouring that humble meal with her presence tomorrow under my roof . . . And we were all indulging in – what is it? – delightful anticipations and dilating on the agreeablenesses of rapid – but not for fear of the police and consideration for one's personal safety *too* rapid – speed over country roads and all, if I may use the expression, was gas and gingerbread when . . . There is a loud knocking on the door and – *avec des yeux effarés* . . .' and here Mr James really did make his prominent and noticeable eyes almost stick out of his head . . . 'in rushes the chauffeur . . . And in short the chauffeur has omitted to lubricate the wheels of the magnificent one thousand two hundred guinea motor-car with the result that its axles have become one piece of molten metal . . .

The consequence is that its master and mistress will

return to Burwash which should be pronounced Burridge by train, and the magnificent one thousand two hundred guinea motor-car will *not* devotedly return here at noon and will *not* in time for lunch convey me and my nephew Billiam to Burwash and will *not* return here in time for me to give tea to my friend Lady Maud Warrender who is honouring that humble meal with her presence to-morrow beneath my roof or if the weather is fine in the garden. . . .'

'Which,' concluded the Master after subdued 'ho, ho, ho's' of merriment, 'is calculated to make Mr Kipling think.'

In 1891, shortly after young Rudyard Kipling – he was barely twenty-five – had settled in England, Henry had written a complimentary critical introduction for a collection of Kipling's Indian stories published in America under the title, *Mine Own People*.

On the whole [he remarked of the author] he presents himself as a strangely clever youth who has stolen the formidable mask of maturity and rushes about, making people jump with the deep sounds, and sportive exaggerations of tone, that issue from its painted lips. . . . Mr Kipling's actual performance is like a tremendous walk before breakfast, making one welcome the idea of the meal, but consider with some alarm the hours still to be traversed. Yet if his breakfast is all to come, the indications are that he will be more active than ever after he has had it. Among these indications are the unflagging character of his pace and the excellent form, as they say in athletic circles, in which he gets over the ground. We don't detect him stumbling; on the contrary, he steps out quite as briskly as at first, and still more firmly. There is something zealous and craftsman-like in him which shows that he feels both joy and responsibility.[32]

When Kipling got married in February, 1892, Henry gave the bride away and saw them off on their round-the-world honeymoon. 'She was poor Wolcott Balestier's sister and is a hard, devoted, capable, characterless little person, whom I don't in the least understand his marrying. It's a union of which

197

I don't forecast the future, though I gave her away at the altar – a dreary little wedding, with an attendance simply of four men, her mother and sister prostrate with influenza. Kipling strikes me personally as the most complete man of genius (as distinguished from "fine intelligence") that I have ever known.'[33]

But Kipling's early promise was not fulfilled in Henry's eyes. Six years later, he was writing:

> His *Ballad* future may still be big. But my view of his prose future has much shrunken in the light of one's increasingly observing how little of life he can make use of. Almost nothing civilised save steam and patriotism – and the latter only in verse, where I *hate* it so, especially mixed up with God and goodness, that half spoils my enjoyment of his great talent. Almost nothing of the complicated soul or of the female form or of any question of shades – which latter constitute, to my sense, the real formative literary discipline. In his earliest time I thought he perhaps contained the seeds of an English Balzac; but I have quite given that up in proportion as he has come steadily from the less simple in subject to the more simple – from the Anglo-Indians to the natives, from the natives to the Tommies, from the Tommies to the quadrupeds, from the quadrupeds to the fish, and from the fish to the engines and screws . . .[34]

Notwithstanding this change in opinion, Henry and the Kiplings continued to keep in touch, and Henry regularly visited them, first at Rottingdean and later after they had moved to Burwash. However, the time came when these visits proved something of a trial. Theodora Bosanquet recalled how, one July day in 1908, Henry was 'much fussed' as he had accepted an invitation to lunch with the Kiplings. 'It rained and he didn't want to go and didn't much expect Mr Kipling to send his motor-car for him. However he did, so Mr James, really rather annoyed had to go.'

Another critic, who analysed Kipling and also Henry James, both in words and caricatures, was Max Beerbohm. But of his two subjects, 'the incomparable Max' was much less kind to

Kipling, whom he always disliked, while he really revered Henry. The dramatic adaptation of *The Light That Failed* by 'George Fleming' in 1903 gave Beerbohm the opportunity in a critique which he wrote of the production to make a neat contrast with Henry, whose view incidentally he shared, that Kipling as a writer was 'uncivilised'.

'George Fleming' is, as we know, a lady. Should the name Rudyard Kipling, too, be put between inverted commas? Is it, too, the veil of feminine identity? If of Mr Kipling we knew nothing except his work, we should assuredly make that conjecture. A lady who writes fiction reveals her sex clearlier through her portrayal of men than through any other of her lapses. And in Mr Kipling's short stories, especially in *The Light that Failed* (that elongated short story which 'George Fleming' has now adapted to the stage), men are portrayed in an essentially feminine manner, and from an essentially feminine point of view. They are men seen from the outside, or rather, not seen at all, but feverishly imagined . . . To him, as to his hero, they typify, in its brightest colours, the notion of manhood, manliness, man. And by this notion Mr Kipling is permanently and joyously obsessed. That is why I say his standpoint is feminine . . . Mr Kipling is so far masculine that he has never displayed a knowledge of women as they are; but the unreality of his male creatures, with his worship of them, makes his name ring quaintly like a pseudonym . . .

For Mr Kipling is nothing – never was anything – if not unsqueamish. The ugly word, the ugly action, the ugly atmosphere – for all these he has an inevitable scent; and the uglier they be, the keener seems his relish of them. Strength, mere strength, is not enough to make a hero for him: the hero must also be a brute and a bounder. Writing of George Sand, Mr Henry James once suggested that she, though she may have been to all intents and purposes a man, was not a gentleman. Conversely, it might be said that Mr Kipling as revealed to us in his fiction, is no lady. But he is not the less essentially feminine for that.[35]

[THREE]

'As a good listener,' Max Beerbohm remarked in a broadcast talk which he gave in 1936 on the subject of speed, 'I rather sigh for the old leisurely repasts and the habit of lingering long after them to hear more from the lips of such talkers as Oscar Wilde or Henry James, Reginald Turner or Charles Brookfield.'[36] It has been stated that Henry first met Beerbohm, then a youngster of twenty-three, at a New Year's Eve party at the Gosse's in 1895. Edmund Gosse and his wife Nelly kept open house every New Year's Eve, and the occasion was marked by some entertainment usually of excellent quality. But on this occasion Gosse had been misled into the choice of a puppet show, which turned out to be very poor. The show was presented in a small upstairs room in Delamere Terrace, packed with celebrities and others not so well known. Henry found himself jammed up against a wall with two young men, one of whom was Max Beerbohm; the other, whom he already knew, was Edward Marsh, just down from Cambridge and about to go into the Colonial Office. As the entertainment proceeded there was a growing sense of failure, and Henry became increasingly bored. Unable to contain himself any longer, he turned towards Marsh, and laying his hand on the younger man's shoulder in a characteristic and familiar gesture, broke out: 'An interesting example of economy, my dear Marsh – economy of means – and er – er –' here a glint of malice came into his eyes – 'economy of *effect*'.[37]

This encounter happened during Henry's bearded period; Beerbohm thought at the time that he looked like 'a Russian Grand Duke of the better type' and was struck by his curious 'veiled' expression. (When he shaved off his beard soon after coming to Lamb House, 'he looked rather like a lay Cardinal'.) After their initial meeting, Beerbohm often found himself in Henry's company, usually in London. He enjoyed this, as he admired Henry's writing. According to his biographer, Lord David Cecil, 'Henry James was all that Max liked a great man to be: majestic, benignant and slightly comical. He equally enjoyed the subtle wisdom of Henry James's remarks

and the extraordinary manner – preliminary sighings, portentous pauses and anxious reassuring gestures – with which he
uttered them. Now and again he noted that Henry James
could be malicious. "But this, though it made him more
formidable, also made him more entertaining".'

Henry, on his side, took to the brilliant young caricaturist,
who had just collected some of his essays into a single volume
which he called, with endearing effrontery, *The Works of Max
Beerbohm*. For Henry liked courteous, elegant, intelligent
youth; he insisted on treating the young Beerbohm as an equal,
and flattered his vanity by doing this in public. Once, at a
wedding reception, a woman acquaintance of Henry's saw the
two of them standing together. 'How terribly distinguished
you look,' she remarked. 'We *are* distinguished,' replied Henry.
'But you need not look so terribly so,' said the woman. 'We
are shameless, shameless!' was Henry's acute rejoinder.[38]

When he read Henry's short story 'The Jolly Corner' when it
came out in the first number of *The English Review* under the
editorship of Ford Madox Hueffer, Max Beerbohm could not
resist writing to Henry about it, and his writings in general.
'I have had such a very lovely letter from him', he told his
friend Reggie Turner. The letter read as follows:

> *Lamb House,*
> *Rye.*
>
> *19 December, 1908*

My dear Max Beerbohm,

I won't say in acknowledgment of your beautiful letter
that it's exactly the sort of letter I like best to receive,
because that would sound as if I had *data* for generalizing –
which I haven't; and therefore I can only go so far as to say
that if it belonged to a class, or weren't a mere remarkable
individual, I *should* rank it with the type supremely gratify-
ing. On its mere lonely independent merits it appeals to me
intimately and exquisitely, and I can only gather myself in
and up, arching and presenting my not inconsiderable back
– a back, as who should say, offered for any further stray
scratching and patting of that delightful kind.

I can bear wounds and fell smitings (so far as I have been ever honoured with such – and indeed life smites us on the whole enough, taking one thing with another,) better than expressive gentleness of touch; so you must imagine me for a little while quite prostrate and overcome with the force of your good words. But I shall recover, when they have really sunk in – and then be not only the 'better', but the more nimble and artful and alert by what they will have done for me.

You had, and you obeyed, a very generous and humane inspiration; it charms me to think – or rather so authentically to know, that my (I confess) ambitious Muse does work upon you; it really helps me to believe in her the more myself – by which I am very gratefully yours

HENRY JAMES

Not long before his death, Sir Max Beerbohm, as he then was, recalled for the benefit of the present writer what he called 'an incident', in which he took part with Henry James and which afterwards seemed to him strangely and exactly like the basis of a short story written by Henry – 'one of the many short stories he wrote on the theme of an elderly and very eminent great writer in relation to an earnest young admirer and disciple'.* It was the early spring of 1909. Max had been to a luncheon party given by Somerset Maugham at the Carlton Hotel, and he was on his way to his club, the Savile, which in those days was housed at the southern end of Piccadilly, with the object of reading Henry's contribution to the latest number of *The English Review*, entitled 'The Velvet Glove'.

There was a keen north-easterly wind blowing and I was wearing a rather thin overcoat and was therefore walking quickly. But I would have been hasting in any case so eager

---

* Sir Max Beerbohm recited these recollections to the present writer in the garden of his villa near Rapallo, in 1954. They were subsequently broadcast by the B.B.C. in 'Recollections of Henry James in his Later Years' in the Third Programme on June 4th, 1956. See H. Montgomery Hyde. 'An Afternoon with Max' in *The Spectator*, October 5, 1956.

was I to read that story. And then, halfway down the slope, I encountered a slowly descending figure which seemed to me vaguely familiar. I must explain that hitherto it was only in drawing-rooms and dining-rooms that I had seen Henry James and that his magnificently massive and shapely brow was what had always most impressed me there. Hence my momentary failure now to recognise him in a very large, old top hat, of which the brim came down almost to the level of his eyebrows; he, however, had identified me and he accosted me in the deeply ruminating manner that was his. He told me that he'd just come up to London from his home at Rye. He said that he was to all intents and purposes a country cousin, and he asked me whether there was any exhibition of pictures for him to see. I was able to tell him that there was a very good one at the Grafton Galleries. He asked me with much circumlocution whether I would be inclined to act as his guide. He was a great hesitator, you know, the greatest of hesitators. He would have been a great Parliamentarian, because in the House of Commons those who hesitate are greatly valued. A fluent speaker is apt to be considered superficial, while a hesitator they think is hesitating because he is deeply pondering the grave issues. Balfour was a great hesitator, and so is Winston.

Max Beerbohm felt much honoured by this invitation. And yet, to his great surprise, he heard himself saying instantly: 'Well, I'm afraid I can't. I have to be in Kensington at half-past three.'

'Ah,' said Henry. 'You young men, always entangled in webs of engagements, yes, yes . . . Some young woman, I suppose.'

And with that he passed on up the slope of the street.

What had prompted me to tell that fib? It wasn't merely the north-east wind and the thin overcoat and the prospect of having to walk slowly up that slope. It wasn't merely shyness and the fear that what I might have to say would sound cheap and tawdry to Henry James, that profoundly fastidious critic of men. Nor was it merely the presentiment

that he would not share my admiration for that picture
which was the outstanding one in the Grafton Galleries,
young Augustus John's 'Woman Smiling'. It was mainly my
aforesaid impatience to be reading 'The Velvet Glove'.

And here I was now in the Savile reading it. It was, of
course, a very good story, and yet, from time to time, I
found my mind wandering away from it. It was not so
characteristic, not so intensely Jamesian a story as James
would have founded on the theme of what had just been
happening between us, a theme of the disciple loyally, or
unloyally, preferring the Master's work to the Master.

Two years earlier, Max Beerbohm had brought out a large
folio volume of drawings of contemporary celebrities, which
he called *A Book of Caricatures*. Of the fifty or so celebrities
Henry was the only one to appear twice, but he did not appear
to take offence at either of these caricatures, although not
merely his figure but also his prose style was caricatured.

The first, entitled 'London in November and Mr Henry
James in London', showed the subject, in top hat and carrying
an umbrella, groping his way through a dense London fog,
his left hand in front of his eyes as if to be reassured by
a familiar landmark. The caption, in Beerbohm's handwriting,
read:

> ... It was, therefore, not without something of a shock
> that he, in this to him so very congenial atmosphere, now
> perceived that a vision of the hand which he had, at a ven-
> ture, held up within an inch or so of his eyes was, with an
> almost awful clarity, being adumbrated. ...

The second drawing, 'Mr Henry James Revisiting America',
showed the returning expatriate surrounded by a heterogene-
ous group of natives, who commented accordingly. 'My!
Ain't he cree-ative?' an admiring young girl exclaimed. 'Hail,
great white novelist!' says an Indian Chief. 'Tuniyaba – the
spinner of fine cobwebs!' Then there is an ecstatic old black
mammy: 'Why, it's Masser Henry! Come to your old nurse's

arms, honey!' Similar remarks are attributed to other characters, including a Beacon Hill hostess, a Harvard Intellectual, and a Westerner in a sheriff's hat. Max's caption is sub-titled 'Extract from His Unspoken Thoughts':

> ... So that in fine, let, without further beating about the bush, me make to myself amazed acknowledgement that, but for the certificate of birth which I have – so quite indubitably – on me, I might in regarding (and, as it somewhat were, overseeing) *à l'oeil de voyageur* these, dear good people, find hard to swallow, or even to take by subconscious injection, the great idea that I am – oh, ever so indigenously! – one of them. ...

Beerbohm did several other drawings of the Master. One, apparently, unpublished, he showed the present writer, as well as Mr S. N. Behrman, whose description of it is worth quoting: 'It is quite dumb but eloquent. James is shown kneeling in the corridor of a country house on a crowded week-end. It is very early in the morning. His eyes are beaded on two pairs of Edwardian shoes – a man's and a woman's. He has been staring at them for a long time; he will continue to do so. He will stare at those four shoes until they have yielded the last drop of their secret to him.'[39] Another amusing sketch, now in the Waller Barrett Collection in the University of Virginia, is entitled 'An Awful Fancy: Mr Henry James subpoenaed as a psychological expert in a *cause célèbre*'. He is shown leaning over the side of the witness box with a puzzled expression, while being fiercely cross-examined by Sir Edward Carson. 'Come, sir,' says Carson. 'I ask you a plain question and I expect a plain answer!' Henry also figures in the famous Edwardian caricature mural in the entrance hall of the Villino Chiaro, Max's villa near Rapallo.* Finally, there was the drawing entitled 'The Old Pilgrim Comes Home', done in 1913 and no doubt inspired by the subject's seventieth birthday; it

---

* The other Edwardians were King Edward VII, the Marquis de Soveral, Joseph Chamberlain, Reggie Turner, Arthur Pinero, William Rothenstein, George Moore, Rudyard Kipling and Winston Churchill.

showed him walking towards the Eternal City whose chief buildings are reflected in the distance by the sun.*

Beerbohm wrote several longer parodies of Henry, but always in good-natured vein. One of them, unpublished during the lifetime of either of them, was in the guise of a specimen chapter of an alleged forthcoming book by Max Beerbohm entitled *Half Hours with the Dialects of England.* The chapter was on Rye and contained a sonnet to Henry in the broadest Sussex supposed to have been written by a dressmaker who had fallen in love with the master of Lamb House. Max began by describing the dressmaker's hopeless and unrequited passion for Henry and the unfortunate consequences it caused.

Persons passing up the steep and cobbled alley that leads from the main street of this town to Mr Henry James's residence will have noted on one of the front-doors a small oval brass plate, inscribed thus:

Miss Peploe,
Dressmaker.

... A stranger in Rye would jump to the conclusion that Miss Peploe was a highly susceptible woman, on whose heart, however, Mr James had made no impression at all. In point of fact, Miss Peploe, till Mr James entered Rye, had been notably impervious to the shafts of Cupid. Her soul had been bounded on the East by her needle, on the West by her yard-measure, on the South, by her scissors, and on the North by her thimble. To please her customers had been her sole aspiration.

On the very day of Mr James's entry into Rye, all was changed. It happened that Miss Peploe was at her window at the moment when he, with the local house-agent, passed up the street to inspect the house where he now resides. As we know he loved it at first sight. Just so did Miss Peploe love *him.* Since then, it must be confessed, she is not the dressmaker she was. The woman in her has emerged, and the poet become vocal; but the *couturière* leaves much to be

---

* Published in *A Survey* (1921).

desired. Dresses are often not delivered within the time specified. Misfits are frequent. Buttons come off. Seams burst. Customers are angry and few.

Let it be said at once that Mr James himself is wholly innocent of this sad state of things. It is not, perhaps, likely that a man so observant as he has failed to remark the face of Miss Peploe flying to the window whenever he fares up or down the street. But never has he paused to make sign of recognition. Nor has Miss Peploe, as yet, had the courage or immodesty to tell her secret to him.

In offering the accompanying 'sample of Miss Peploe's racier Muse', Max hoped of it, 'apart from its importance to the purpose of his book, that it may chance to meet the eye of Mr James, and so, perhaps, pave the way to Miss Peploe's future happiness'.

The last two lines of the sonnet read:

> Wings o' the Dove! No dove do be for bein'
> More dove than me when I do thee be zeein'.

There were explanatory notes to the sonnet written in the style of a scholarly editor of classical poetry. The explanation of 'Wings o' the Dove!', for instance, was 'an expletive much favoured by the fishermen of Rye since Mr James made his home in their midst'.[40]

The whole thing was a piece of good-humoured banter on Beerbohm's part. Whether Henry ever saw it is not recorded. We do know, however, that he read the parody of him called 'The Mote in the Middle Distance' which Max included in his *Christmas Garland*. Henry ate his Christmas dinner in 1913 with the Gosse's, when he brought up the subject and, according to Gosse, 'discussed it with the most extraordinary vivacity and appreciation'.

He was full of admiration [Gosse wrote to Beerbohm]. I told him that you had a certain nervousness about his acceptance of your parody of him, and he desired me to let you know at once that no one can have read it with more wonder and delight than he. He expressed himself in superlatives. He called the book 'the most intelligent that has been produced in England for many a long day'. But he says you have destroyed the trade of writing. No one, now, can write without incurring the reproach of somewhat ineffectively imitating – *you!* What could be more handsome. And alas! my dear Max, what can be more true?[41]

Max Beerbohm's literary perception was most sensitive, a fact not lost upon Henry, for the two men really had a great deal in common. It has been pointed out that both were literary dandies, who saw the arts 'linked inevitably with polite society', and both believed in 'the importance of the finer shades in conveying intensity of emotion'.[42]

The dramatic review which Max wrote of the matinée production of *The High Bid* in 1909 gave him an opportunity to bring in the corpus of Henry's writing in the Collected Edition, then nearing completion. What Max wrote must surely stand high among the many hundreds of thousands of words of literary criticism of Henry James during the past sixty years or so.

When I think of Mr James's books, and try to evaluate the immense delight I have had in that immense array of volumes, it seems to me that in my glow of gratitude the thing I am most of all grateful for is not the quality of the work itself, but the quality of the man revealed through that work. Greater than all my aesthetic delight in the books is my moral regard for the author. This confession, if it chance to meet his eye, may startle him. He was not in Paris in the early 'seventies for nothing. His 'form' in fiction rigidly forbids self-assertion. Not his to button-hole us and tell us what he thinks of his characters. We must find out about them for ourselves. No philosophics will be expounded to us, no morals pointed for us. . . .

'E.A.B.' of the 'Daily News' pronounces that Mr James whose books he has read, is 'a clever man' – a remark that gives me somewhat the impulse that Charles Lamb had in regard to a gentleman who had fired off precisely that remark about Shakespeare. How much more than clever Mr James is, how many qualities unrelated to cleverness are in him, is measured for us by the fatuous inadequacy of this remark from a man who is, as 'E.A.B.' is, himself a very clever man. 'Subtle,' adds 'E.A.B.', as a make-weight. It is the Gradus epithet for Mr James, and saves time. But I am sorry for any one who, having read even but one or two of Mr James's earliest short stories, could find no other epithets to affix. And you need search heart and brain for epithets to describe the later James – the James who has patiently evolved a method of fiction entirely new, entirely his own, a method that will probably perish with him, since none but he, one thinks, could handle it; that amazing method by which a novel competes not with other novels, but with life itself; making people known to us as we grow to know them in real life, by hints, by glimpses, here a little and there a little, leaving us always guessing and wondering, till, in the fulness of time, all these scraps of revelation gradually resolve themselves into one large and luminous whole, just as in real life.

To read (say) 'The Golden Bowl' or 'The Wings of the Dove' is like taking a long walk uphill, panting and perspiring and almost of a mind to turn back, until, when you look back and down, the country is magically expanded beneath your gaze, as you never saw it yet; so that you toil on gladly up the heights, for the larger prospects that will be waiting for you. I admit, you must be in good training. People often say 'Oh, what a pity it is that dear Henry James won't write the sort of books he *used* to write. Do you remember "The Portrait of a Lady"?' etc., etc. I always hint to these people, as politely as possible, that an artist's business is not to keep pace with his admirers, and that their business is to keep pace, if possible, with *him*; and that, if they faint by the way, they will be safer in blaming themselves than in blaming *him*. Mr James, that very conscious and devoted artist, may be trusted, he especially, to have followed the right line of progress – to have got the logical development of his own peculiar gifts. I know no fictionist so evidently steeped as he is in the passion for literature as a fine art –

209

none who has taken for his theme writers and writing so often, and with such insight.

[FOUR]

'Yes, indeed, I am at Rye – where else should I be? For I am here pretty well always and ever, and less and less anywhere else.' So Henry wrote to a woman friend of long standing in the autumn of 1909. 'There are advantages preponderant in that; but there are also drawbacks; one of which is that I am liable to go so long without seeing you.' He went on to refer to 'my homely and solitary state, my limited resources, my austere conditions, and frugal though earnest hospitality', and added: 'I am more and more aged, infirm, and unattractive, but I make such a stand as I can, and shall be very glad to see you if you can brave the adventure or face such a tiresome displacement on such meagre terms.'[44]

This invitation, by no means her first, to spend a week-end at Lamb House, was addressed to the novelist Violet Hunt. Henry had first met her as a child in the Kensington House of her parents, Alfred Hunt, the landscape painter, and his wife, the original of Tennyson's 'Margaret', who also wrote novels. 'Mamma,' she had said, 'he looks as if he ought to be wearing earrings!' Such was the impression made on the child by 'this Elizabethan', as she described Henry, 'with his dark, silky beard and deep wonderful eyes'. Violet grew up to be a pretty and vivacious girl – 'the sweetest Violet in England I think her', so Oscar Wilde told her mother when she was eighteen, although less kind friends used to refer to her behind her back as 'the immodest Violet'. Her early novels, which she wrote in the eighteen-nineties following her mother's example, earned warm praise from Henry for they were regarded as 'daring' when they appeared. Their authoress had imported a vein of French realism into them, and soon she was regarded as a kind of English Colette, with whom she shared a passion for cats as well as emotional entanglements with the opposite sex. As another friend of hers put it, 'popular rumour credited her with being very French and fast, a fashionable and faintly

210

TEA IN THE STUDIO BOOKBINDERY
Mary Weld (centre), Marion Lane (right)
'Glory in your femininity, Miss Weld!'
From a photograph by courtesy of Miss C. F. Kingdon

THEODORA BOSANQUET
'excellent emanuensis'

BURGESS NOAKES
'very gentle, punctual and desirous
to please'

From photographs at Lamb House

VIOLET HUNT

'I deeply regret and de-
plore the lamentable
position in which I gather
you have put yourself in
respect to divorce pro-
ceedings about to be
taken by Mrs Hueffer'

FORD MADOX
HUEFFER
(Ford Madox Ford)

'I wish for you very heartily that your complica-
tions may work out for
you into some eventual
"peace with honour"'

From photographs in The
Flurried Years *by Violet
Hunt (Hurst & Blackett,
Ltd)*

vicious blue-stocking'. No doubt French literary influence was responsible for the element of 'nastiness' in what she wrote, as it was in the case of her young male contemporary and devoted admirer Somerset Maugham. After she had sent Henry her novel *The Human Interest* and he had 'absorbed' it 'in its totality', he wrote to her: 'I am extremely struck with its cleverness and expertness – your acuteness of mind and skill of hand. Of course I don't in my battered and wrinkled stage of life and reflection read any fiction *naïvement* and unquestioningly, the eternal critic within me insisting on his rights and taking his cake, or his fun, as he goes.' At the same time he admitted that in this instance he was 'under the charm of your wonderfully observant talent and singularly neat execution'.[45]

While Violet Hunt contrived to get herself 'talked about', Henry had no objection to being seen in public with her in London, or having her as a guest in Rye, so long as she was not involved in any openly scandalous association. 'I hope your brave life is winning most of its battles', he wrote to her on one occasion. 'You strike always in the thick of the fray, and I look at you through a hole in the curtain of a broken-down ambulance pulled off into a distant field.' She would invite him to literary dinners and suchlike in London, but he always fought shy of such gatherings. 'Do let us have a little table and be obscure and happy,' he wrote to her after receiving an invitation which somewhat alarmed him. 'But I fear I *can't* come to a thing of speeches and other things: it is with me an absolute and insurmountable rule.' On another occasion she tried to get him to come to supper in a restaurant after a lecture he gave to the Royal Literary Society, on whose council he sat, but without success. 'Since you kindly ask me,' he answered her, 'I boldly, even brutally, reply: "No, I *don't* go out to supper. It's a proceeding, in all the current London conditions (I mean the Berkeleys, Carltons, Cecils, Princes and *tutti quanti*) that I have utterly forsworn and unspeakably abhor." There you are for a civil answer – and I would go to the stake on it. I've done them all, and when once last summer I was entrapped into that hideous "midnight sun" of the Carlton electric glare lighting,

211

green women and thrusting one into the pillory of a kind of livid destructiveness (you see it's my complexion and Facial Beauty I'm thinking of) I swore a mighty oath. "No more, no more!" '[46]

Her first stay at Lamb House was in the summer of 1903. 'I shall be alone,' Henry had told her beforehand, 'and I feel I should mention, with homely conscientiousness, that I inveterately work, and should even with *all* the Graces, Wits, Beauties and Celebrities, crowding my lordly halls all at once from 10.15 a.m. to 1.30 p.m.' She went walks with him across the Rye golf links, accompanied by Max on a long chain, the Dachshund getting his lead wrapped round the lamp-posts on their way. When she left, she borrowed a book on Shakespeare by someone who seems to have shared Henry's doubts about the authorship of the plays. In acknowledging the book's return, Henry wrote to her:

> I am 'a sort of' haunted by the conviction that the divine William is the biggest and most successful fraud ever practised on a patient world. The more I turn him round and round the more he so affects me. But that is all – I am not pretending to treat the question or to carry it any further. It bristles with difficulties, and I can only express my general sense by saying that I find it *almost* as impossible to conceive that Bacon wrote the plays as to conceive that the man from Stratford, as we know the man from Stratford, did.[47]

For the next five years Violet was a regular and welcome guest of the Master. By this time she was 'My dear Violet' or 'My dear Authoress', or his 'Purple Patch', from the colour of the coat and cap she used to wear. During one of her visits to Lamb House he gave her a photograph of himself which he inscribed from 'her faithful old friend'. Finally there came the invitation for which she proposed herself to stay in November, 1909. Everything was arranged, and then suddenly something happened in her private life which made it impossible in the circumstances for Henry to receive her. By the same mail as Violet accepted the invitation a letter arrived from Ford

Madox Hueffer informing Henry that his wife Elsie had insti-
tuted a matrimonial suit against him and that he hoped to
marry Violet if and when he was free to do so. Henry was horrified at the prospect of being mixed up in any way with such
unpleasantness. 'I deeply regret and deplore the lamentable
position in which I gather you have put yourself in respect to
divorce proceedings about to be taken by Mrs Hueffer,' he
wrote to Violet with pained feelings; 'it affects me as painfully
unedifying and that compels me to regard all agreeable
and unembarrassed communication between us as impossible. I can neither suffer you to come down to hear me utter
these homely truths, nor pretend at such a time to free and
natural discourse of other things, on a basis of avoidance of
what must now be most to the front in your own consciousness
and what in a very unwelcome fashion disconcerts mine.'
Furthermore, the letter began 'Dear Violet Hunt' instead of
the usual friendly and familiar 'My dear Violet'.[48]

It was in vain for Violet to protest that she was 'innocent'
of any misconduct with Hueffer. Henry did not see that her
protest at all invalidated his previous expression of opinion.

> What sort of a friend is it that would say less? I wasn't for
> a moment pretending to characterize the nature of the
> relations that may conduce to that possibility – relations, on
> your part, I mean, with the man to be divorced, which in
> themselves are none of my business at all. But your *position*
> as a result of those relations – if I had it to speak of again I
> am afraid I could only speak of it so.
>
> That is not the point, however; the ground of my writing
> to you as I did was another matter, as to which your letter
> again makes me feel how right I was. I could see you, after
> so hearing from Mr Hueffer only on a basis of impossibly
> avoiding or of still more impossibly hearing of, his or his
> wife's private affairs, of which I wish to hear nothing what-
> ever; and you immediately illustrate this by saying 'as you
> know' they have been separated for years. I neither knew
> nor know anything whatever of the matter; and it was exactly
> because I didn't wish to that I found conversing with you to
> be in prospect impossible.

That was the light in which I didn't – your term is harsh! –
forbid you my house; but deprecated the idea of what would
otherwise have been so interesting and welcome a *tête à tête*
with you. I am very sorry to have had to lose it, and am
yours in this regret

HENRY JAMES[49]

Henry repeated his argument to Hueffer, but he put it more
briefly. 'What I wrote to her that I deplored and lamented,'
he told him, 'was the situation in which, whatever it had or
hadn't been, her general relation with you had landed her –
the situation of her being exposed to figure in public proceedings. I don't see how any old friend of hers can be indifferent
to that misfortune. But these things surely are your affair
together, and I wish for you very heartily that your complications may work out for you into some eventual "peace with
honour".'[50]

It was true that Hueffer had been living apart from his wife
for some time – actually months not years – and refused to
return to her. In fact, Mrs Elsie Hueffer was about to petition
the courts for the restitution of conjugal rights, sometimes a
preliminary to divorce but more frequently to a judicial separation. When the case came on, two months later, before the
President of the Divorce Division of the High Court, Hueffer
was formally ordered to return to his wife within fourteen days.
Since he did not do so, he was then ordered to pay her £25
alimony and thereafter at the rate of £3 a week *pendente lite*.
Hueffer, who was already allowing his wife rather more than
twice that amount, became indignant and foolishly attempted
to resist the alimony order by refusing to pay anything more.
This resulted in his being imprisoned for contempt of court,
an unpleasant and humiliating experience for a man in his
position. At the same time, he had been careful to keep Violet's
name out of the proceedings, and in order to give his wife the
necessary evidence to go on with the divorce he took a German
girl to live with him temporarily. But Mrs Hueffer, who was a
Catholic and had born her husband two daughters, was persuaded by her Catholic relatives to drop the contemplated

divorce. To add further to his troubles, *The English Review*, which Ford Hueffer had edited with skill and which he had filled with brilliant articles from well-known writers, collapsed owing to the withdrawal of a financial backer; although Violet Hunt found another rich backer, the latter's first move was to eject Hueffer from the editorial chair.

Violet, who was forty-seven and eleven years older than Hueffer, would have been glad of him as a husband. No doubt she was partly prompted by self-interest, but to do her justice it must be said that she took over his affairs, arranged the sale of his collection of pictures and rare books, thereby rescuing him from bankruptcy. At the same time she took the precaution of obtaining a Bill of Sale on his furniture, which was transferred to South Lodge, the house on Campden Hill where she lived with her mother and which had been the scene of many literary parties, particularly in the heyday of *The English Review*. Hueffer also went to live at South Lodge, nominally as a paying guest. Shortly afterwards Hueffer took Violet to Germany, where they spent some months together. The object of this exercise was for Hueffer, whose father was a German-born naturalized Englishman, to acquire German nationality and then procure a divorce and get married to Violet under German law. Although there is nothing to show that anything came of this ingenious idea, nevertheless both Hueffer and his mistress let it be known on their return to England that they were now man and wife.

Consequently, when a journal called *The Throne* printed a publicity paragraph announcing the forthcoming publication of a novel, *The Governess*, said to have been written jointly by Mrs Alfred Hunt, 'one of the popular novelists of the old days', and her daughter, Miss Violet Hunt ('now Mrs Ford Madox Hueffer'), one of the most successful of the 'modern school', Mrs Elsie Hueffer, who regarded herself as still legally married, sued *The Throne* for libel and was awarded £300 damages. As judgment was being entered by Mr Justice Avory, counsel who held a watching brief for Violet rose to say that the 'lady whose name has been mentioned on both sides . . . wished him to state that she believed herself to be Mrs Ford Madox Hueffer

and intended so to call herself'. But the judge stopped him
from going any further. 'I decline to allow this Court to be
made a medium of advertisement,' he remarked testily.[51]

Violet, who fortunately had some money of her own, had
again fled abroad with her physically ailing lover and she
stayed on the Continent until the scandal had died down. The
affair, which did both her reputation and Hueffer's a great deal
of harm, further upset her friends. But Henry, who had long
since made up his difference with her once more addressed her
as 'My dear Violet' and wrote again in the old friendly strain,
'Well, patch with purple if you must,' he told her after the
libel action, 'so long as the piece holds.'[52]

[FIVE]

Henry had another woman friend, who resembled Violet Hunt
in that she was the same age, possessed private means, wrote
novels and had a lover, with whom Henry used to correspond
amicably. But she managed her affairs and her particular
affair with considerably more skill and discretion than the luck-
less Violet. This was Edith Wharton, born Edith Newbold
Jones, a fellow American, who was perhaps Henry's closest
literary woman friend in his later years. Indeed it was sometimes said, though without any foundation in fact, that their
relationship extended to a more intimate field. Once, at a
dinner party she gave at which Henry was among the guests, a
message came from a newspaper asking her if she would verify
a rumour. She read the message aloud to the assembled company – 'Are you and Henry James engaged to be married?'
The astonished silence was broken by Henry exclaiming, 'And
yet they say truth is stranger than fiction!'[53]

To Henry, Edith was 'the all-imperative Mrs Wharton' and
he devised a variety of names for her, such as 'the whirling
princess', 'the devil-dancer', 'the gyrator', 'the golden eagle',
'the incomparable one' and 'the Angel of Devastation'. If she
complained of his exacting use of her motor during her visits,
for his part he used to feel utterly worn out by her overpowering personality. '"The Angel of Devastation" has become a

mere agitating memory', he wrote after one of her visits to Lamb House, 'but nothing could have exceeded the commotion and exhaustion produced by her actual prolonged stay. Devoted as I am to her, I feel even as one of those infants of literary allusion whom their mothers trust to terror by pronouncing the name of the great historic ravagers of their country, Bonaparte, or Attila, or Tamarlane'.[54] Gerard Hopkins remembered her at Lamb House as 'a very dominant and frightening figure, full of metallic jangles and very trim clothes, with a very determined manner'. It was a hot Sunday afternoon, when she suddenly told Henry that he must come for a walk with her round the garden.

> The poor old man obviously didn't want to go at all, but she set off, James behind her, looking a curious mixture of an extremely dignified and respectful butler and a rather round old dog, toddling slowly. He must have made some protest, I think, because across the garden came the clear voice of Mrs Wharton saying, 'Nonsense, Henry, it will do you good!'

'Dear admirable Edith, where am I going to take her?' Henry would ask his friends. 'We've motored to see all the beautiful old houses and gardens within motoring distance from Rye that can be reached between tea and dinner.'[55]

They first met in the late 1880s in the house of a mutual friend in Paris – Mrs Boit, who will be remembered as the tenant of Lamb House during the first of Henry's two absences in America. They met again from time to time casually, but it was not until some years after Henry had settled in Rye and her visits to Europe became more frequent and prolonged and she acquired a house in Paris that they became such close friends. Incidentally, it was Edith Wharton who, when he was staying with her in Paris in 1908, introduced him to the French painter Jacques-Emile Blanche, who painted what is perhaps the best portrait of 'the Master' in existence.

Edith Wharton regarded herself as a literary disciple of Henry's, being like him concerned with artistic form in her novels and looking to moral values behind the upper class social scene of which she wrote. But it was a case of the disciple outstripping the Master, certainly from the point of view of the commercial success of her books, which sold far better than his. That he was painfully aware of the difference may be gathered from Henry's reaction to a remark she made one day when they were driving together in her large new limousine. The magnificent vehicle had, she said, been bought with the proceeds of her last novel. 'With the proceeds of *my* last novel,' said Henry with wry irony, 'I purchased a small go-cart, or hand-barrow, on which my guests' luggage is wheeled from the station to my house. It needs a coat of paint. With the proceeds of my next novel, I shall have it painted.'[56]

Edith Wharton's description of the Lamb House establishment has already been quoted. Of her own visits and the excursions she used to make with her host in the surrounding countryside, 'great loops' of exploration, as he called them, she wrote:

At Lamb House my host and I usually kept to ourselves until luncheon. Our working hours were the same, and it was only now and then that we went out before one o'clock to take a look at the green peas in the kitchen-garden, or stroll down the High Street to the Post Office. But as soon as luncheon was despatched (amid unnecessary apologies for its meagreness, and sarcastic allusions to my own supposed culinary extravagances) the real business of the day began. Henry James . . . had a passion for motoring. He denied himself (I believe quite needlessly) the pleasure and relaxation which a car of his own might have given him, but took advantage, to the last drop of petrol, of the travelling capacity of any visitor's car. . . .

James was as jubilant as a child. Everything pleased him – the easy locomotion (which often cradled him into a brief nap), the bosky softness of the landscape, the discovery of towns and villages hitherto beyond his range, the magic of ancient names, quaint or impressive, crabbed or melodious. These he would murmur over and over to himself in a low chant, finally creating characters to fit them, and sometimes whole families, with their domestic complications and matrimonial alliances, such as the Dymmes of Dymchurch, one of whom married a Sparkle, and was the mother of little Scintilla Dymme-Sparkle, subject of much mirth and many anecdotes. Except during his naps, nothing escaped him, and I suppose no one ever felt more imaginatively, or with deeper poetic emotion, the beauty of sea and sky, the serenities of the landscape, the sober charm of villages, manor-houses and humble churches, and all the implications of that much-storied corner of England.

One perfect afternoon we spent at Bodiam – my first visit there. It was still the old spell-bound ruin, unrestored, guarded by great trees, and by a network of lanes which baffled the invading charabancs. Tranquil white clouds hung above it in a windless sky, and the silence and solitude were complete as we sat looking across at the crumbling towers, and at their reflection in a moat starred with water-lilies, and danced over by great blue dragonflies. For a long time no one spoke: then James turned to me and said solemnly: 'Summer afternoon – summer afternoon; to me those have always been the two most beautiful words in the English language.' They were the essence of that hushed scene, those ancient walls; and I never hear them spoken without seeing the towers of Bodiam mirrored in their enchanted moat.[57]

Another memorable afternoon was when Edith Wharton was taken to call on the octogenarian George Meredith at Box Hill shortly before his death. Edith was reluctant to intrude upon him in his cottage, but Henry insisted. 'I want you to know Meredith,' he said. They found the invalid author, 'white of head and beard, and statuesquely throned in a Bath chair', attended by his daughter, Mrs Henry Sturgis, the novelist Morley Roberts and a trained nurse, who astonished the visitors by calmly eating her supper only a foot or two from her patient's chair. After Edith had been introduced and 'the great man' grasped who she was, he lifted a book which lay open at his elbow and held it out with a smile. To Edith's delight, it turned out to be her recently published *Motor Flight through France*, which by coincidence Meredith had been reading when she came in, although he had had no advance notice of her visit. 'As they sat there,' Edith recalled, 'James benignly listening, Meredith eloquently discoursing, and their old deep regard for each other burning steadily through the surface eloquence and the surface attentiveness, I felt I was in great company and was glad.'

On another occasion, when Edith and Henry were staying at a mutual friend's house in the country, their host suggested taking them to call on a charming neighbour, who had once been a celebrated music-hall artist. Henry had met her at a theatrical supper party, when he first came to London, and he now declared himself delighted to renew the acquaintance. The lady, who remembered their meeting, welcomed him cordially. After a while, she drew Edith Wharton aside and expressed her pleasure at seeing dear Mr James again after so many years, and added: 'I've so often wondered what had happened to him since. Do tell me – *has he kept up his writing?*'[58]

On her earlier visits, Edith was accompanied by her husband Edward, from whom she later separated and was divorced, and Henry often went along with them on their motor tours of England ('Your silver-sounding toot that invites me to the car – the wondrous cushioned *general* car of your so wondrously india-rubbertyred and deep-cushioned fortune – echoes for me but too mockingly in the dim, if snug, cave of my permanent *retraite*.')[59] According to Edith, Henry was convinced that because he lived in England and their American chauffeur, whose name was Cook, did not, it was necessary that Cook should be guided by him through the intricacies of the English countryside. 'Signposts were rare in England in those days, and for many years afterwards, and a truly British reserve seemed to make the local authorities reluctant to communicate with the invading stranger!' However, Cook was not only a skilful driver but a born path-finder, while James's sense of direction was non-existent, or rather actively but always erroneously alert; and the consequences of his intervention were always bewildering and sometimes extremely fatiguing. The first time Edith and her husband visited Lamb House, they

came over from France with their car and chauffeur, and
Henry went by train to Folkestone to meet them. On the
drive, Henry insisted on seating himself beside Cook on the
plea that the roads across Romney Marsh formed such a tangle
that only an old inhabitant could guide the visitors to Rye.
'The suggestion resulted in our turning around and around
in our tracks till long after dark,' Edith afterwards recalled,
'though Rye, conspicuous on its conical hill, was just ahead of
us, and Cook could easily have landed us there in time for
tea.'

Another year they had been motoring together in the west
of England, and on their way back to Rye had arranged to
spend a night at Malvern. It was a dark rainy afternoon, and
as they approached the spa, Edith who was sitting at the back
of the car with Henry noticed her friend was growing restless.
At last, unable to contain himself any longer, he broke out, 'My
dear, I once spent a summer at Malvern, and know it very
well; and as it is rather difficult to find the way to the hotel, it
might be well if Edward were to change places with me and let
me sit beside Cook.' Edward obligingly did so, though with
doubt in his heart, as his wife was quick to observe. Malvern
was encircled by a kind of upper boulevard or ring road, as it
would be called today, and for an hour they circled about
above the outspread town, while Henry vainly tried to
remember which particular street led down most directly to
their hotel. He would stop the motor literally at every corner,
while the Whartons would hear a muttering, at first confident
and then anguished. 'This – this, my dear Cook, yes . . . this
certainly is the right corner, But no; stay! A moment longer,
please – in this light it's so difficult . . . appearances are so
misleading. . . . It may be . . . yes! I think it *is* the next turn . . .
"a little further lend thy guiding hand" . . . that is, drive on;
but slowly, please, my dear Cook; *very* slowly!' And the same
agitated monologue would be repeated, until at length the
hard-tried chauffeur would gently interrupt; 'I guess any
turn'll get us down into the town, Mr James, and after that I
can ask –' And so Henry reluctantly yielded to this suggestion,
and eventually the party arrived at their destination, late,

hungry and exhausted, while Henry was still convinced that the next turning would have been the right one, if only his friends had been more patient.

What Edith Wharton regarded as the most absurd of these episodes occurred on another rainy evening, when they arrived at Windsor to stay with Howard ('Howdie') Sturgis, an eccentric American dilettante and bachelor, who wrote one outstanding novel called *Belchamber*, did embroidery, and entertained his friends at Queen's Acre ('Qu'Acre'), his luxurious house in King's Road near Windsor Great Park.[60] On this occasion, the long suffering Cook was on holiday and his substitute was unable to find the way. Peering out of the car window into the darkness, Henry spied a doddering old man who had stopped to gaze at the stationary motor. 'Wait a moment, my dear,' Henry reassured Edith, 'I'll ask him where we are.' Leaning out of the window, he beckoned the old man to approach.

'My good man, if you'll be good enough to come here – a little nearer – so.' Then, as the old man came within hearing distance, Henry continued: 'My friend, to put it to you in two words, this lady and I have just arrived here from Slough; that is to say, to be more strictly accurate, we have recently *passed through* Slough on our way here, having actually motored to Windsor from Rye, which was our point of departure; and the darkness having overtaken us, we should be much obliged if you would tell us where we are now in relation, say, to the High Street, which, as you of course know, leads to the Castle, after leaving on the left hand the turn down to the railway station.'

Edith was not surprised when this extraordinary appeal was met by silence and a dazed expression on the old man's wrinkled face. Meanwhile Henry rambled on. 'In short' – Edith squirmed, since she knew that these two words were his invariable prelude to a fresh series of explanatory ramifications – 'in short, my good man, what I want to put to you in a word is this: supposing we have already (as I have reason to think we have) driven past the turn down to the railway station (which, in that case, by the way, would probably not have been on our left hand, but on our right), where are we now in relation to —'

Edith, now fast losing her patience felt herself utterly unable to sit through another parenthesis. 'Oh, please,' she interrupted, 'do ask him where the King's Road is.'

'Ah –? The King's Road? Just so! Quite right! Can you, as a matter of fact, my good man, tell us where in relation to our present position, the King's Road exactly *is*?'

'Ye're in it,' said the aged face at the window.

So they eventually reached Queen's Acre, where Edith Wharton used to say that some of the happiest hours of her life were passed and some of her dearest friendships formed or consolidated. Henry also enjoyed the congenial intellects and temperaments of those he met there. 'Our dear Howard is like a cake – a richly sugared cake – always on the table,' Henry remarked of their host. 'We sit round him in a circle and help ourselves. Now and then we fling a slice over our shoulder to somebody outside; occasionally we draw our chairs closer together to make room for a new-comer.' In her entertaining book of reminiscences, *A Backward Glance*, Edith Wharton has left a vivid picture of these gatherings. The company included several Cambridge dons. There was Gaillard Lapsley, Fellow of Trinity College and a distant American relative of Henry's, his 'long-limbed' young friend Percy Lubbock, Pepysian Librarian at Magdalen, and sometimes, too, Arthur Benson, Master of the College. Benson, it must be admitted, found the intellectual going pretty hard to take. 'I felt as if I would never be able to talk again,' he wearily confided to his diaries after one of these tea-time sessions. 'It seems to me exactly like eating meal after meal . . . That is the worst of these great talkers, that they can't *stop*.'

> . . . dominating the hearth, and all of us [wrote Edith Wharton] Henry James stands, or heavily pads about the room, listening, muttering, groaning disapproval, or chuckling assent to the paradoxes of the other tea drinkers. And then, when tea is over, and the tray has disappeared, he stops his prowling to lean against the mantelpiece and plunge into reminiscences of the Paris or London of his

youth, or into some slowly elaborated literary disquisition, perhaps on the art of fiction or the theatre, on Balzac or Tolstoy, or, better still, on one of his contemporaries. I remember, especially one afternoon when the question: 'And Meredith —?' suddenly freed a 'full-length' of that master which, I imagine, still hangs in the mental picture-galleries of all who heard him. . . .

He himself, James said, when he read Meredith, was always at a loss to know where he was, or what causes had led to which events, or even to discover by what form of conveyance the elusive characters he was struggling to identify moved from one point of the globe to another (except, Howard interpolated that the heroines always did so on horseback); till at last the practical exigencies of the subject forced the author to provide some specific means of transport, and suddenly, through the fog of his verbiage, the reader caught the far-off tinkle of a bell that (here there was a dramatic pause of suspense) – that turned out to be that of a mere vulgar hansom-cab: 'Into which,' James concluded with his wicked twinkle, 'I always manage to leap before the hero, and drive straight out of the story.'

Another guest both at Qu'Acre and Lamb House was an able but somewhat selfish and supercilious American lawyer named Walter Berry. Edith Wharton fell desperately in love with him. Their affair was at its height in the summer of 1908, just at the time that Edward Wharton's mental health broke down. The rival demands of her lover and her husband were a severe trial to Edith, who took Henry into her confidence. He comforted her, just as he had comforted Edmund Gosse in his trouble twenty years earlier.

Only sit tight yourself *and go through the movements of life.* That keeps up our connection with life; behind which, all the while, the deeper and darker and unapparent, in which things *really* happen to us, learns, under that hygiene, to stay in its place. Let it get out of its place and it swamps the scene; besides which its place, God knows, is enough for it! Live it all through, every inch of it – out of it something valuable will come – but live it ever so quietly; and – *je maintiens mon dire* – waitingly![62]

Edith hoped that Walter Berry would marry her after her divorce had gone through, but he did not choose to do so, although he was to remain her friend and adviser in her strikingly successful literary career. Meanwhile Henry was able to congratulate her on her 'definite liberation' from a man who was 'truly as slatedly, swaggeringly, and extravagantly mad as he can be'. For Teddy Wharton now spent most of his time, according to Henry, dashing about in 'his prodigious and unique American motor-car – 100 miles an hour in which it is quite open to him to kill himself', and asking his friends whether they had seen his gold garters, upon which he would 'whisk up his trousers and show them in effect his stockings held up with circles of massive gold!' What Henry thought so 'very wonderful' in her at this time was that she was able to write such an 'exquisite' novel as *The Reef*, 'with that amount of harum-scarum banging about her ears'.

In gratitude for his sympathy, Edith Wharton busied herself with various mutual friends such as Edmund Gosse, William Dean Howells and her sister-in-law Mary Cadwalader Jones, in trying to get Henry awarded the Nobel Prize for Literature in 1912. But nothing came of the idea, of which Henry was probably ignorant, and the prize for that year went to Gerhart Hauptmann. This was a pity, for Henry could have done with the substantial sum of money which was part of the award. 'As you know, he has never been a "best-seller",' Mrs Cadwalader Jones told Howells, 'and his personal property has dwindled in value, as property will if one lives in Europe and has less than no business ability.'[63]

Six 🦋 Chelsea

After his return from America in 1911, Henry spent no more winters in Rye. The first one he spent in London, living in the Reform Club, as we have seen, and working on his autobiography with Theodora Bosanquet, in the rooms she had taken for him in the house where she lodged in Chelsea. Arthur Benson, who dined with him in the Athenaeum in November, 1911, noted a distinct change. 'There is something about him which was not there before, something stony, strained, anxious. But he was deeply affectionate and talked very characteristically.' They spoke of the new and rising generation of writers like Arnold Bennett and Hugh Walpole.

Henry discussed Bennett almost contemptuously. 'The fact is that I am so *saturated* with impressions that I can't take in new ones,' he remarked. 'I have lived my life, I have worked out my little conceptions, I have an idea how it all ought to be done – and here comes a man with his great voluminous books, dripping with detail – but with no scheme, no conception of character, no *subject* – perhaps a vague idea of just sketching a character or two – and then comes this great panorama, everything perceived, nothing seen *into*, nothing related. He's not afraid of masses and crowds and figures – but one asks oneself what is it all for, where does it all end, what's the *aim* of it?'

By this time we had dawdled and pecked through our dinner – he ate a hearty meal, and there was much of that delicious gesture, the upturned eye, the clenched upheld

226

'LONDON IN NOVEMBER AND MR HENRY JAMES IN LONDON'

'. . . It was, therefore, not without something of a shiver, that he, in this to him so very congenial atmosphere, now perceived that a vision of a hand which he had, at a venture, held up within an inch or two of his eyes was, with an almost awful clarity, being adumbrated. . . .'

From A Book of Caricatures *by Max Beerbohm (Methuen & Co Ltd)*

'MR HENRY JAMES REVISITING AMERICA'

'So that in fine, let, without further beating about the bush, me make to myself amazed acknowledgement that, but for the certificate of birth which I have – so quite indubitably – on me, I might in regarding (and, as it somewhat were, overseeing) *à l'oeuil de voyageur* these, dear good people, find hard to swallow, or even to take by subconscious injection, the great idea, that I am – ever so indigenously! – one of them . . .'

From A Book of Caricatures *by Max Beerbohm (Methuen & Co Ltd)*

hand, and that jolly laughter that begins in the middle of a
sentence and permeates it all. . . .

Henry had much more time for Hugh Walpole, whom he
described as 'charming in his zest for experience and his love
of intimacies'. They had met about three years previously as
the result of a 'fan-letter' the younger man had written to him,
had become warm friends, Walpole now being a frequent and
welcome visitor to Lamb House when the Master was in residence. 'I often think,' Henry went on, 'if I look back at my
own starved past, that I wish I had done more, reached out
further, claimed more – and I should be the last to block the
way. The only thing is to be there, to wait, to sympathize, to
help if necessary.'

Benson concluded his account of this meeting:
He joined all this with many pats and caressing gestures;
then led me down by the arm and sent me off with a blessing.
I felt he was glad that I should go – had felt the strain – but
that he was well and happy. He is a wonderful person, so
entirely simple in emotion and loyalty, so complicated in
mind. His little round head, his fine gestures, even to the
waiters – 'I am not taking any of this – I don't need this' –
his rolling eyes, with the heavy lines round them, his rolling
resolute gait, as if he *shouldered* something and set off with
his burden – all very impressive. . . .[1]

In replying to the bread-and-butter letter which Hugh
Walpole had sent him after his first 'wonderful week-end' at
Lamb House, Henry had suggested that Hugh should address
him as '*Très chère Maître*' or 'My very dear Master' and this
injunction was always strictly obeyed. Hugh had been thrilled
by this visit. 'The house and garden are exactly suited to him,'
he had written at the time. 'He is beyond words. I cannot speak
about him.'[2] But with the passing of time he was to view the
Master in clearer and cooler perspective.

Immature though I was I perceived instantly his inevitable loneliness. He was lonely in the first place because, an
American, he was never really at home in Europe. Nor was he

at home in America for when he was there he longed for the age, the quiet, the sophistications of Europe. He was lonely in the second place because he was a spectator of life. He was a spectator because his American ancestry planted a reticent Puritanism in his temperament and this was ever at war with his intellectual curiosity. Sexually also he had suffered some frustration. What that frustration was I never knew, but I remember him telling me how he had once in his youth in a foreign town watched a whole night in pouring rain for the appearance of a figure at a window. 'That was the end . . .' he said, and broke off.[3]*

With the exception of a few days at Easter, which he spent at Rye with his younger nephew William ('Billy') James and his bride, to whom he lent Lamb House for a prolonged honeymoon, Henry stayed on in London until the following July. His increasing sense of loneliness – and even London clubs can be lonely at week-ends – appears from a letter he wrote at this time to the novelist Rhoda Broughton, with whom it is said he had once been in love:

Reform Club, Pall Mall, S.W. June 2, 1912. . . .
This is a dark moist Sunday a.m. and I sit alone in the great dim solemn library of this Club (Thackeray's Megatherium or whatever,) and say to myself that the conditions now at last *ought* to be auspicious – though indeed that merely tends to make me but brood inefficiently over the transformations of London as such scenes express them and as I have seen them growing. Now at least the place becomes an utter void, a desert peopled with ghosts, for all except three days (about) of the week – speaking from the social point of view. The old Victorian *social* Sunday is dust and ashes, and a holy stillness, a repudiating blankness, has possession – which however, after all, has its merits and its conveniences too. . . .[4]

He returned to Rye in the middle of a heat wave to 'feel intensely, after so long an absence, the blest, the invaluable,

---

* He told Edmund Gosse this story in greater detail: see above p. 181.

little old refuge quality of dear Lamb House at this and kindred seasons', and to hope that he was over the 'pulls and breaks, sometimes disheartening ones, through the recurrence of bad physical conditions'.

The main thing to say about these [he wrote to his nephew Harry] is that they tend steadily, and most hopefully, to diminish, both in intensity and duration, and that I have really now reached the point at which the successful effort to work really helps me physically – to say nothing of course of (a thousand times) morally. It remains true that I do worry about the money question – by nature and fate (since I was born worrying, though myself much more than others!) – and that this is largely the result of these last years of lapse of productive work while my expenses have gone more or less (while I was with you all in America less!) ruthlessly on. But of this it's also to be cheeringly said that I have only to be successfully and continuously at work for a period of about ten days for it all to fall into the background altogether (all the worry) and be replaced by the bravest confidence of calculation.[5]

As it turned out, he had 'quite a Devil of a summer, a very bad and damnable July and August, through the renewal of an ailment that I had regarded as a good deal subdued'. This as 'a most deplorable tendency to chronic pectoral, or, more specifically, anginal pain'. No sooner had he got 'more or less the better of' this trouble 'in a considerably reassuring way' than he was 'smitten with a violent attack of the atrocious affliction known as "Shingles"' – 'my impression of the nature of which had been vague and inconsiderate, but to the now grim shade of which I take off my hat in the very abjection of respect. It has been a horrible visitation. . . .' This painful complaint, as well as a recurrence of his heart trouble, kept him in bed in Lamb House for much of the time until the middle of December, when he determined 'to break into the vicious circle and dissipate the blight, by going up to town – almost straight out of bed and dangling my bedclothes about me'. Also he had found what promised to be the ideal flat and he was anxious to get into it at the earliest possible moment after the present occupant had moved out.[6]

The flat was No. 21 Carlyle Mansions, in a block quite recently built in Cheyne Walk, 'a bit of the old-time stretch of riverside Chelsea'. Two large 'reception' rooms looked south over the Thames, there were three bedrooms and good servants' quarters. Also the unfurnished rent was reasonable, £125 a year for a three-year lease with the option to renew. When he saw it for the first time before leaving London that summer, it seemed to be 'within my powers' and just what 'I am looking to for a more convenient and secure basis of regularly wintering in London, for the possibly brief remainder of my days, than any I have for a long time had'.

He was greatly amused by an incident which occurred when he met the outgoing woman tenant. She expressed interest on hearing his name.

'Are you any relation of the writer, Mr James?' she asked him.

'Writer? What writer?'

'Oh, I meant the novelist, Henry James – the novelist. Are you perhaps, by any chance, his son?'

'Well, no,' replied Henry, with marked enjoyment. 'The novelist hasn't got a son. But I feel somehow that if he *had* a son, I should be!'[7]

Carlyle Mansions belonged to a property company, and in due course Henry was asked to supply the customary two references, a banker's reference and a 'social' reference. The landlords laid particular stress upon the latter, and when Henry gave the name of John Sargent, they did not appear to have heard of him, or possibly the designation of 'artist' may have put them off, since it was intimated that this reference was not satisfactory. Then he gave 'Edmund Gosse, Esq., House of Lords', where Gosse was now the official Librarian. 'I want, in response to a letter just received from the proprietors,' Henry told his friend, 'to floor that apparently rather benighted and stupid body, who are restless over the question of a "social reference" (in addition to the reference to my Bankers), by a regular knock-down production of the most eminent and exalted tie I can produce; whereby I have given them your distinguished name as a voucher for my respectability – as distinguished from my solvency; for which latter I don't hint that you shall, however dimly, engage!' What he really wanted to do, he explained, was 'to create for our ironic intelligence the harmless pleasure of letting loose a little, in a roundabout way, upon the platitude of the City and West End Properties Limited, the dread effulgence of their Lordships; the latter being the light and you the transparent lantern that my shaky hand holds up'.

Gosse responded quickly to this appeal, though with some astonishment. 'But what kind of asses they must be who ask *you* for any proof of quality?' he wrote. 'They shall go down to posterity with the bailiff who asked Miss Wordsworth whether it was true that her aged father wrote verses! And with the young lady who exclaimed "What are *Keats*?" They must be men of evil lives; and irresistibly the question surges up "Can they be themselves respectable?"'

In due course 'the foolish creatures' applied to Gosse. 'I have answered them according to their folly,' he told Henry, 'expressing in one breath reverence for you and contempt for them.' This had the desired effect.

'Clearly, they were to be hurled to their doom,' Henry wrote a few days later; 'for the proof of your having, with your potent finger, pressed the merciless spring, arrived this morning in the form of a quite obsequious request that I will conclude our transaction with a signature. This I am doing . . .' Gosse was equally gratified. 'I am delighted at having brought the silly landlords fluttering, like pheasants, to your feet.'[8]

[TWO]

Henry moved up from Rye together with his domestic staff, helped by the faithful Theodora Bosanquet, early in the New Year (January 5th, 1913). Theodora could see that he obviously liked the two large front rooms with their good view over the greenery of Carlyle Gardens and the width of Cheyne Walk to the river. The typewriter was placed near the window

of the more westerly room, which he had chosen as his work
room; the other front room was the dining-room. Henry's
bedroom was at the back and, although it was smaller than the
front rooms, it was quiet. On the day after he settled in he went
to pay a call on Pinker, his literary agent, where he met Arnold
Bennett, apparently for the first time. Bennett noted that he
was 'a very slow talker' but spoke 'beautiful French'. Henry
talked with feeling about his recent illness, and was grateful
that he had 'one or two faithful dependable servants' to look
after him. 'An old man waning', was Bennett's snap judgment
'but with the persistent youthfulness that all old bachelors
have'. After he had been in the flat for a fortnight, he wrote
with some of his old enthusiasm: 'I feel singularly justified of
this basis for my winter times in London; so much does it
appear, now that the preliminary and just post-preliminary
strain of it is over, the very best thing I could have done for
myself. My southward position (as to the rooms I most use)
immediately over the River is verily an "asset", and not even
in the Garden Room at Lamb House, of summer mornings,
have I been better placed for work. With which, all the detail
here is right and pleasant and workable; my servants extremely rejoice in it. . . .' He continued to write of 'these admirable
and ample two rooms southward over the River, so still and
yet so animated' as being ideal for work. Indeed, as he told his
nephew Harry, 'this apartment grows in grace – nothing really
could have been better for me!'[9]

At the end of the first month, he summed up how he felt in a
letter to his old friend Edward Warren:

*21, Carlyle Mansions, Cheyne Walk, S.W. February 4,
1913.* . . . Lamb House, with its solitude and confinement,
has definitely become a quite impossible place for hiberna-
tion, and the large area and conversational resources of
London (even on the mild scale on which I am able to deal
with them) are a precious, in fact quite a remedial resource.
On the other hand, my little perch of these dozen years in
Pall Mall had become equally impossible in illness and for
any long stretch of time.

This Chelsea perch, the haunt of the sage and the seagull, as you so happily term it (though I feel scarcely more like one of these, than like the other) proves, even after brief experiment, just the right thing for me; and though I have but a couple of ample rooms straight on the River, which I pay for by a much dimmer rearward residuum, such a fine scrap of a front, given what it is on fine days or on almost any days, very decently suffices and makes me more than content.

When I have got, with improving conditions, a little less rudely installed, you must absolutely come, and bring Margaret or Dorothy or both, to see for themselves how absolutely interesting it is. Meanwhile I thank the mysterious Powers, it is almost better than anything else for me to get out in the afternoon and ventilate and circulate as far as I may, especially without more pre-committal than I can help to a definite presence anywhere at a definite hour; and this all the more that up to now I have been regularly subject to such aggravations of pain toward the real close of day as to have to tear off my clothes for very anguish and tumble into bed by 8 o'clock. This wipes out my evenings for any social purpose, and I feel, not without relief, that to such complicated ends they will never again be sketched in.[10]

The truth was that he was still very much of an invalid, 'having to reckon with so much chronic pectoral pain, now so seated and settled – moreover too it is astonishing with how much pain one can with long practice learn constantly and not too defeatedly to live'. 'My difficulty still is that I am "up against" answering for myself in advance at a given hour and day', was how he put it to Warren; 'which is what has kept me perforce very shy and detached, very much on the outer edge of things, during this no great time that I have been in London. London means, alas, too much, appointments, engagements, pledges and coming up to the scratch in general all round and all the time. That is the one defect of an otherwise so delightful place.'[11]

'My beginnings of going out again have consisted, up to

today, in four successive excursions in a Bath chair' he wrote to his sister-in-law Alice James on March 5th, 1913, '. . . and the Bath chair habit or vice is, I fear, only too capable of marking me for its own. This of course not "really" – my excellent legs are, thank heaven, still too cherished a dependence and resource and remedy to me in the long run, or rather in the long (or even the short) crawl; only, if you've never tried it, the Bath chair has a sweet appeal of its own, for contemplative ventilation; and I builded better than I knew when I happened to settle here, just where, in all London, the long, long, smooth and really charming and beguiling Thames-side Embankment offers it a quite ideal course for combined publicity (in the sense of variety) and tranquillity (in the sense of jostling against nobody and nothing and not having to pick one's steps). Add to this that just at hand, straight across the River, by the ample and also very quiet Albert Bridge, lies the very convenient and in its way also very beguiling Battersea Park. . . .'

Alice James now pressed him to come over to America for the summer and spend it with her and his nephews and nieces. But he had to decline this invitation.

You can see, can't you? how strange and desperate it would be to 'chuck' everything up, Lamb House, servants, Miss Bosanquet, *this* newly acquired and prized resource, to come over, by a formidable and expensive journey, to spend a summer in the (at best) to me torrid and (the inmost inside of 95 apart) utterly arid and vacuous Cambridge. Dearest Alice, I could come back to America (could be carried back on a stretcher) to die – but never, never to live. To say how the question affects me is dreadfully difficult because of its appearing so to make light of you and the children – but when I think of how little Boston and Cambridge were of old ever *my* affair, or anything but an accident, for me, of the parental life there to which I occasionally and painfully and losingly sacrificed, I have a superstitious terror of seeing them at the end of time again stretch out strange inevitable tentacles to draw me back and destroy me. And then I could never either make or afford the journey (I have no margin at all for *that* degree of effort).

Happily by this time he had been able to 'dismiss' the Bath chair and in a limited measure to resume his old social habits. 'I am wintering and staying on in London on a more settled basis than for a long time back,' he told Violet Hunt, 'and London is on the whole propitious to me.' This marked the beginning of the Indian summer of his life, which was to be full of action and excitement.[13]

[THREE]

The coming of spring brought the prospect of Henry's seventieth birthday, which fell on April 15th, 1913. Towards the end of March, he heard that groups of friends, on both sides of the Atlantic, were planning to celebrate the event with presentations and gifts. The project originated in London with Edmund Gosse, who proposed that he should be presented with his portrait, to be painted by Sargent, together with a suitable letter announcing the gift and timed to reach him on the morning of his birthday. A committee was formed by Gosse with Percy Lubbock as its secretary, and a circular appeal was sent out inviting subscriptions. When he heard about it, Henry wrote to Lubbock asking him to put a stop to it. He could not refuse to sit for his portrait, he told him, but he could not accept it as a gift. His refusal produced a closely written protest of fifteen pages from Mrs Lucy Clifford, one of the signatories of the circular appeal, scolding him for 'coldly, callously and ungratefully' rejecting a gift from his friends.

The receipt of this communication, which reached Carlyle Mansions on April 2nd, threw him into a state of great excitement. He could do nothing for most of the morning except talk to Theodora Bosanquet about how his letter to Percy Lubbock had been 'misinterpreted'. Eventually he sent his secretary off to the Post Office with a telegram to Mrs Clifford asking her to meet him the same afternoon, 'but not for much business which I can't stand'. He had also heard that a similar circular appeal had gone out to his American friends under Edith Wharton's signature, suggesting that in view of the shortness of time, their contribution 'might most appropriately take the form of a sum of money (not less than $5000) for the purchase of a gift, the choice of which would be left to him'. His immediate reaction was to cable his nephew Harry in New York, asking him to stop this presentation too.[14]

So far as the proposed English presentation went, a compromise was reached following his meeting with Mrs Clifford. He agreed to sit for the portrait and to accept it on the understanding that he would be free to bequeath it in his will to a public gallery such as the Metropolitan Museum of Art in New York. Since the response to the English appeal had been 'so warm and general', Mrs Clifford told him, and a sum in excess of the amount of the £500 artist's fee had been received, he also agreed to accept the addition of a birthday present 'in the form of a reproduction, in silver-gilt, of a fine Charles II porringer and dish', or the 'Golden Bowl', as he afterwards like to call it from the title of his novel.

The outcome of the proposed American gift was not so satisfactory. According to Edith Wharton, 'Mr James's family apparently represented to him that I was trying to raise a fund for the support of his old age', with the result that 'he has made it known that he prefers not to accept it'. The contributions were therefore returned to the donors. To one of them, Charles Scribner, who was his American publisher, she wrote with some bitterness:

> It is difficult to understand how any one can have so maliciously misrepresented the circular, which was certainly explicit enough – and the net result has been to cause great distress to Mr James when he learned the facts, and to put his compatriots in the rather sorry position of making no sign on his birthday, while his English friends have offered him the equivalent – or more – of what we proposed to ask him to apply to the purchase of some birthday remembrance.[15]

The English appeal went out under the signatures of J. M. Barrie, Lucy Clifford, Edmund Gosse, Percy Lubbock, W. E.

Norris, Margaret Prothero, John S. Sargent, and Hugh Walpole. Edith Wharton's name was also to have appeared, but just as the circular was about to go to the printers, she asked Lubbock to remove it, as she did not wish to appear in both the English and the American scheme. Unfortunately, as has been seen, the latter collapsed after she wrote to Lubbock; this caused her considerable chagrin, and Henry had a decidedly wounded letter from her. It made him extremely sorry, since, as he told his personal secretary, Mrs Wharton was 'perhaps his best friend'.

Whether Sargent should properly have appeared among the signatories was questioned in an amusing letter from Max Beerbohm in Rapallo:

> I have signed a birthday letter to Henry James – a letter to be sent to him on his seventieth birthday by a number of friends and admirers; and I have subscribed two guineas towards a birthday present to him. The present will (it is 'earnestly hoped' by the committee which is organising the sending of the letter and the buying of the present) 'take the form of a painting of Henry James himself by Mr John Sargent'. And among these earnest hopers who sent out his appeal is Sargent himself! . . .
>
> Poor Sargent, most sensitive and correct of men, can't have known that his name was going to be included among the names of this committee. But anyway, as he is such a devoted old friend of H.J., I think he might have done the thing gratis – else better not do it at all. However, I hope he will buy himself something nice with my two guineas.* H.J. arriving at J.S.'s studio to have a sitting would be a lovely theme for a caricature – with appropriate dialogue; but this I must forego as the circular was marked 'private and confidential'. . . .[16]

If the inclusion of Sargent's name on the circular caused some eyebrows to be raised, the omission of others caused annoyance in the quarters concerned. According to Hugh Walpole, Gosse deliberately left out Sydney Colvin and his

---

* In fact, Sargent had offered to do the portrait for nothing.

wife and Mrs Humphry Ward, who were old friends of Henry's
and they were furious. 'At first I was miserable because I
thought they'd be furious with my being on,' wrote Walpole
at the time, 'but apparently it's felt that someone of the
younger generation ought to be there. But there's been the
most awful fuss.'[17]

After Henry had talked with Mrs Clifford, the committee
arranged for the dispatch of a printed letter to the subscribers,
informing them that, 'as soon as may be, Mr Sargent will make
arrangements for painting the portrait' and also letting them
know about the 'Golden Bowl'. Walpole was deputed, as the
youngest committee member, to take the letter down to the
printers in the City, and when he heard this Henry accompanied him 'so that nothing might be wrong'. But something
did go wrong, although it was not a matter of very great
moment. The pro forma letter began 'Dear', leaving the name
of the recipient blank, to be filled in before each one was sent
off. This Walpole forgot to do and Henry failed to notice the
omission, with the result that all the subscribers were addressed
as 'Dear' without their names. Gosse was extremely angry with
Walpole when he discovered what had happened, particularly
as there were several members of the House of Lords on the
list, such as Haldane and Rosebery. However, Henry insisted
on taking the blame entirely upon himself.

Fortunately everything went off as planned on the day. 'I
had yesterday a Birthday, an extraordinary, prodigious, portentous, quite public Birthday, of all things in the world,' he
wrote to his sister-in-law on April 16, enclosing the accounts in
The Times and the *Pall Mall Gazette* and a copy of the birthday
letter, 'ushering in the quite wonderful array of signatures (as
I can't but feel) of my testifying and "presenting" friends', who
described him as 'the writer, the master of rare and beautiful
art, in whose work creation and criticism meet as they have
never met before in our language'.

What I wish I *could* send you is the huge harvest of exquisite, of splendid sheaves of flowers that converted a
goodly table in this room, by the time yesterday was waning,

into such a blooming garden of complimentary colour as I
never dreamed I should on my own modest premises, almost
bewildered stare at, sniff at, all but quite 'cry' at. I think I
must and shall in fact compass sending you a photograph
of the still more glittering tribute dropped upon me – a
really splendid 'golden bowl' of the highest interest and
most perfect taste, which would, in the extremity of its
elegance, be too proudly false a note amid my small belong-
ings here if it didn't happen to fit, or to sit, rather, with
perfect grace and comfort, on the middle of my chimney-
piece, where the rather good glass and some other happy
incidents of tone most fortunately consort with it. It is a
very brave and artistic (exact) reproduction of a piece of
old Charles II plate; the bowl or cup having handles and a
particularly charming lid or cover, and standing on an
ample round tray or salver; the whole being wrought in solid
silver-gilt and covered over with quaint incised little figures
of a (in the taste of the time) Chinese intention. In short it's
a very beautiful and honourable thing indeed . . .

'I think you are enormously congratulated on your idea,'
Lubbock wrote to Gosse the same day, 'and I am proud to
have had a share in carrying it out. I can't thank you enough
for your help and encouragement at all stages, at some of which
it was certainly needed. I had to the last a slight fear that he
might be overwhelmed and oppressed, even though gratified.
But not a bit of it. He seemed to thrive and grow vigorous on
our homage.'[19]

[FOUR]

A few days later Percy Lubbock lunched with Henry in the
flat to discuss the letter of thanks to the subscribers which he
had drafted. 'Read it and tell me . . . whether you think it will
do,' he had written beforehand to the younger man, 'as being
on the one hand not too pompous or important and on the
other not too free and easy. I have tried to steer a middle way
between hysterical emotion and marble immortality! To any
emendation you suggest I will give the eagerest ear, though I

have really considered and pondered my expressions not a little, studying the pro's and con's as to each *tour*.' In fact, Lubbock had no substantial emendations to put forward; his only suggestion, which Henry adopted, was that the list of the subscribers should follow the text of the letter instead of preceding it, as Henry at first felt it should.[20]

The letter, which the subscribers' committee thoughtfully had printed and circulated at their expense, read as follows:

> *21 Carlyle Mansions,*
> *Cheyne Walk, S.W.*
>
> *April 21st, 1913.*

Dear Friends All,

Let me acknowledge with boundless pleasure the singularly generous and beautiful letter, signed by your great and dazzling array and reinforced by a correspondingly bright material gage, which reached me on my recent birthday, April 15th. It has moved me as brave gifts and benedictions can only do when they come as signal surprises. I seem to wake up to an air of breathing goodwill the full sweetness of which I had never yet tasted; though I ask myself now, as a second thought, how the large kindness and hospitality in which I have so long and so consciously lived among you could fail to act itself out according to its genial nature and by some inspired application. The perfect grace with which it has embraced the just-past occasion for its happy thought affects me, I ask you to believe, with an emotion too deep for stammering words.

I was drawn to London long years ago as by the sense, felt from still earlier, of all the interest and association I should find here, and I now see how my faith was to sink deeper foundations than I could presume ever to measure – how my justification was both stoutly to grow and wisely to wait. It is so wonderful indeed to me as I count up your numerous and various, your dear and distinguished friendly names, taking in all they recall and represent, that I permit myself to feel at once highly successful and extremely proud. I had never in the least understood that I was the one or signified that I was the other, but you have made a great difference. You tell me together, making one rich tone of your many voices, almost the whole story of my social experience, which I have reached the right point for living over again, with all manner of old times and places renewed, old wonderments and pleasures reappeased and recaptured – so that there is scarce one of your ranged company but makes good the particular connection, quickens the excellent relation, lights some happy train and flushes with some individual colour.

I pay you my very best respects while I receive from your two hundred and fifty pairs of hands, and more, the admirable, the inestimable bowl, and while I engage to sit, with every accommodation, to the so markedly indicated 'one of you,' my illustrious friend Sargent. With every accommodation, I say, but with this one condition that you yourself, in your strength and goodness, remain guardians of the result of his labour – even as I remain all faithfully and gratefully yours,

HENRY JAMES

P.S. And let me say over your names.

There followed the list, in alphabetical order, of the two hundred and sixty-nine subscribers. It was remarkably varied in composition, the literary profession being naturally strongest. Celebrities like Bennett, Galsworthy, Kipling, Shaw and Wells appeared along with sager Establishment writers like Arthur Benson, Lord Esher, Gosse, Sir Sidney Lee, Pinero, Sir George Trevelyan, Rhoda Broughton, Mrs Belloc Lowndes and Mrs Humphry Ward. Besides Hugh Walpole, the younger generation of writers included Rupert Brooke, Maurice Hewlett, Logan Pearsall Smith and Virginia Woolf. Among the authors whose names one might expect to find in the list, E. F. Benson, Joseph Conrad, Thomas Hardy, Violet Hunt and Ford Madox Hueffer were notably absent. The first three were almost certainly written to by the committee, so that their absence is something of a mystery, particularly in the case of Fred Benson, both of whose brothers subscribed. Violet Hunt and Ford Hueffer, on the other hand, were living together abroad after unwelcome publicity in the law courts, and they may well not have been asked to contribute. By way of contrast, Wharton and her lover Walter Berry both figured in the list, and as persons of considerable private means, who had both pressed expensive presents upon Henry in the past, it no doubt amused him to reflect, as he put it, that they were now able to 'come in on the cheap'. Besides Barrie, Pinero and Shaw, the theatre was represented by Granville Barker, Elizabeth Robins, Alfred Sutro, Ellen Terry and George Wyndham, but not by George Alexander or Johnston Forbes-Robertson, who had both produced plays of Henry's. (Forbes-Robertson's absence was not altogether surprising in view of Henry's description of him as '*the* typical mountebank'.) His publishers included Sir Frederick Macmillan, William Heinemann and George Duckworth, but not Algernon Methuen; George du Maurier and Joseph Pennell, illustrators of his books, also appeared, but his literary agent, James B. Pinker, did not. Still, all in all, it was an impressive and goodly list.

[FIVE]

Shortly afterwards, Henry began to sit for his portrait to Sargent at his studio in Tite Street. 'He likes one to have a friend there to talk with and to be talked to by, while he works – for animation of countenance, etc. I didn't have one today and we perhaps a trifle missed it.' So Henry wrote to his Irish friend Jocelyn Persse, after the first sitting. 'Will you, and should you care to, come for this helpful purpose the next time?'[22]

The sittings were spread over the next two months, so that his summer sojourn in Lamb House did not begin until July. His Rye neighbours, George Prothero and his wife, had begged him to come down for the Whitsun holiday, but he declined. He had now reduced his domestic establishment to three – a cook-housekeeper named Joan Anderson, a house-parlour maid, Minnie Kidd, and, of course, the ever faithful Burgess Noakes. He did somewhat half-heartedly broach the subject to the two women in their 'luminous kitchen, which somehow let

EDITH WHARTON

'"The Angel of Devastation" has become a mere agitating memory, but nothing could have exceeded the commotions and exhaustion produced by her actual prolonged stay.'

From a photograph by courtesy of Constable Publishers, London, and Laurence Pollinger Ltd.

WITH MRS HUMPHRY WARD

'irrepressible'

From a photograph at Lamb House

HENRY JAMES BY JOHN SARGENT (1913)

'. . . nothing less, evidently, than a very fine thing indeed, Sargent at his very best and poor old H. J. not at his worst; in short, a living breathing likeness and a masterpiece of painting.'

By permission of the Trustees of the National Portrait Gallery in a derisive glare upon every cranny and crevice of the infatuated scheme'.

Before their attitude I lowered my lance [he wrote to Mrs Prothero] – easily understanding moreover that their round of London gaieties is still so fresh and spiced a cup to them that to feel it removed from their lips even for a moment is almost more than they can bear. And then the coarse and brutal truth is, further, that I am oh so utterly well fixed here for the moment and so void of physical agility for any kind of somersault. A little while back, while the Birthday raged, I did just look about me for an off-corner; but now there has been a drop and, the blest calm of Whitsuntide descending on the scene here, I feel it would be a kind of lapse of logic to hurry off to where the social wave, hurrying ahead of me, would be breaking on a holiday strand. . . .

Forgive my beastly rudeness. I will write more in a day or two. Do loll in the garden yourselves to your very fill; do cultivate George's geniality; do steal any volume or set of volumes out of the house that you may like; and do still think gently of your poor ponderous, and thereby, don't you see? so permanent, old friend,

HENRY JAMES[23]

He had sat twice before to Sargent for drawings – the first being for the *Yellow Book* twenty years before and the second for a charcoal impression secretly commissioned by Edith Wharton in 1912. On this third occasion he was fascinated by Sargent's work in oils and as pleased with its progress as were his friends.

One is almost full-face, with one's left arm over the corner of one's chair-back and the hand brought round so that the thumb is caught in the arm-hole of one's waistcoat, and said hand therefore, with the fingers a bit folded, entirely visible and 'treated'. Of course I'm sitting a little askance in the chair. The canvas comes down to just where my watch-chain (such as it is, poor thing!) is hung across the waistcoat: which latter, in itself, is found to be splendidly (poor thing though it also be) and most interestingly treated. Sargent *can* make such things so interesting – such things as my coat-lappet and shoulder and sleeve too! But what is most interesting, every one is agreed, is the mouth – than which even he has never painted a more living, and, as I am told, 'expressive'! In fact I can quite see that myself; and really, I seem to feel, the thing will be all that can at the best (the best with such a subject!) have been expected of it. [24]

The portrait took ten sittings to complete. On June 25th, he wrote to Rhoda Broughton:

. . . it is now finished, *parachevée* (I sat for the last time a couple of days ago;) and is nothing less, evidently, than a very fine thing indeed, Sargent at his very best and poor old H.J. not at his worst; in short, a living breathing likeness and a masterpiece of painting. I am really quite ashamed to admire it so much and so loudly – it's so much as if I were calling attention to my own fine points. I don't alas, exhibit a 'point' in it, but am all large and luscious rotundity – by which you may see how true a thing it is. And I am sorry to have ceased to sit, in spite of the repeated big bites it made in my precious mornings: J.S.S. being so genial and delightful a *nature de grand maître* to have to do with, and his beautiful high cool studio, opening upon a balcony that overhangs a charming Chelsea green garden, adding a charm to everything. He liked always a friend or two to be in to break the spell of a settled gloom in my countenance by their prattle; . . . [25]

His old friend Edward Warren's praise of 'Sargent's masterpiece' gave him particular pleasure. The more Henry looked at the portrait the more he admired it. Indeed his delight was almost childish; as he told Warren, 'I can't help being proud of my so limited connection with it, I take comfort at any rate in feeling that I should find it exactly as fine and interesting (and the extent to which it is these things strikes me as quite wondrous), if I were wholly unacquainted with either of the gentlemen concerned.' [26]

The portrait was on exhibition to the subscribers for three days in the artist's Chelsea studio, together with a bust of Henry by Derwent Wood, which Sargent had himself commissioned. Henry stood beside the portrait and, as each person approached, explained that 'the slight flaw in the title' had been his fault and neither Gosse's nor Hugh Walpole's that the names had been omitted in the circular letter. His explanations took a very long time, Walpole recalled afterwards. 'And the queue grew ever longer and longer. And I stood for hours blushing and confused. It was an amazing scene but a beautiful one.' On December 18th, 1913, Henry wrote to Edmund Gosse:

> The exhibition of the Portrait came to a most brilliant end to-day, with a very great affluence of people. (There have been during the three days an immense number.) It has been a great and charming success – I mean the View has been; and the work itself acclaimed with an unanimity of admiration and, literally, of *intelligence,* that I can intimately testify to. For I really put myself on exhibition beside it, each of the days, morning and afternoon, and the translation (a perfect Omar Khayam, *quoi!*) visibly left the original nowhere. I *attended* – most assiduously; and can really assure you that it has been a most beautiful and flawless episode. The slight original flaw (in the title) I sought to bury under a mountain of flowers, till I found that it didn't in the least do to 'explain it away', as every one (like the dear Ranee*) said: they exclaimed too ruefully 'Ah, don't tell me you didn't *mean* it'. After which I let it alone, and speedily recognised that it was really *the* flower – even if but a little wayward wild flower! – of our success.

Two people are known to have disliked the Sargent portrait, though for widely different reasons. The first was the French artist Jacques-Emile Blanche, who had painted Henry in Paris

* Margaret Brooke, who married Sir Charles Vyner Brooke, the 'white' Rajah of Sarawak.

five years earlier. He complained that the work lacked psychological insight. 'Of his model, so complex and finely shaded in his sensibility, he [Sargent] has made a business man from the provinces.'[28]* The other person was an aged 'militant' suffragette with white hair, Mrs Mary Wood, who appeared at the Royal Academy, where the portrait figured in the Summer Exhibition, and slashed it with a chopper, which she had concealed in the ample folds of her cloak. 'If they only gave women the vote,' she shouted as she was dragged protesting before a magistrate, 'this would never have happened.' Apparently she was not moved by any hatred of the subject – indeed Henry was on the whole sympathetic towards 'women's rights' – but simply because the portrait happened to be the most notable and valuable canvas in the exhibition. 'I have tried to destroy a valuable picture,' Mrs Wood said afterwards, 'because I wish to show the public that they have no security for their property nor for their art treasures until women are given political freedom.'†

The incident, which Theodora Bosanquet noted that he took 'very calmly', produced a deluge of sympathetic letters. Among them was one from Mrs Humphry Ward, to whom he replied:

> But figure me as a poor thing additionally impaired by the tomahawk of the savage, and then further see me breasting a wondrous high tide of postal condolence in this doubly-damaged state . . . And let me say at once that I gather the sense of the experts to be that my wounds are really curable – such rare secrets for restoration can now be brought to bear! They are to be tried at any rate upon Sargent's

---

* This opinion was echoed by the art critic of *The Times* (May 2nd, 1914), who described the portrait as 'a wonderful likeness; but it is a likeness of Mr James as anyone might see him casually in the train. Mr Sargent does not of course fall into the vulgar error of painting him according to his own notion of how a great novelist ought to look, but as he looks to eyes that have got no emphasis from the mind, and so his portrait lacks the intensity of design which only that emphasis can give. It is a likeness and nothing more.'

† Mrs Wood was committed for trial and immediately went on hunger strike, which resulted in her being released from prison under the 'Cat and Mouse' Act.

admirable work, and I am taking the view that they *must* be effective.

As for our discomfort from *ces dames,* that is another affair – and which leaves me much at a loss. Surely indeed the good ladies who claim as a virtue for their sex that they can look an artistic possession of that quality and rarity well in the face only to be moved bloodily to smash it, make a strange appeal to the confidence of the country in the *kind* of character they shall bring to the transaction of our affairs.[29]

The incident also produced a characteristic letter from Edmund Gosse in *The Times*:

There is, no doubt, a fiendish ingenuity in the skill with which these wicked women have chosen as the victim of their senseless malice the picture which, more than any other in the Royal Academy, was the emblem of private affection and regard expended, with the tenderest solicitude, by a body of personal admirers in paying honour to a great man who has nothing whatever to do with politics.

The artist himself took charge of the restoration. 'I . . . am able to tell you that, quite extraordinarily, the consummate restorer has been able to make the injuries good, desperate though they at first seemed,' Henry informed a friend two weeks later, 'and that I am assured (this by Sargent himself) that one would never guess what the canvas has been through. It goes back at once to the Academy to hang upon its nail again, and as soon as it's in place I shall go and sneak a glance at it.'[30] Certainly the restorers did a good job, helped no doubt by the newness of the paint, 'the whole surface more plastic to the manipulator's subtle craft than if it had been hardened with time', as Henry put it, and more than half a century was to elapse before the picture again needed some attention.*

---

* In 1966, a 'greyish blob' appeared by the nose, according to Mr David Piper, the then Director of the National Portrait Gallery, where the portrait now hangs, but this was put right by 'conservation treatment' and 'Henry James is on show again as rubicund as ever': *Evening Standard,* April 24th, 1966.

Henry's pleasure that the portrait had suffered no lasting damage was increased by the news which reached him at this time that the bust by Derwent Wood had been bought with the aid of the Chantrey Bequest for the Tate Gallery. 'When Derwent Wood's work was seen by a great many people in the autumn,' he told Gosse, 'I didn't quite feel it adequately appreciated, and greatly admiring it myself, was rather disappointed. I was *sure* it was fine, and I now greatly rejoice for him that the judges and even the jealous colleagues have done him such signal justice – besides rejoicing for myself and for the vision of my "long rest" here (or hereabouts) by the Thames-side of which these two years have made me so fond.'[31]

[SIX]

His Chelsea apartment proved as congenial a place for work as Henry had anticipated. He was able to continue his autobiography. The first volume, *A Small Boy and Others*, which had been completed before he moved into Carlyle Mansions, came out in 1913, to be followed a year later by *Notes of a Son and a Brother*. He also began work on a third volume, *The Middle Years*, as well as on a novel, *The Ivory Tower*, but the outbreak of the Great War caused him to lay both of them aside, and they were never finished. 'I am not, meanwhile, very well, thank you!' Henry told H. G. Wells '– with fairly chronic pectoral (anginal – though not strictly cardiac) distress, and have to live too carefully for any joy of freedom that the like of you (if there *be* any like of you!) knows and practices. But I go sometimes to the Reform – though almost only for victualling and in the evening – the relief of dining a little on other food than my cook's; for I never dine elsewhere.' He told Arthur Benson the same thing one afternoon at tea in the Athenaeum, 'very portly and gracious' and talking 'very richly', as Benson noted at the time. 'But you look well,' said Benson. Henry laughed. 'I *look*, my dear Arthur, I admit I *look* – but at that point I can accompany you no further. It's a look, I allow.'[32]

Since he could not make the journey to America, Harry and Billy and Peggy, his nephews and niece, crossed the Atlantic to him. 'They infinitely comfort and sustain me,' he told Gosse. Other young people would call at Carlyle Mansions to enliven his days, such as his god-daughter Dorothy Warren and the budding young actress Ruth Draper, whose sister was to marry his nephew Harry. At one of their meetings Ruth asked the Master whether he would advise her to go on the stage or whether she should try to write, as she had some literary aptitude. He took a long while to answer, as she stood quietly looking up at him to hear what he was going to say. At last the words came, punctuated by his customary pauses. 'No, my dear child, you – you have woven – you have woven your own – you have woven your own beautiful – beautiful little Persian carpet. Stand on it!'

Ruth Draper has also recalled an occasion when she called for him one morning at Carlyle Mansions and they went shopping together.

On the way – we were going in a four-wheeler – he asked me if I'd mind stopping at the Athenaeum to get a little money, and I shrank back in the back of the cab, having been told that I must never look at the outside of a gentlemen's club. Presently he came out and he said: 'My dear child, would you like to see the Athenaeum?' I was terrified and very shy and I said: 'Oh, Mr James, would I be allowed to go in?'

I was very much embarrassed. He said: 'Come with me', so I believe I am one of the few women who has ever been in the inside of the Athenaeum Club. He took me all over the library and into the room where the beautiful books are and showed me Thackeray's chair and I was duly impressed of course. It was a great thrill.

Well, after he got his money at the Athenaeum, we got into the cab again and went to the stores. He had a list which his housekeeper had given him before we left his flat. I remember we bought a sponge, and we bought some rice and some prunes and some ink and various household commodities, and I was so amused that he did this himself.[33]

Ruth Draper had already begun to experiment with writing

the type of 'monologue', which was to make her famous as a *diseuse*. Her flair prompted Henry to compose one for her to deliver on the subject of an American woman visitor to England who asked the American Embassy to arrange for her to be 'presented' at Court. 'It's the fatuous, but *innocently* fatuous, female compatriot of ours let loose upon a world and a whole order of things, especially this one over here which she takes so serenely for granted,' he wrote in sending Miss Draper the script. 'The little scene represents her being pulled up in due measure; but there is truth, I think, and which you will bring out, the small climax of her not being too stupid to recognize things when they are really put to her – as in America they so mostly are *not*. They are put to her over here – and this is a little case of it. . . . But I needn't carry coals to Newcastle or hints to our Ruth; who, if she takes to the thing at all, can be trusted to make more out of it by her own little genius than I can begin to suggest.'

Henry begged Ruth Draper to preserve his anonymity, but although she was impressed by the monologue she felt she could not do it as one of her 'acts' without revealing his authorship, since it 'bore his peculiar stamp'. Consequently it was never produced. 'I think he was disappointed,' she said afterwards, 'but I never learned it or tried it on anyone.' In some ways this was a pity, since it was an amusing sketch.[34]

In the spring of 1914, there was a considerable sensation – Compton Mackenzie goes so far as to say that 'the literary world was shaken to its foundations' – when Henry accepted an invitation from the *Times Literary Supplement* to contribute two articles on 'The Younger Generation' of English writers. The first of these was devoted to Joseph Conrad, Maurice Hewlett, John Galsworthy, H. G. Wells and Arnold Bennett, who, he said, 'have not quite perhaps the early bloom of Mr Hugh Walpole, Mr Gilbert Canaan, Mr Compton Mackenzie and Mr D. H. Lawrence; but the spring unrelaxed is still, to our perception, in their step'.[35] Of the four others who formed the subject of the second article, Henry had first asked Hugh Walpole about Lawrence ('Who is D. H. Lawrence, who, you think, would interest me?')[36] while his agent Pinker had drawn his attention to the first volume of Mackenzie's *Sinister Street*. At this time Mackenzie was living in Capri, but he returned on a visit to England soon after the articles appeared and he called at Carlyle Mansions to renew the acquaintance with the Master, which had begun when he was a boy twenty-three years before. He told Henry how grateful he was for what he had written about him, but added that some of his pleasure had been spoilt because, as he put it afterwards, 'I'd got the impression from his article that he thought Hugh Walpole was on the same level as the other three of us – an arrogant thing, I suppose, for a young man to say, but there it was.' According to Mackenzie, Henry held up his hands in a great gesture of consternation and said to him, gasping for the words he wanted as if they were moths fluttering round him, 'You, you amaze me, you, you astound me. All I thought I'd said about our excellent, our dear young friend Hugh Walpole was that up to the present moment he had written absolutely nothing!'[37]

'And now,' Henry continued, 'I want to hear all about your work.' Just as he said this, his housekeeper came in with the news that a man from the Army and Navy Stores had arrived, and would Mr James send an order for some marmalade?

The rising young novelist was at a loss to understand why the housekeeper could not give the order herself, but apparently Henry had to give it in writing.

'Forgive me, my dear, my dear young friend this appalling intrusion from the great outside world, and . . .' – he turned towards the housekeeper – 'marmalade, did you say, Mrs Anderson?'

'Marmalade, Mr James.'

'Well what will engage you for a moment, my dear boy, while I go into this complicated question!' He picked up two books from the table. 'Now here's our dear H.G.'s last book,' he went on. 'I wasn't quite sure whether our dear H. G. – or here's our dear Arnold Bennett's last book – perhaps you'd like to turn the pages of that or . . .'

'Mr James, the man is waiting.'

'Aha, ah yes – yes, yes!'

Henry thereupon sat down at the table, took a pen and dipped it in the ink and held it poised over the paper. 'Marmalade,' he murmured to himself. 'How, how should one address the directors of this vast emporium – this huge agglomeration – on marmalade?'

'Six jars, Mr James,' said the housekeeper, who had noticed the Master's hesitation.

'Please, Mrs Anderson. I must give attention to this. It's not one of those – um –' At this, he broke off and turned again to his young visitor. 'Are you sure, my dear boy? If you don't find that book, dear H.G.'s interesting or Arnold Bennett's, there's another here by –'

'Mr James, Mr James,' the housekeeper beseeched him. 'Please, the man is waiting.'

'Ah, marmalade!'

According to Mackenzie, this performance went on without exaggeration for quite five minutes before Henry got down to ordering from the Army and Navy Stores six two-pound pots of Oxford marmalade, eventually dismissing his housekeeper with a characteristic lament for 'these co-operative stores which our Frankenstein of a civilization has created to destroy the amenity of existence'.[38]

Another book, which Henry may well have recommended to young Mackenzie, knowing his ancestry, was *Twelve Scots Trials* by William Roughead. Its lawyer author had recently sent him this volume of criminal trials, and the gesture resulted in an amicable correspondence between them on the literature of crime, especially murder, in which Henry had come to take an intense interest. He was fascinated by the personalities of criminal trials, as his letters to Roughead show. Nor could he understand why other lawyers did not always share his interest. Once, when walking along the Rye High Street with a friend, he encountered the principal local solicitor, Mr Dawes. He immediately buttonholed him and eagerly inquired his opinion of a murder case which was being prominently reported in the papers. The old gentleman, who had the usual country solicitor's conveyancing practice, replied in his leisurely manner that he had not given any thought to the subject. Henry was amazed. 'The man's a damned fool,' he exclaimed to his companion as they went on their way.[39]

'I am not sure I enter into such matters best when they are *very* archaic or remote from our familiarities,' he told Roughead, 'for then the testimony to manners and morals is rather blurred for me by the *whole* barbarism. But I can more or less swallow a couple of centuries. The thrilling in the comparatively modern much appeals to me – for there the *special* manners and morals become queerly disclosed.' The cases of Madeleine Smith, Oscar Slater and Frederick Seddon, in particular, fascinated him, and when Roughead told him that he had been to a dinner of The Crimes Club in London where the Seddon case was discussed and had sat beside Edward Marshall Hall, K.C., Henry was filled with envy. 'I find it in me to wish verily that I had been present,' he wrote, '– I could, perhaps presumptuously, have so felt it in me to be – at that fond criminological feast of which you give me so appetizing an account. I have never in my long life had the good fortune of a chance of talk with a great defender or arraigner of murders – and there *are* such things I should have liked to ask Marshall Hall, for instance, especially perhaps about that prodigious young man – a glassmaker's designer, or something of that sort – whom he defended four or five years ago and who was so amazingly acquitted and acclaimed in consequence. I want always to know what happens to such glorified persons *afterwards*: their escape is so much more interesting than their punishment.'*

Henry believed with Roughead that Oscar Slater had been wrongly convicted of the murder of Connie Gilchrist, and he urged Roughead to continue his researches into this amazing case, although he had a feeling, which he expressed to his correspondent, that he himself would not live to see Slater's

---

* The reference was to the 'Camden Town murder' in 1907, when Marshall Hall secured the acquittal of Robert Wood, who had been accused of murdering a prostitute named Phyllis Dimmock. Some years later the successful advocate was accosted outside a provincial Assize court by a smart, happy-looking little man and asked whether he did not remember him. 'Why, isn't your name Wood?' said Marshall Hall. 'No, it's not,' replied the other, 'but I'd like you to know that I'm doing very well, and owe it all to you.'

vindication. Roughead's book on the trial of Mary Blandy at Oxford Assizes in 1752 for murdering her father with arsenic at her lover's instigation, also earned Henry's warm praise. ('I devoured the tender Blandy in a single feast.') 'Keep on with them *all*, please,' he wrote to the author, 'and continue to beckon me along the gallery that I can't tread alone and where, by your leave, I link my arm confraternally in yours: the gallery of sinister perspective just stretches in this manner straight away.'[40]

Seven ❧ War and Death

The fateful fourth of August, 1914, found Henry at Lamb
House with his niece Peggy. The invasion of Belgium despite
Germany's guarantee of her neutrality convinced Henry,
when he heard the first news, that a deep conspiracy for
violence and wrong had been brewing in the 'councils of the
two awful Kaisers' for a good while back. 'The plunge of
civilization into this abyss of blood and darkness by the
wanton feat of those two infamous autocrats,' he wrote to
Howard Sturgis, 'is a thing that so gives away the whole long
age during which we have supposed the world to be, with
whatever abatement, gradually bettering, that to have to take
it all now for what the treacherous years were all the while
really making for and *meaning* is too tragic for any words.'
And to his nephew Harry: 'For myself, I draw a long breath
that we are not to have failed France or shirked any shadow of a
single one of the *implications* of the Entente: for the reason
that we go in only under the last compulsion, and with cleaner
hands than we have ever had, I think, in any such matter
since such matters were. (You see how I talk of "we" and
"our" – which is so absolutely instinctive and irresistible with
me that I should feel quite abject if I didn't!).'[1]

In those first days, when he could hear the distant boom of
the big German guns across the Channel, he was thankful to be
in Rye, 'in this sympathetic little old house, which has somehow assuaged in a manner the nightmare'. At the end of
August, his faithful manservant Burgess Noakes decided that
he must join up, which he did to become one of the gallant
band of 'Old Contemptibles'.

My own domestic plot here rocks beneath my feet, since yesterday afternoon [Henry wrote to Edith Wharton on September 1] with the decision at once to volunteer of my invaluable and irreplaceable little Burgess! I had been much expecting and even hoping for it, but definitely shrinking from the responsibility of administering the push with my own hand: I wanted the impulse to play up of itself. It now appears that it had played up from the first, inwardly – with the departure of the little Rye contingent for Dover a fortnight ago. The awfully decent little chap had then felt the pang of patriotism and martial ardour *rentrés*; and had kept silent for fear of too much incommoding me by doing otherwise. But now the clearance has taken place in the best way in the world, and I part with him in a day or two. [2]

Edmund Gosse has given a vivid impression of his friend at this time:

At Lamb House he sat through that gorgeous tawny September, listening to the German guns thundering just across the Channel, while the advance of the enemy through those beautiful lands which he knew and loved so well filled him with anguish. He used to sally forth and stand on the bastions of his little town, gazing over the dim marsh that became sand-dunes, and then sea, and then a mirage of the white cliffs of French Flanders that were actually visible when the atmosphere grew transparent. The anguish of his execration became almost the howl of some animal, of a lion of the forest with the arrow in his flank, when the Germans wrecked Rheims Cathedral. He gazed and gazed over the sea southeast, and fancied that he saw the flicker of the flames. He ate and drank, he talked and walked and thought, he slept and waked and lived and breathed only the War. His friends grew anxious, the tension was beyond what his natural powers, transfigured as they were, could be expected to endure, and he was persuaded to come back to Chelsea, although a semblance of summer still made Rye attractive.

The end of September saw him back in Carlyle Mansions, 'having very blessedly this perch to come to'. Peggy had gone home with other American nationals, as their Government had urged, and Henry felt desperately lonely. 'I could no longer endure the solitudinous (and platitudinous) side of my rural retreat,' he confessed to Rhoda Broughton. 'I found I simply ate my heart out in the state of privation of converse (any converse that counted) and of remoteness from the source of information – as our information goes.'[3]

There is a conflict of opinion among Henry's biographers and literary critics and even members of his family as to the quality of his letters at this time. That they made a great impression upon Percy Lubbock is evident from the fact that Lubbock devoted more than one hundred pages to them in his edition of *The Letters of Henry James*. Harry James thought this was too much. 'What was written after the war began,' he told Lubbock, 'will, I think, pale and come within a short time to seem to be a part, not so much of Uncle Henry as of the general emotion of the hour. Don't think that when I say this I mean that his immediate and absorbed and highly individual expression of that emotion should not have justice done to it. It is very interesting, revealing, and in a way splendid, but I think it would be as clear and would perhaps be more fully revealing if there were less repetition.' Henry's biographer F. W. Dupee went further. 'His war letters, to which Percy Lubbock gave so much space in his collection, are not among James's best,' Dupee has written; 'like Proust's Mme Verdurin in her military phase, he rejoiced too much in the belated privilege of saying "we".' On the other hand, Leon Edel regards them as 'among the most eloquent of all his utterances'.[4] Whatever one may think about them, they certainly reflect the enthusiasm and energy, surprising in view of his impaired health, with which he devoted himself and his pen to the support of the allies, helping the Belgian refugees, comforting the bereaved, and visiting sick and wounded soldiers in hospital, besides writing articles and letters to the press. He wrote to James Pinker, his literary agent, at this time:

I am unable really to care for anything but what happens to, and above all by, our armies. What is happening through the arrival of the Indian troops at Marseilles, as wonderfully described in this morning's papers, has agitated me to the extremity of joy. I am usually resigned to be out of the hustle of great shows but had the seeing of that one been in the least in question for me, I should have found myself unspeakably inconsolable not to have assisted. I feel quite like one of the French old ladies described as trying to pat them tremulously on the back or otherwise desperately caress them!

According to Mrs Lucy Clifford, 'he spent hours every week comforting the soldiers in hospital – especially the French ones who were lonely in strange surroundings and found the language difficult'. He even took a convalescent to his own dentist, and put up a volunteer from Rye in his Chelsea flat. The English literary critic John Bailey described a call he made at Carlyle Mansions at this time: 'Old Henry James asked me to come and see him and was most extraordinarily affectionate, kissing me on both cheeks when I arrived and thanking me enormously for coming. He is passionately English and says it is almost good that we were so little prepared, as it makes our moral position so splendid. He almost wept as he spoke.'[5]

Edith Wharton, who had come over from Paris, gave a luncheon party in the house she had taken in Grosvenor Place. Logan Pearsall Smith remembered how Henry burst into the room, 'his great eyes ablaze', and greeted his hostess.

'My hands, I must wash them!' he cried. 'My hands are dripping with blood. All the way from Chelsea to Grosvenor Place I have been bayoneting, my dear Edith, and hurling bombs and ravishing and raping. It is my day-dream to squat down with King George of England, with the President of the French Republic and the Czar of Russia, on the Emperor William's belly, until we squeeze out of it the last irrevocable drops of bitter retribution.'

Mrs Wharton, who shared Henry's patriotic feelings, said that she must have a seat with the others. 'No, Edith,' was the stern reply. 'That imperial stomach is no seat for ladies. This is a war for men only: it is a war for me and poor Logan.'

American-born Pearsall Smith, who had recently become a naturalized British subject, now gave Henry an idea. 'This is certainly my war,' he said to him. 'Why don't you come into it? Why don't you enrol yourself as a British subject?'

Henry said nothing, but he was to ponder the question deeply over the next few months. From time to time Pearsall Smith would ring him up on the telephone and taunt him. 'When are you coming into the war? How long are you going to sit with the Roumanians on a back seat in the Balkans?'[6]

Presently Henry made the unwelcome discovery that he could no longer freely travel down to Rye. If he wished to stay at Lamb House, he must register as an alien with the police and be under police supervision – 'an alien friend of course, which is a very different thing from an alien enemy,' as he told his nephew Harry, 'but still a definite technical outsider to the whole situation here, in which my affections and my loyalty are so intensely engaged.'[7]

Meanwhile, an important war task which he set himself was to raise funds for the American Volunteer Motor Ambulance Corps, which had been formed by Richard Norton, a son of his old friend the President of Harvard. He was encouraged, as he told Walter Berry, 'by the chance of my having lately, with rather a rush, dined and lunched successively with several high in authority – the Prime Minister,* Lord Chancellor,† Winston Churchill, Ian Hamilton, people I don't in my sequestered way, often see'.[8]

He composed a vigorous appeal for publication in the American papers; it also appeared as a pamphlet in England. In characteristic Jamesian style, he cited a typical example of the work of the Corps in a small town in northern France, which had been under heavy German attack:

> Just as our Volunteers arrived a fresh bombardment began, and though assured by the fleeing inhabitants, including the mayor of the place, who was perhaps a trifle over-responsibly in advance of them, that there were no

---

* Mr Asquith.
† Lord Haldane.

wounded left behind – as in fact proved to be the case – we nevertheless pushed on for full assurance. There were then no wounded to bring out, but it was our first happy chance of bearing away all the hopeless and helpless women and children we could carry.[9]

His meetings with various politicians led to his being invited to join the Anglo-French Parliamentary Committee 'for the relief of the invaded Departments', and his remarks at one of the Committee meetings were subsequently printed as the opening contribution to *The Book of France*, a collection of essays by well-known French writers with translations by their English colleagues.[10] Henry, who also translated the essay by Maurice Barrès entitled 'The Saints of France', took the greatest pains with his opening contribution, trying it out beforehand upon several of his friends, including Violet Hunt. 'Perhaps you would be kind enough to tell me if I am comprehensible?' he asked Violet. 'They tell me' – turning his head away – 'that I am obscure.'

Violet admitted to having been stirred beyond measure by what she heard. 'Mr James!' she said, with genuine awe. 'I did not know you could be so – *passionate!*'

It was now Henry's turn to be taken aback. He walked to a bookcase at the other end of his study in Carlyle Mansions and turned round, fixing the 'Purple Patch' with his piercing eyes. 'Ah, madam,' he said, 'you must not forget that I am addressing – not a woman but a nation!'[11]

Great pleasure was afforded him by the regular letters he received from Burgess Noakes at the Front. In one letter Burgess had written that all the men in his regiment, the Royal Sussex, had been ordered to grow moustaches, to make them look older, he supposed. 'Anyway, that's where I come in,' he added, 'for I can grow more in two days than what most of the other men can grow in two months.' Burgess went on to say that he was finding the long marches very trying but he 'hadn't fallen out yet'.[12]

In return he would send Burgess fatherly advice as well as parcels of foodstuffs and ointment for his feet.

I shall pack off to you some more food and chocolates as soon as I can get again to the Stores [he wrote to Burgess on March 22nd, 1915]. I judge that is more 'comforting' to you, under your wear and tear, than anything else. But remember that if there is any particular thing you want and will mention it to us, even by a simple post card, you shall have it at once. The jolly plucky spirit of your letters gives me the greatest pleasure, and makes me feel that you are seeing life indeed. It is an immense adventure, truly, and one in which, if things go well with you, as I so heartily hope they will, you will always be glad and proud to have played your part. Play it up to the very notch and take all the interest in it you possibly can. I like immensely your telling me how you hold out in marches, under whatever drawbacks, when longer legs have to fall out; this does you the greatest honour. What a lot you must be seeing, feeling and above all hearing – with that terrific artillery always in your ears! Notice and observe and remember all you can – we shall want to have every scrap of it from you on your return. . . .

Make, by the way, very free use of that ointment we sent you – I hope you will find it a really good preventive; if you do we shall keep you supplied with it without interruption. . . .

Cultivate good relations with the French whenever you come in contact with them – which must be, in one way and another, pretty often; they are a wonderfully clever and intelligent, a highly civilized people when you come to know them; though of course you see them now under the most tremendous strain and burden that ever a nation had to bear. Like them, admire them and fraternise with them as much as you can; I used to see much of them in my younger time, and I take the most enormous satisfaction in their Alliance with this country. So do all you can to contribute your mite to the success of that![13]

Burgess was to return alive and well, but there were others who did not come back and Henry was to feel their loss, as if they had been his own children, so deeply attached to them had he become. Above all, there was the young poet Rupert

Brooke, 'a creature on whom the gods had smiled their brightest', in Henry's words, not yet twenty-eight at the time of his death while on his way with the Royal Naval Division to Gallipoli. Henry had made his acquaintance when on a visit to Cambridge during May Week in 1909, 'in that splendid setting of the river at the "backs"'. The poet had come over from The Old Vicarage in Grantchester, where he was living, and he had suggested giving Henry the experience of a punt; this the latter did not readily forget, as another member of the river party dropped the pole as he was pushing off and this had struck the Master a smart blow on the head.[14] In the following years they kept in touch, for Henry greatly admired the young man's writings, both in prose and verse, particularly his gift of combining humour with poetic beauty and tenderness of feeling. 'What it comes to, I suppose, is that he touches me most when he is whimsical and personal, even at the poetic pitch, or in the poetic purity, which he perpetually is. And he penetrates me most when he is most hauntingly – or hauntedly – English; he draws such a real magic from his conscious reference to it.'[15]

The last time they met was early in 1915, when Brooke was on leave and staying with the Asquiths in Downing Street. One night Henry came over from Chelsea to sit at the poet's bedside. The result of this meeting was Henry's agreeing to write an introduction to a volume of Brooke's impressions of a trip he had made two years previously to America, Canada, and the South Seas, and which in the event was to be the last thing Henry himself ever wrote.[16] Then, too, he was enraptured by the poet's sonnets. 'This evening, alone by my lamp,' he told Eddie Marsh on March 28th, 'I have been reading them over and over to myself aloud, as if fondly to test and truly to try them; almost in fact as if to reach the far-off author, in whatever unimaginable conditions, by some miraculous, some telepathic intimation that I am in quavering communion with him . . . Splendid Rupert – to be the soldier that could beget them on the Muse! and lucky Muse, not less, who could have an affair with a soldier and yet feel herself not guilty of the least deviation!'[17]

Henry was stunned by the news which reached him barely four weeks later from the Aegean. 'This is too horrible and heartbreaking,' he wrote to Marsh the same day. 'If there was a stupid and hideous disfigurement of life and outrage to beauty left for our awful conditions to perpetrate, those things have been now supremely achieved, and no other brutal blow in the private sphere can better them for making one just stare through one's tears.' He wrote again a few weeks later when Marsh sent him an advance copy of Rupert's posthumously published *1914 and other Poems*: 'His place is now very high and very safe – even though one walks round and round it with the aching soreness of having to take the monument for the man. . . . He seems to me to have had in his short life so much that one may almost call it everything. And he isn't tragic now – he has only stopped. It's we who are tragic – you and his mother especially, and whatever others; for we can't stop, and we wish we could.'[18]

[TWO]

One day, towards the end of April, 1915, Henry encountered Arthur Benson by chance in the Athenaeum, and they had lunch together for what was to be the last time. According to Benson, Henry 'kept on being entangled by voluble persons' in the club dining-room. Benson noted that he looked ill, changed colour and was dark under the eyes, but at the same time was 'very tremendous' and was in 'a cheerful and pontifical mood'. He ate a plentiful meal of veal and pudding, but he spoke to his old friend 'very gravely' of his health and chronic angina. 'We went down together and he made me a most affectionate farewell. He is slower and more *soigneux* in utterance than ever, but leaves a deep impression of majesty, beauty and greatness. He said that his life was now one flurried escape from sociability . . .'[19]

By mid-summer, Henry felt that he could no longer delay taking action on the question posed to him by Logan Pearsall Smith at Edith Wharton's the previous autumn. So he picked up the telephone, and instead of 'the elaborations of phrase, the

parentheses, the polybyllabic evasions, which made a talk on
the telephone with Henry James so amazing an adventure',
there was a terse query.

'Logan, how – you know what I mean – how do you do
it?'

'You go to a solicitor,' was Logan's equally terse reply.

'Of course,' the Master rejoined. 'I know just the right
person.' And with that he rang off with a bang, which, it
seemed to Pearsall Smith, must almost have smashed the
receiver.[20]

The same afternoon Henry rushed off to see his solicitor in
Gray's Inn. 'What,' he asked, 'is the exact modus operandi of
my becoming naturalized in this country?' He was told that
he would have to apply to the Home Office in prescribed form
and that he must produce four householders to vouch for his
personal respectability and for his ability to speak and write
English. Thereupon he instructed the solicitor to proceed with
the preparation of the application, which he himself undertook
to draft, besides finding the necessary sponsors.[21]

First, he went to Edmund Gosse as his oldest literary friend.
Gosse immediately agreed to be a sponsor. 'It is splendid of you
and beautifully like yourself, to make this sacrifice for us,'
was Gosse's spontaneous reaction. 'You give us the most intimate thing you possess. It is most moving, and most cheering,
a *grande geste* indeed. . . . How I rejoice to think of you about to
be *of* us in this anxious time, as you have been *with* us without
fail ever since the trouble began.'[22] Having taken his friend's
advice, Henry next approached 'our admirable friend the
Prime Minister', who he said, 'had always been so beautifully kind and charming to me', although he thought that
Asquith practised 'a rigid intellectual economy' outside
his office. Henry had recently spent a weekend at Walmer
Castle with the Asquiths, and Mrs Asquith had lent him her
intimate diary to read. ('Saint Simon is in forty volumes –
why should Margot be put in one?') The Prime Minister's
signature on the document, Henry felt, 'would enormously
accelerate the putting through of the application and the
disburdening me of the Sussex "restricted area" alienship,

which it distresses me to carry on my back a day longer than I need'.[23]

In his letter to the Prime Minister, Henry explained what had prompted him to take the step of renouncing the citizenship of his birth:

> I have assiduously and happily spent here all but 40 years, the best years of my life, and I find my wish to testify at this crisis to the force of my attachment and devotion to England, and to the cause for which she is fighting, finally and completely irresistible. It brooks at least no inward denial whatever. I can only testify by laying at her feet my explicit, my material and spiritual allegiance, and throwing into the scale of her fortune my all but imponderable moral weight – 'a poor thing but mine own'. Hence this respectful appeal. It is necessary (as you may know!) that for the purpose I speak of four honourable householders should bear witness to their kind acquaintance with me, to my apparent respectability, and to my speaking and writing English with an approach of propriety. What I presume to ask of you is whether you will do me the honour to be the pre-eminent one of that gently guaranteeing group? Edmund Gosse has benevolently consented to join it.[24]

Asquith replied that he would be delighted to become one of the sponsors who had formally to vouch for the eligibility to British citizenship of 'this distinguished American and personal friend', although he afterwards added in a jocular aside to his secretary that 'the bonds of friendship were strained to cracking when I had to subscribe to the proposition that he could both write and talk English'.[25] The other two sponsors were Sir George Prothero, the historian and editor of the *Quarterly Review*, who was his neighbour in Rye, and James Pinker, his literary agent.

'You probably won't be surprised to learn that the force of events has brought to a head the disposition I have strongly felt, ever since the beginning of the war, to apply for naturalization in this country,' Henry wrote to Pinker. 'I find myself

July 1915.

21 CARLYLE MANSIONS
CHEYNE WALK
S.W.

TELEPHONE 2417 KENSINGTON.

My dear Gosse.

The undersigned applicant for naturalization in this country applied .... "because of his having lived & worked in England for the best part of forty years; because of his attachment to the country & his sympathy with it & its people; because of the long friendships & associations & interests he has formed here — these last including the acquisition of some property; all of which things have brought to a head his desire to throw his moral weight & personal allegiance, for whatever they may be worth into the scale of the contending 'nations' present & future fortune."

Henry James.

LETTER TO EDMUND GOSSE
From the original at Lamb House

266

so exceedingly wanting to do so that the question simply settled itself for me, and I have taken preliminary steps.'

And so the matter was 'beautifully expedited', going through in five or six days from the time the papers were sent in.* Besides the Prime Minister, who 'has been most kind about backing me', Henry received the 'kindest possible' personal and private letter from the Home Secretary, Sir John Simon, telling him that 'he has just decreed the issue of my certificate of Naturalization, which will at once take effect . . . He gives me his blessing on the matter, and all is well'.[26]

'It does not fall to a Home Secretary's lot every day to authorize a certificate of naturalization on the recommendation of the Prime Minister, Prothero and Gosse', Sir John Simon had written. 'I am glad to think that "in spite of all temptations to belong to other nations" you are to be one of *us*.'

Henry replied the same day:

I thank you more than I can say for the signal kindness and sympathy of your letter which greatly touches me and brightly lights my path. Your having found *time* in all your storm and stress is a beautiful fact to me. For myself the case was of the simplest – like Martin Luther I could do no other!' I *had* to testify and at the point things had come to there was but one manner that sufficiently relieved my feelings. If my own country and *their* own! – had testified a little more *for* me, that would doubtless have served, but as she has distinctly not so acted, collectively, I could but act for myself; and it will remain a proud and I hope not a fatuous, thought to me that I shall have set her a little an example and shown her something of the way![27]

The business was completed a week later – to be exact, at 4.30 p.m. on July 26th, 1915 – when Henry took the Oath of

---

* The explanation which Henry James gave in his application for naturalization was, at Pinker's suggestion, communicated to *The Times,* which published it on July 28th, 1915. 'I not only haven't, as I say, any objection to its being made public,' Henry James told Pinker, 'but quite desire that this should be the case – for the sake of what I feel as the good example!' MS letter in Yale University Library cited by Leon Edel and Dan H. Laurence in *A Bibliography of Henry James* (1961) at p. 352.

Allegiance to King George V, before a Commissioner in his solicitor's office, and at last could say '*Civis Britannicus sum*'. 'The odd thing is that nothing seems to have happened and that I don't feel a bit different,' he told Gosse afterwards; 'so that I see not at all how associated I have become, but that I was really too associated for any nominal change to matter. The process has only shown me what I virtually *was*.' . . .[28]

[THREE]

While Henry was engaged in the business of becoming a British subject, something most unpleasant occurred to affect a personal and literary friendship of long standing. One day, when he happened to be in the Reform Club, the hall porter handed him a new book by H. G. Wells entitled *Boon*, with a note to the effect that it had been left there for him by the author. Glancing through the pages, Henry saw that it was a satire on some aspects of contemporary society and that the opening chapter was headed 'Of Art, of Literature, of Mr Henry James'. He had not read very far before he realized that this chapter consisted for the most part of a devastating lampoon upon himself and his literary method expressed through the lips of the author's fictional hero, Boon. In acknowledging the gift, Henry wrote to Wells that he had found the volume 'very curious and interesting, after a fashion – though it has naturally not filled me with a fond elation'.[29] Indeed he could hardly expect to be elated, for example, by the following:

> Having first made sure that he has scarcely anything left to express, he then sets to work to express it, with an industry, a wealth of intellectual stuff that dwarfs Newton. He spares no resource in the telling of his dead inventions. He brings up every device of language to state and define. Bare verbs he rarely tolerates. He splits his infinitives and fills them up with adverbial stuffing. He presses the passing colloquialism into his service. His vast paragraphs sweat and struggle; they could not sweat and elbow and struggle more if God Himself was the processional meaning to which they sought to come. And all for tales of nothingness . . . It

is leviathan retrieving pebbles. It is a magnificent but painful hippopotamus resolved at any cost, even at the cost of its dignity, upon picking up a pea which has got into a corner of its den. Most things, it insists, are beyond it, but it can, at any rate, modestly, and with an artistic singleness of mind, pick up that pea. . . .[30]

Wells replied to Henry's letter of mild protest in a tone of half-apology, in which he admitted to 'an immense embarrassment', while at the same time offering a somewhat lame explanation on the basis of the 'real and very fundamental difference' in their inate and developed attitude towards life and literature. 'To you literature like painting is an end,' Wells wrote, 'to me literature like architecture is a means, it has a use. Your view was, I felt, altogether too dominant in the world of criticism, and I assailed it in lines of harsh antagonism. And writing that stuff about you was the first escape I had from the obsession of this war. *Boon* is just a waste-paper basket. Some of it was written before I left my house at Sandgate [in 1911] and it was while I was turning over some old papers that I came upon it, found it expressive and went on with it last December.'[31]

Henry was neither amused nor convinced by Wells's arguments. He came back with a stinging rejoiner which put an end to their friendship once and for all.

21, Carlyle Mansions, Cheyne Walk, S.W. July 10, 1915.
I am bound to tell you that I don't think your letter makes out any sort of case for the bad manners of 'Boon', as far as your indulgence in them at the expense of your poor old H.J. is concerned – I say 'your' simply because he has *been* yours, in the most liberal, continual, sacrificial, the most admiring and abounding critical way, ever since he began to know your writings: as to which you have had copious testimony. Your comparison of the book to a wastebasket strikes me as the reverse of felicitous, for what one throws into that receptacle is exactly what one doesn't commit to publicity and make the affirmation of one's estimate of one's contemporaries by. I should liken it much

rather to the preservative portfolio or drawer in which what is withheld from the basket is savingly laid away. . . .

Meanwhile I absolutely dissent from the claim that there are any differences whatever in the amenability to art of forms of literature aesthetically determined, and hold your distinction between a form that is (like) painting and a form that is (like) architecture for wholly null and void. There is no sense in which architecture is aesthetically 'for use' that doesn't leave any other art whatever exactly as much so; and so far from that of literature being irrelevant to the literary report upon life, and to its being made as interesting as possible, I regard it as relevant in a degree that leaves everything else behind. It is art that *makes* life, makes interest, makes importance, for our consideration and application of these things, and I know of no substitute whatever for the force and beauty of its process. If I were Boon I should say that every pretence of such a substitute is helpless and hopeless humbug; but I wouldn't be Boon for the world, and am only yours faithfully.

HENRY JAMES

His heart condition, which became acute towards the end of July, prevented him from going down to Rye as he had done the year before, so he stayed on in London through August and September, though feeling that the medical treatment he received did him little good. 'There is no Rye for me this summer, alas,' he wrote at the end of August. 'I have lent my house there for a longish succession of weeks, and many reasons moreover make the conveniences of town more sustaining to me in these difficult days – days for which the difficulties are augmented for me, I am sorry to say, by my being much more unwell than I should like.' Instead he tried to find company 'in the mild hum of waterside Chelsea' where 'all this quarter of the town bristles with soldiers and for the most part extremely good-looking ones'.[33]

But he was still able to take some exercise and to go out for short walks. One day, in the middle of August, he ran into Ford Madox Hueffer in St James's Park. Hueffer was wearing the uniform of the Welch Regiment, having just been commissioned as a subaltern. He expected to be off to France soon, he told Henry.

'*Ah*,' observed Henry gravely. '*Tu vas te battre pour le sol sacré de Madame de Stael!*' Then, with an air of passionate sincerity, he put his hand on his chest, bowed, and assured his companion that he 'loved and had loved France as he had never loved a woman!' It was indeed true, for had he not written to Edith Wharton, who was doing war work in France, condemning the German bombardment of Rheims Cathedral in language that created such a powerful impression that his letter was read before the *Académie Française* and ordered to be published?

His friends and the sons of his friends were all volunteering for military service or some other form of war work. 'I admire the parents as much as the sons,' he told Edward Warren, whose son Christopher had joined up, 'and I can't say more than it brings home to me the rather ignominiously safe side of my own failure of consanguinity here.' And when Warren himself announced his departure for France with an ambulance unit, Henry wrote: 'I do think it admirable of you to go out to that scene of comparative relief and mercy, where, however you will doubtless have miseries enough brought closely home to you. That's what those there seem mostly to feel to be the case, though with an interest and an inspiration that sustains and reinforces. . . . I applaud so the high quality of conscience that you bring to your effort, easier as it must be to make than not to make it.'[34]

Of his young friends who perished in the war, above all, after Rupert Brooke, he felt the loss of Wilfred Sheridan. This young fighting soldier, descended from the Irish dramatist Richard Brinsley Sheridan, had married the beautiful and gifted sculptress Clare Frewen, whose father Moreton Frewen was Henry's Sussex neighbour at Brede Place. Lieutenant Wilfred Sheridan fell in action at the battle of Loos, on the very day that he heard the news that his wife had borne him a son. 'The thought of coming into your presence, and into Mrs Sheridan's with such empty and helpless hands is in itself paralysing,' he wrote to Clare on learning the dreadful news; 'and yet, even as I say that, the sense of how my whole soul is full, even to its being racked and torn, of Wilfred's beloved-est image and the splendour and devotion in which he is all radiantly enwrapped and enshrined, makes me ask myself if I don't really bring you something, of a sort, in thus giving you the assurance of how absolutely I adored him! Yet who can give you anything that approaches your incomparable sense that he was yours, and you his, to the last possessed and possessing radiance of him?'[35]

The prospect of his own death, which he had a feeling was not far off, prompted him to pay another visit to his solicitor at this time. He had made a valid will when he was in America in 1910, describing himself as 'a citizen of the United States now domiciled in London'. He now added a codicil to the will, referring to the fact of his British naturalization and making certain additions and alterations to the will. Of these the principal was the disposition of the Sargent portrait, which had been presented to him by a large body of friends and was legally his, although he had at first tried to disclaim ownership. He accordingly bequeathed the painting to the National Portrait Gallery in London with the direction that, should that Gallery's governing body not accept it within six months of his death, then it should go to the Metropolitan Museum of Art in New York.* He further directed that, should he die in England, his remains were to be cremated at Golder's Green Crematorium and 'my ashes afterwards laid near those of my parents, my elder Brother and my Sister, in the Cemetery of Cambridge, Massachusetts'.[36]

In October he went down to Rye for what was to prove to be his last visit to 'the dear little house'. Looking round the garden, he was saddened by the disappearance of the old mulberry tree, over against the south wall, victim of a recent gale. 'Once the fury of the tempest really descended he was bound to give way, because his poor old heart was dead, his immense

---

* The painting was accepted by the National Portrait Gallery, where it now hangs.

old trunk hollow. He had no power to resist when the south-wester caught him by his vast *crinière* and simply twisted his head round and round. It's very sad, for he was the making of the garden – he was *it* in person; and now I feel for the time as if I didn't care what becomes of it – my interest wholly collapses.' It was a depressing omen.[37]

When he was at Rye, Henry had 'a very bad time' with his angina, and after a fortnight he returned to Carlyle Mansions so as to be nearer a heart specialist. 'The past year has made me feel twenty years older, and, frankly, as if my knell had rung', he wrote to Hugh Walpole, who had just come back from a war mission to Russia and had telephoned him at Rye. 'Still, I cultivate, I at least attempt, a brazen front. I shall not let that mask drop until I have heard *your* thrilling story . . . I have "seen" very few people – I see as few as possible, I can't stand them, and all their promiscuous prattle, mostly; so that those who have reported of me to you must have been peculiarly vociferous. . . . I think I shall know your rattle of the telephone as soon as ever I shall hear it.'[38]

Walpole was staying in Cornwall when he received this letter. Unfortunately by the time he returned to London some three weeks later, the Master had largely lost the power of speech and was too ill either to receive visitors or to talk on the telephone.

What may well have been the last occasion on which he went out to a meal in mixed company arose out of a conversation he had with his friend and Chelsea neighbour Logan Pearsall Smith during one of the walks they habitually took together in 'this riverside suburb'. Pearsall Smith happened to ask Henry whether he knew the Spanish-American philosopher George Santayana. Oh, of course, replied Henry, wasn't he a great friend of his brother William at Harvard? Did he not admire his crystal-clear prose never found in other contemporary writers? And had he not spent days and months in his company, and listened long to the sound of his enchanting conversation? But, he went on, 'to answer your question, my dear Logan, as plainly – and I may say, as brutally – as you put it, I have *not* personally (to use your blunt adverb) met

273

Santayana, nor shall I ever meet him. He has never rung my doorbell, nor will he ever ring it. He wouldn't ring it even if he were in London, and now he isn't seen in London any more.'

'But I saw him yesterday,' said Pearsall Smith. 'He is now in London, and is lunching with me tomorrow. Though you don't like blunt questions, I shall permit myself bluntly to ask you, will you come to luncheon to meet him?'

'Come?' Henry cried, raising his hands to heaven. 'I would walk across London with bare feet on the snow to meet George Santayana. At what time? One-thirty! I will come. At one-thirty, I shall inexorably make my appearance.'

He was only a minute or two late. As Pearsall Smith and his sisters, Mrs Bernard Berenson and Mrs Bertrand Russell, were shaking hands with Santayana, they saw a taxi drive up. Then they heard heavy footsteps on the stairs. There was a pause before the drawing-room door opened and Henry entered, 'the most portentous of all the personalities I have ever encountered', as his host described him. Ignoring the others, he gravely approached the other male guest, and laying his arm on his shoulder, inquired, almost reproachfully, 'Now tell me, are you really George Santayana?' When fully reassured on this point he turned to the rest of the company 'with greetings of elaborate but quite unapologetic courtesy', and they all went in to luncheon.

The table talk was about England. Pearsall Smith expressed his lifelong satisfaction in being domiciled with so admirable a race as the English. 'Yes,' Santayana agreed, 'in my opinion the most superior white race, since the Greeks, which has peopled this planet.' Then, remembering his own qualms about acquiring British citizenship, not to mention Henry's experience over *Guy Domville* in the theatre and the incident of his portrait at the Royal Academy, their host wondered whether there was any loyalty or transfer of allegiance which could be wholeheartedly rushed into without reservation. 'Mustn't such things, like all that is mortal, be subject to qualifications, to occasional drawbacks, and even to moments, at least of disillusion?'

Never did Henry impress his host as more awe-inspiringly

portentous. 'Disillusion' – no, that was not the word to be used of his experiences with regard to 'these decent and dauntless people'. But he still hesitated over the word 'drawback'. Well, perhaps there were drawbacks, or rather qualifications; and especially the one which had forced Edith Wharton to depart from the shores of this island. 'The numbness and dumbness of the tongue-tied people of England! No good talk, no good general conversation, none of that famous cooperative criticism of life which was the solace of existence in France and in Italy. No house any longer in London where fine spirits could gather and wag their tongues freely . . . No tirades, no denunciations; nothing but dreary mumblings and grumblings about politics, diseases, and dentists, and insipid duologues automatically switched on and turned off at vapid luncheons and dinners.'

Henry's voice dropped to a conversational level, as he led up to what seemed at first an anti-climax, but in a way was really a climax. 'I am now going to tell you a story,' he said. 'It's a story I have never told before, and shall never tell again; a story that in decency I oughtn't to tell. But now I shall indecently tell it! Some years ago my friend Alphonse Daudet was in London; he often came to see me, and we met at dinners and luncheons. On the last of these occasions, when he came to say farewell, "My dear friend," he remarked, "I have been observing you carefully for some months; I have met almost all your friends and acquaintances; and I see that you are living among people less fine than yourself." That was what he said when he left England for Paris. Oh, for the wings of a dove, I sigh sometimes to follow after him, and after Edith to that conversational city!

'But I see that I have lingered too late in this pleasant society; at my age one is apt to prolong one's happiest moments. I hadn't the slightest notion how the clock had been ticking. Do you think, Logan, you could ring up for a taxi for me?'[39]

[FOUR]

On getting back from Rye, Henry was able to complete his introduction to Rupert Brooke's *Letters from America*. He then planned to resume work on an unfinished novel, *The Sense of the Past*, which he had laid aside a dozen or so years before and which Theodora Bosanquet had found in a drawer in Lamb House. He spent the evening of December 1st, reading through what he had written, intending to go on with it next morning. Then he went to bed. Burgess Noakes, who was on leave and staying in Carlyle Mansions, called him as usual about eight o'clock and noticed nothing amiss. But about half an hour later, Minnie Kidd, the maid, who was in the dining-room laying the table for breakfast, thought she heard the Master shout. She immediately went into his bedroom where she found him lying in a state of collapse on the floor. Her immediate thought was that he had had another heart attack, but it was soon apparent that his left leg was powerless. She and Burgess then managed to get him back into bed. Henry's doctor was sent for, and the maid went round to Theodora Bosanquet's flat near by to tell her she thought the Master had had a stroke.

So indeed it turned out to be. Theodora immediately went over to Carlyle Mansions, where she saw Henry who spoke to her quite lucidly. He apparently had suffered a paralytic stroke 'in the most approved fashion', so he told her. He had enjoyed a much better night than for some time past, he went on, and felt that his sleep had been particularly refreshing. But when he got up and crossed the room, he had fallen down. It was particularly distressing, he said, to find himself in a state of mental confusion, fumbling with the cord of the electric lamp under the mistaken impression that it would in some way connect with the bell. Then he called out for Minnie Kidd and she came quite soon. He elaborated on the premonitory sensation of the stroke to his old friend Lady Prothero, when she called later in the day to inquire how he was. As he was in the very act of falling, he heard a voice in the room, not his own, saying: 'So here it is at last, the distinguished thing!'[40]

The following night Henry had a second stroke, which caused further paralysis. It was now evident that he was seriously ill. Two trained nurses were engaged and a cable was sent to Mrs Alice James with the news of her brother-in-law's condition. She immediately decided to come over and she took the first available ship, to be followed by her children Harry and Peggy. But it took her ten days to reach London, and by the time she arrived the patient's condition had considerably deteriorated, embolic pneumonia having developed with a blood clot on the brain and another on the lung.

On December 11th, he woke up from a sleep and asked the nurse to fetch his secretary. This the nurse did, asking Theodora to go into his room because he was so delirious. He looked at her as she entered the room and appeared to see her and recognize her, speaking to her very clearly though not with any relation to the immediate circumstances of his illness. His words were all about going out to dinner 'at Lady Hyde's' and wanting to take Burgess Noakes with him. His idea seemed to be that Burgess should come back to let Theodora know he had arrived safely at Lady Hyde's. Then he asked: 'Where am I? What is this address?' When Theodora answered, '21 Carlyle Mansions,' he said, 'How very curious. That's Lady Hyde's address too!' After this colloquy, which was most touching and pitiful to Theodora, he went to sleep again.

The same evening he again sent for his secretary, because he wished to dictate. At this request the typewriter was moved into the bedroom, and he proceeded to dictate a series of rambling sentences, forming a strangely moving vision in which he appeared to see his own dedicated life as in some way paralleled by the career of Napoleon Bonaparte. 'They pluck in their terror handfuls of plumes from the Imperial Eagle, and with no greater credit in consequence than that they face, keeping their equipoise, the awful bloody beak that turns upon them. . . . Everyone looks haggard, and our only wonder is that they succeed in looking at all. . . .'[41]

Next morning he went on with his dictation, as if motivated by some deeply rooted empathy to penetrate the mind of Napoleon, giving his secretary two letters as if written by the French Emperor. One was on the subject of the redecoration of the Louvre and Tuileries, and the other to his brother Joseph and his wife urging them to accept the throne of Spain. The second letter was as follows:

277

My dear brother and sister,

I offer you great opportunities in exchange for the exercise of great zeal. Your position as residents of your young but so highly considered Republic, at one of the most interesting minor capitals, is a piece of luck which may be turned to account in the measure of your acuteness and your experience. A brilliant fortune may come to crown it, and your personal merit will not diminish that harmony, but you must rise to each occasion. The one I now offer you is of no common cast, and please remember that any failure to push your advantage to the utmost will be severely judged.

I have displayed you as persons of great taste and judgment. Don't leave me a sorry figure in consequence, but present me rather as your fond but not infatuated relation, able and ready to back you up.

Your faithful brother and brother-in-law,

HENRY JAMES

Fits of delirium continued intermittently for the next few weeks, followed by lucid intervals. 'He is better this morning but talking wildly,' wrote Mrs Clifford on December 13th. 'If he recovers we fear one side will be paralysed.' Once he imagined himself in Cork. Then he inquired if the plumbers had carried out the alterations to his bathroom and he spoke about 'the curious annexation of Chelsea to Cork'. On another occasion, he asked Theodora whether everything he had told her was clear. When she assured him it was, this seemed to put his mind at rest. Then he suddenly said to her: 'This place in which I find myself is the strangest mixture of Edinburgh and Dublin and New York and some other place I don't know.' At other times, he would ask for Burgess and would say, 'I want Burgess' or 'Isn't Burgess working for me any more?' Once he asked if he could be moved to Rye and apparently made the journey in his imagination since he spoke to Burgess of the pleasure of being back at Lamb House. On December 15th, his sister-in-law wrote to Edmund Gosse, who had sent a sympathetic inquiry with an offer of help:

There is really very little to do save to hope for better days. And I think there is some prospect of them. Henry knew and welcomed me and today he is distinctly better. Only the coming days can show how much – or how little – this improvement specifies.

Unfortunately this optimism was mere wishful thinking. On Boxing Day he was wheeled into the dining-room in his Bath chair after a restless night. But he was equally restless there, needing frequent help in being moved about the room from one chair to another. By the evening, Theodora noted, the whole household was pretty well exhausted, Minnie and Burgess flat out in the kitchen, the nurse hysterical in the passage and Mrs James 'even more hysterical than before'. Mrs James told Theodora that she was doing her best to persuade the doctor to administer enough morphia to keep the patient quiet.[42]

Meanwhile the proofs of his Introduction to Rupert Brooke's *Letters from America* had arrived from Edward Marsh, who had edited the collection, but Henry was too ill to look at them or to have them read aloud. 'It will distress him to know he can't attend to them himself,' Theodora Bosanquet wrote to Marsh. However, since he had dictated the whole work twice, she did not feel that there could be any faults of carelessness. She suggested that Marsh should keep in touch by telephone ('The phone does not seem to disturb him.'), which Marsh agreed to do. Marsh then sent a copy of what Henry had written to Brooke's mother. 'His tribute to Rupert will almost certainly be the last thing he will write – if so, it makes a beautiful end to his work.'

At this time, Marsh was working in the Prime Minister's Private Office in Downing Street, and he immediately took the opportunity to raise the question of making some public recognition of Henry's work. At the time of his naturalization Asquith had considered recommending him for the Order of Merit, the highest civilian distinction which it is within the power of the Sovereign to confer. But the idea had run into opposition from Lord Morley on the apparent ground that Henry's novels were confined to the doings of the 'idle rich', and had been temporarily dropped. However, when Marsh asked the Prime Minister whether he would not reconsider it, Asquith told him to put up a minute on the subject addressed to him personally. Marsh accordingly set to work and was able to produce what he thought was 'a cogent plea'. Such indeed it proved to be.[43]

May I write a few words in the hope that the question of the O.M. for Mr Henry James has not been irrevocably set aside?

I think there should be little doubt of his right to stand beside George Meredith and Thomas Hardy – the only novelists yet admitted to the Order. If they have qualities which he has not, the converse is also true. It has been said that the great French novelists are conscious artists, the English inspired amateurs. Henry James is the exception. No writer of his time gives the same impression of knowledge and mastery in the architectural structure of his works, and in the gradual building up of atmosphere, character, and situation. . . .

He's sometimes blamed for dealing only with characters drawn from the hothouse life of the leisured classes, hypertrophied in intellect and emotion; but an artist should be judged not by his choice of material but by his treatment. It would be equally fair to rule out Thomas Hardy for his complete failure to represent any educated person.

Henry James's shorter stories are certainly not inferior to those of any English writer. His style may be criticized as mannered, and sometimes obscure; on the other hand it is one of the most individual that has ever been evolved; it is infinitely expressive, except when it defeats itself by trying to express too much; and it rises at times to the height of beauty.

Apart from fiction, his critical work is of the highest order; and his introductions to his own novels in the Library Edition are I think a uniquely illuminating account of an artist's creative processes.

Marsh went on to deal with Henry's influence on his own

and the succeeding generation of novelists – 'Arnold Bennett and H. G. Wells would recognize him as their master, as R. L. Stevenson would if he were alive' – and finally mentioned Morley's obstructive attitude, in addition to two extraneous considerations.

His recent naturalization was a generous and impressive gesture of adherence to our national cause, and deserves some grace of recognition. And the compliment would no doubt be appreciated in America.

I understand that Lord Morley is against the proposal; but with the greatest respect for him I could wish that some opinion might be taken which would be representative of a later epoch in taste.

In the face of these arguments, Asquith hesitated no longer and immediately forwarded the recommendation to Lord Stamfordham, the King's Private Secretary. Lord Stamford-ham replied two days later, on December 28th, conveying His Majesty's approval, and the information was sent to Carlyle Mansions the same day.

As one of his oldest and closest friends, Edmund Gosse asked leave to be the first to tell Henry of the award, to which Mrs Alice James agreed. Accordingly on New Year's Day, Gosse called early at Carlyle Mansions and on entering the sick room found Henry lying with closed eyes in the light of a single flickering candle. Kidd, the maid, told Gosse that she was afraid the patient was past hearing anything. Then, leaning over the bed, Gosse whispered, 'Henry, they've given you the O.M.' Not a sign of interest showed in Henry's still face, and Gosse quietly left the room. Directly the door closed, however, the patient opened his eyes and said to the maid: 'Kidd, turn off the light to spare my blushes.'[44]

When Theodora Bosanquet called later in the morning, she found Henry much more like his old self and obviously pleased with the news. His sister-in-law had a bundle of congratulatory telegrams in her hand which she proceeded to read out. These caused Henry to remark, 'What curious manifestations such occasions call forth.' When Theodora added her congratulations, he waved a friendly hand towards her.

He was pleased, too, by the anonymous official tribute which appeared in *The Times*, probably the handiwork of Edward Marsh:

> The high honour now conferred on him will give the keenest satisfaction to lovers of literature all over the world, and not least in France, with whose national spirit and national culture he is deeply imbued. For Mr James, though American by birth and British by adoption, is a citizen of the world. The variety and subtlety as well as the fertility of his genius have placed him with Mr Thomas Hardy unquestionably at the head of living masters of English. Now he joins Mr Hardy in the Order, membership of which is the highest distinction attainable by a writer, and in which they are the only two representatives of pure English.

A further improvement in his condition took place during the next fortnight, greatly to the doctor's surprise. But it was not maintained, and he began slowly and perceptibly to sink. 'The poor old fellow is going,' the doctor told Theodora on January 13th. He was now living in the past and his mind would wander across the years to such incidents as the day his father took him to tea with Carlyle. By this time it was painfully evident that he would be unable to go to Buckingham Palace to receive the Cross and insignia of the Order of Merit at the King's hands. Permission was therefore given for Lord Bryce, an old friend and a former British Ambassador in Washington, to confer the Order on the King's behalf in Carlyle Mansions. This simple ceremony took place a few days later, on January 19th, by which time Henry was barely conscious.

Yet he lingered on for another six weeks. His nephew Harry, who arrived at the end of January, wrote on February 2nd:

> Physically, he's nearly helpless, being completely paralysed on the left side. Since he's been under the constant supervision of the nurses his heart and other functions have been kept in order and he's no worse than 10 days ago. But

he's very confused in mind – drowsily wandering almost all the time and cognizant of nothing except that he's ill. He usually recognizes his servants, the members of his family and his doctor – the only people who see him.

I don't think he's at all acutely aware of his condition, and that's a blessing. He suffers no pain and no more mental distress than is inseparable from a stage of drowsy muddle. But I'm glad to have seen him again, even so; there never was a gentler more considerate and careful patient. His fragmentary speech abounds in amplified courteousnesses – sometimes more ample than ever – and in broken but solicitous enquiries about the welfare of anyone beside him. He also wanders a great deal in the past, and seems often to think that my father is here, tho' not in the same room.[45]

'But he is never coming back to us,' Alice James wrote to Gosse on February 11th. 'He does not suffer and the mental confusion which distressed him at first no longer weighs on him. He thinks he is in foreign cities, among old friends, and that his brother William, the only one he asks for, will be coming in ere long. Such serenity of spirit shines through the wrecked brain that his presence is still a comfort to us.'

Two weeks later, he had what the nurses thought was another stroke and fell into a coma. In one of his last conscious moments, in which his mind was dwelling on his work, he said to Alice James: 'Tell the boys to follow, to be faithful, to take me seriously.'

His sister-in-law was at his bedside when he died, shortly before seven o'clock in the evening of February 28th, 1916, quite painlessly and peacefully without ever regaining consciousness. 'He just gave three sighs and went,' said Mrs James afterwards.

[FIVE]

Next day Alice James and her daughter Peggy began to make arrangements for the funeral service, to be held in Chelsea Old Church, once Sir Thomas More's private chapel, since in giving directions for the strictly private cremation at Golder's Green, they felt that Henry had not perhaps realized how many of his friends would wish to pay their last respects to his memory. Meanwhile a number of those friends, notably Bailey Saunders, Lucy Clifford and Mrs Prothero approached the Dean of Westminster with the object of having the funeral service in the Abbey. The Dean did not appear very willing but eventually said that it could be done, and incidentally it would cost £100. In the circumstances Peggy and her mother felt that it would be 'more dignified' to go on with the arrangements for Chelsea Old Church. It was 'more in accord with his life', Mrs James said '– better befitted the New Englander'. She told the Dean: 'We should love to remember that among his friends there were those who thought of the great Abbey. But my daughter and I, as these friends know well, have not wavered in our preference for the "simple funeral" he asked for and Chelsea Old Church which he loved.' Announcements were accordingly sent to the press that the service would be held there on March 3rd.

When the undertakers had completed their work, a plaster cast or death mask was made of the face. Minnie Kidd then took Theodora Bosanquet into the drawing-room, where the Master lay in his coffin, which was covered with a black pall, while there was a white square over the face. This the maid folded back, but Theodora could not see anything but the actual face, which was bound round with a bandage. It looked very fine, Theodora thought, like a great work of art fashioned in ivory wax, perfectly peaceful but entirely dissociated from everything that was his personality. When Theodora called again next day, the maid again took her in to see the Master. This time, noted Theodora, he looked a little more like himself, because the face was not quite so bandaged, though they still had to keep the bandage under the chin, the housemaid explained, because the mouth fell open when they took it off. The following morning, which was the day of the funeral, Theodora received 'a very kind note' from Mrs James asking if she would not like to go and see him just once more 'because he was looking so beautiful'. So Theodora went, but she did not notice much difference from the previous afternoon except that 'the upper lip and chin were just the least bit glistening with the growth of hair since death'.

Several people who had seen the Master in his coffin were struck by the likeness of the face to Napoleon, which seemed to Theodora Bosanquet 'certainly great', though Mrs James thought that it was more like the head of Goethe. A comment of a rather different kind was made by the gardener, George Gammon, who had come up from Rye for the funeral. He too was taken into the drawing-room and after he had viewed his dead master was asked by Mrs James if he did not think him beautiful, to see him so at peace. 'Yes, ma'am,' replied George. 'He has kept very well, hasn't he?' This remark greatly intrigued Mrs James. 'Henry would have loved to hear it,' she told Theodora.[46]

It rained hard on the day of the funeral, but the weather did not deter Henry's friends and admirers from the little old church by the river. Mrs James asked Theodora to go along early so as to see that the wreaths from the family were 'properly placed'. The service had been announced for two o'clock, but when Theodora arrived, shortly before half past one, there were numbers of people waiting for the doors to open, including the choir boys. Theodora went off in search of the verger, who eventually arrived and let the people in. Theodora noticed Mrs Clifford and the Ranee of Sarawak sitting comfortably in the Ranee's car, but others who came on foot got quite wet. Newspaper reporters were stationed at the church door and took the names of the distinguished mourners, who included the American Ambassador (W. H. Page), Augustine Birrell, John Sargent, Viscount Bryce, Sir Frederick Macmillan and Mrs Rudyard Kipling. The Prime Minister was represented by his Private Secretary, Mr Maurice Bonham-Carter. Edmund Gosse, who was looking about for a good seat, was not at all pleased when Theodora suggested that he should go to the side. 'But I came *early*,' he protested, evidently expecting a reserved place in one of the front pews. Eventually Mrs James arrived with Harry and Peggy, also Mr Sargent and his two daughters, who together occupied the first pew, while Bailey

Saunders and Theodora squeezed into the row behind. Henry's valet and the two women servants and the gardener sat beside them across the centre aisle. Then the coffin was carried in and placed in the chancel and the service began. Theodora liked the 'mellow old tone' of the church, and felt that if the organ had been better and the choir more effective, 'it would have been quite a good place for the funeral service'. Mrs James, on the other hand, was pleased with the service. 'How kind and welcoming the Old Church was to our Pilgrim,' she told Gosse afterwards, 'and how one felt the spiritual atmosphere of affection for the friend who had gone.'[47]

Theodora Bosanquet waited behind until everyone had left the church, and the family had departed with the coffin to the crematorium, accompanied by Bailey Saunders, who insisted on going too, 'though Mrs James quite begged him not to'. Afterwards Theodora found the two press men examining the names on the wreaths, 'There aren't many, are there?' one of them observed, not realizing that 'No flowers by request' had been generally intimated.

Edmund Gosse paid a further tribute in a letter which he wrote to *The Times*, when he returned home later in the afternoon, and which appeared the following morning. He began by recalling 'the mysterious and poignant story', which Henry had contrived to publish twenty-five years previously after it had knocked in vain 'at half a dozen editorial doors impenetrably closed to it'.

Some of us must have thought that 'The Altar of the Dead' of our wonderful friend had been found in the beautiful old dim church of All Saints which stood almost at his door, and into which, he too burdened with unutterable regrets, he often silently slipped. As we stood round the shell of that incomparable brain, of that noble and tender heart, it flashed across me that to generations yet unawakened to a knowledge of his value the Old Chelsea Church must forever be the Altar of the Dead.

No man has awakened greater or penetrated so many shy spirits with affection. But we want to proclaim to the sensual world that when the war with Germany broke out he ceased to be merely the idol of an esoteric group. He became a soldier; he belonged to England. No one has suffered more in spirit, no one was more tensely agitated by the war, than Henry James. Not that he doubted of our victory. In the deadliest trances of the night he never questioned the end. But his nature was like a violin-string, and it was strained until it snapped.

He was a supreme artist; but what we must remember and repeat is that he was a hero. He belonged to a neutral nation that he was attached to by a thousand ties. Yet he broke them all to devote himself, heart and brain and vibrating nerves, entirely to his passionate love of England. He was a volunteer in our great cause. Quite in the beginning of August, 1914, he said to two English friends, 'However British you may be, I am more British still.' He has died before we celebrate the catastrophe of wickedness, and perhaps it is as well, for his great heart might have been broken with joy in the midst of the huzzas.

But let those who knew Henry James and those who knew him not approach the Altar of the Dead with reverence, for he was an English hero of whom England shall be proud.[48]

Mrs James was much touched by Gosse's 'beautiful letter'. She felt that the writer had shown that he took the Master seriously, as Henry had asked in one of his last lucid moments that he should be. 'My children will never forget or cease to be grateful to you for so doing,' she wrote to Gosse. 'I find it easy to think of Henry in the Heavenly Country towards which he has journeyed, never more faithfully than during these weeks of bewildered helplessness. His great spirit revealed itself as never before through the physical ravage and disarray through which it took its way.'[49]

Incidentally Gosse's letter prompted Bailey Saunders to recall that, when he was visiting Rye some years previously he asked Henry which of his writings he would himself put first. 'After much playful disparagement of them all he settled finally on "The Altar of the Dead" as the one with which he was least dissatisfied.'[50]

An Englishwoman also paid a sincere tribute to his memory.

'He was a great personality in London and everybody who knew him seemed to have felt his personal note,' wrote Mrs Lucy Clifford, 'and of course were so immensely touched at his becoming one of us in the darkest time our country has known for centuries. It was the most supreme proof he could give us of his sympathy and affection. But his own country must not for a moment think that he forgot it, for he didn't; and he left directions that his ashes, after cremation, were to be taken back to it.'[51]

In accordance with his wishes, his ashes were taken across the Atlantic and laid beside those of his parents, his elder brother William and his sister Alice, in the family burial ground in the cemetery of Cambridge, Massachusetts. On the headstone of the grave he was described simply and truly as 'novelist and interpreter of his generation on both sides of the sea'. Afterwards the family arranged for the erection of a memorial tablet in Chelsea Old Church; this described him as 'lover and interpreter of the fine amenities, of brave decisions and generous loyalties: a resident of this parish who renounced a cherished citizenship to give his allegiance to England in the first year of the Great War'. His residence in Rye was similarly commemorated by a plaque on the outside wall of Lamb House, with lettering designed by Sir Reginald Blomfield, R.A. and recording the fact that 'Henry James, author, lived here, 1898–1916'.[52] The house itself, which was left in his will to his nephew Harry, was eventually presented in the latter's name to Britain's National Trust, 'to be preserved as an enduring symbol of the ties that unite the British and American peoples'.[53]

There was some surprise when his will was published and the relatively small value of his estate was seen – less than £9000, including the Lamb House property, which was valued at just over £2100, but excluding his share in the family property in New York State. This modest fortune was distributed between the various members of the family in America, except for a few small legacies – £100 each to his friends Lucy Clifford, Jocelyn Persse, and Hugh Walpole, and the same to his three indoor servants and gardener. As has already been seen, he bequeathed the Sargent portrait of himself to the National Portrait Gallery in London.

The last word on the Master may be left to Theodora Bosanquet, who though she survived him by forty-five years could never be persuaded to publish anything about her former employer apart from a brief essay and two magazine articles, in spite of the detailed diaries she kept at the time. It would be difficult to improve upon her summing-up. 'The essential fact is that wherever he looked Henry James saw fineness sacrificed to grossness, beauty to avarice, truth to a bold front. He realized how constantly the tenderness of growing life is at the mercy of personal tyranny and he hated the tyranny of persons over each other. His novels are a repeated exposure of this wickedness, a reiterated and passionate plea for the fullest freedom of development, unimperilled by reckless and barbarous stupidity.[54]

❦ The Lamb House Library

When Henry James died, in 1916, his library consisted of some 2000 volumes housed in his Sussex home, Lamb House, Rye. These ranged from Dean Milman's *History of Latin Christianity* (9 vols, 1867) Mathew Arnold's *God and the Bible* (1875) and *The Foundations of Belief* by A. J. Balfour (3rd edition, 1895) to E. W. Lane's translation of *The Arabian Nights' Entertainments* (3 vols, 1839–41), the complete works in French of the Abbé de Brantôme, including his *Vies des Dames Galantes* (15 vols, 1779) 'nicely bound in full contemporary calf, gilt tooled backs', and the *Memoires* of Jacques Casanova (8 vols, Paris n.d.) 'nicely bound in three-quarter brown calf'. The first volume of the latter bore the inscription in James's hand: 'Henry James, New York, Aug. 21st, 1883.' The majority of the books in the library had similar inscriptions, since the Master was in the habit of autographing his books with the date and place where they were acquired, even in the case of fellow authors' presentation copies to him of their works. Almost all the books were acquired during his forty years' residence in England, although there were a few of earlier date. The earliest would appear to be Moxon's Illustrated Edition (1857) of the *Poems* of Alfred Tennyson, the Poet Laureate, bound in half-morocco and given to Henry by his father during the family's stay in St John's Wood in 1858.[1]

The library was not immediately dispersed on James's death, since the house and contents passed under his will to his nephew Henry James, Jr., who lived in New York and preferred to let Lamb House furnished to a succession of tenants. The latest of these, E. F. Benson, died early in 1940, and before another tenant could be found the house was severely damaged in an air raid on August 18th, 1940, which completely destroyed the adjacent Garden Room or Garden House, where James used to work in the summer months, incidentally spoiling many of the books, between 250 and 300, usually kept there. Lamb House was consequently rendered uninhabitable for the remainder of the war, and it was some time afterwards before the damage could be repaired. Meanwhile Henry James, Jr., had died in 1948, and two years later his widow, who was a sister of the actress Ruth Draper, presented the house in her late husband's name to the National Trust. Unfortunately the gift did not include the contents which together with most of the furniture had already been sold for the benefit of the James estate. 'Personally I felt very badly that the books in the Library were dispersed,' wrote Miss Draper at the time, 'but I hope a few will be kept for the Garden House which I hear is ultimately to be rebuilt.'[2] Although the Trust eventually decided not to rebuild the Garden Room, it did succeed in recovering about 140 volumes from the library, including author's presentation copies of works by A. C. Benson, Edmund Gosse, W. D. Howells, Rudyard Kipling, Logan Pearsall Smith, Hugh Walpole, Mrs Humphry Ward, H. G. Wells and Edith Wharton. These are now preserved in the Henry James Room at Lamb House. Apart from a few of the books which had previously been removed by Henry James, Jr., for himself and other members of the family, the bulk of the library which survived the bombing was bought by a Rye antiquarian bookseller, Mr Gilbert H. Fabes, who in turn sold them over a period to a wide circle of individual customers on both sides of the Atlantic, including Dr Leon Edel and the present writer.

From the catalogue of the library prepared in 1931, on the instructions of Henry James, Jr., supplemented by three of Gilbert Fabes's catalogues (Nos. 17–19, Rye, 1949–51), containing detailed descriptions of the books bought by Fabes, it is possible to get a good idea of the contents of the library as it was at the time of the original owner's death. Henry James was not a book collector and the library which seems to have been somewhat haphazardly assembled appears largely utilitarian in content. English, French and Italian literature, biography, literary criticism, history, drama, crime, belles-lettres, philosophy, theology, topography and travel are the subjects principally represented. As one might expect, there are few books published before the middle of the last century, and apart from the authors' presentation copies few rarities. Among the latter was the 3-volume edition of Congreve's *Works* published by J. Baskerville (Birmingham, 1761); also G. Borrow's *Celebrated Trials*, with plates (6 vols, 1825). Some books, notably a set of French translations of Turgeniev (Paris, 1887), had previously belonged to James's friend Constance Woolson and were evidently left to him at her death.

The collection was richest in modern first editions, Mathew Arnold, J. M. Barrie, Browning, Carlyle, Austin Dobson, Edmund Gosse, Kipling, George du Maurier, Walter Pater, Swinburne and J. A. Symonds and Tennyson being well represented among the English writers, and Balzac, Paul Bourget, Alphonse Daudet, Flaubert, Anatole France, Maupassant and Zola among the French. The American writers included Emerson, James Fenimore Cooper, William Dean Howells, Washington Irving, Edith Wharton, Walt Whitman and C. F. Woolson. A note by James in the first English edition of Fenimore Cooper's *The Monikins* (3 vols, 1835) records that this work was 'given me oddly and charmingly by Anne [Thackeray] Ritchie'.[3] Some of the authors' inscriptions in their presentation copies are also worth noting. Logan Pearsall Smith's first book, *The Youth of Parnassus and Other Stories* (1895) was inscribed 'To Mr Henry James, in the study and admiration of whose work this slight attempt has been made'.[4] H. G. Wells, with less modesty presented his *Mankind in the Making* (1903) 'from the ingenious author'. Edith Wharton's *Italian Backgrounds* (1905) was inscribed 'in memory of Berkshire foregrounds'.[4] Mrs W. K. Clifford's *Woodside Farm* (1902) was given to Henry James 'from his devoted Lucy Clifford'. Similar devotion came from Hugh Walpole, whose first novel, *The Wooden Horse* (1909) was inscribed 'with love from the author', while *The Duchess of Wrexe* (1914) went 'To the Master from his affecionate servant the Author – who sends this, not with pride nor with expectation, but with devotion'.[5]

Although he habitually autographed his books, Henry James rarely added annotations. A terse inscription in the front papers of George Gissing's *New Grub Street* (1898) – 'George Gissing at Lamb House with H. G. Wells' – records the only occasion on which James and Gissing met, in June 1901, when Wells brought Gissing to the house and they stayed the night. Sometimes, when James lent a book to a friend or neighbour, he would write in the fly leaf as with *Old Standards: South Country Sketches* by John Halsham (1913) – 'Dear Mrs Ford, This *Sussex* book is *exceedingly* charming. H.J.'[6] Occasionally he would write something in a book given to him, as in *The Soul of a People* by H. Fielding (1899), which he got from Margaret, Ranee of Sarawak. 'All that is beautiful in life is founded on compassion and kindness and sympathy. Nothing of great value can exist without them.'

It cannot be said that Henry James had read all the books in his library. For instance, although they contain his autograph signature, the six monumental volumes of S. R. Gardiner's *History of the Great Civil War* (1888–91) and *History* of the *Commonwealth and Protectorate* (1894–1901) remained with their pages unopened; at least they passed into the present writer's possession in that state. After the First World War, the soldier-poet Robert Nichols, who had somehow acquired Henry James's copy of the Fowlers' four-volume translation of Lucan, gave the work to Arnold Bennett. 'Looking through the volumes in bed last night,' Bennett wrote in his *Journal* for April 19th, 1920, 'I found that the only part of which the leaves were cut was the Dialogues of Courtesans. Swinnerton and I agreed this morning that it was a very pretty stiff problem whether these pages were cut by Henry James or by Robert.'[7] On this occasion, I think, it was the Master who used the paper-knife.

❧ Sources and Notes

The following abbreviations are used:

Ashley = The Ashley Library of T. J. Wise, British Museum.

B.B.C. = British Broadcasting Corporation Sound Archives. 'Recollections of Henry James in his Later Years.' London, 1956.

Barrett = The Clifton Waller Barrett Library, University of Virginia.

Berg = The Berg Collection, New York City Public Library.

Brotherton = The Brotherton Collection, Brotherton Library, University of Leeds.

Houghton = The Houghton Library, Harvard University.

Lamb = The Lamb House Collection, Rye, Sussex.

Letters = *The Letters of Henry James*, edited by Percy Lubbock. 2 vols. London, 1920.

Notebooks = *The Notebooks of Henry James*, edited by F. O. Matthiessen and Kenneth B. Murdock. New York, 1947.

Selected Letters = *Selected Letters of Henry James*, edited by Leon Edel. London, 1956.

Yale = Yale University Library.

CHAPTER ONE · *Mayfair*

1 *Letters*, I. 49.

2 *Letters*, I. 51.

3 *Letters*, I. 50.

4 Robert C. Le Clair. *Young Henry James*, 184–5.

5 *id.* 189.

6 *Essays in London*, 6–7.

7 *The Middle Years*, 42–4. The Albany figures as the Red Lion in the opening pages of *The Passionate Pilgrim* (1875), Henry James' first story to be published in book form.

8 *Letters*, I. 26–7.

9 *Notebooks,* 27.

10 MS. letter to Alice James, December 13th, 1876: Houghton. E. S. Nadal. 'Personal Recollections of Henry James' in *Scribner's Magazine,* LXVIII, 89. (July, 1920.)

11 MS. letter to Alice James. March 26th, 1879: Houghton. Leon Edel. *Henry James: The Conquest of London,* 349–50.

12 *Notebooks,* 28.

13 *The Education of Henry Adams,* 124. Edel, 287.

14 MS. letter Henry James to Lord Houghton, April 15th, 1877; Trinity College Library, Cambridge. James Pope-Hennessy, *Monckton Milnes: The Flight of Youth,* 206.

15 T. Wemyss Reid. *The Life, Letters and Friendships of Richard Monckton Milnes, first Lord Houghton,* II, 359.

16 MS. letter to William James, March 29th, 1877: Houghton. Partly quoted in *Letters,* I, 53.

17 *Letters,* I. 55–6.

18 *Letters,* I. 54–5, Edel, 277.

19 *Selected Letters,* 103–8; Edel, 316-17.

20 *Letters,* I. 69–70.

21 *Notebooks,* 29.

22 Edmund Gosse. *Aspects and Impressions,* 27–8.

23 *Notebooks,* 28.

24 MS. letter to Alice James, June 5th, 1878: Houghton. Justin M'Carthy. *Reminiscences* (1899), II, 74–5.

25 Nadal. *loc. cit.* Edel, 320, 326-7.

26 *Letters,* I. 62–4.

27 Edel, *The Conquest of London,* 318, 362. MS. letter to Alice James, December 31st, 1878: Houghton.

28 *Letters,* I. 76–7.

29 *Letters,* I. 75.

30 *Letters,* I. 74.

31 Typescript copy letter Henry James, Jr., to Percy Lubbock, May 20th, 1919: Brotherton.

32 *The Letters of Mrs Henry Adams.* ed. Ward Thoron, 320; Edel, 462.

33 *id.* 329 note.

34 *id.* 338.

35 *Notebooks,* 40–1.

36 *id.* 44–5.

37 F. O. Matthiessen. *The James Family,* 129.

38 *id.* 131; *Letters,* I. 97.

39 Matthiessen, 130, 132–3.

40 *Letters,* I. 99.

41 Edel. *Henry James. The Middle Years,* 18–19.
42 *Letters,* I. 113–14.
43 MS. Letter December 26th, 1883: Brotherton. The article first appeared in the *Atlantic Monthly,* January, 1884. It was republished in book form in *Partial Portraits* (1888).
44 MS. letter April 24th, 1887: Brotherton.
45 *London Mercury,* April–May, 1920. Reprinted in Edmund Gosse, *Aspects and Impressions* (1922), pp. 17–53.
46. *The Letters of William James,* ed. Henry James. I, 288.

CHAPTER TWO · *Kensington*

1 MS. letters to William James, March 9th, April 7th, 1886: Houghton. Partly quoted in *Letters,* I. 120. Edel, *The Middle Years,* 97.
2 Edith Wharton. *A Backward Glance,* 247, Edel, 97.
3 MS. letter undated (*c.* 1888): Brotherton.
4 *A Catalogue of the Gosse Correspondence in the Brotherton Collection . . . with an Introduction by Philip Gosse,* at p. vii. MS. letter July 17th, 1907: Brotherton.
5 *Letters,* I. 88–9.
6 Diary of Sir Edward Hamilton, Vol. XLVI: British Museum. Add. MSS. 48644.
7 Nadal. *loc. cit.* MS. letter to William James, March 9th, 1886: Houghton. Partly quoted in *Letters,* I. 119–22. Edel. *Henry James. The Middle Years,* 106.
8 Vincent O'Sullivan. *Aspects of Wilde* (1936), 224. This story was told by Maupassant to Oscar Wilde, who repeated it to Vincent O'Sullivan.
9 Janet Adam Smith. *John Buchan,* 176, 472; *Notebooks,* 181.
10 MS. letters May 16th, 26th, 1910: Lamb.
11 *Letters,* I. 107. *Notebooks,* 57.
12 MS. letters to William James, February 15th, 1885; to Edmund Gosse, June 9th, 1884: Brotherton; Phyllis Grosskurth. *John Addington Symonds,* 270. Gosse's page reference must be to the MS. of the story, since the magazine version begins at p. 563.
13 MS. letter January 7th, 1893: Brotherton. The words 'a queer place' accidentally appear as 'your place' in Mrs Grosskurth's biography of Symonds (at p. 282). See letter from Leon Edel in the *Times Literary Supplement,* June 17th, 1965.

14 MS. letter April 23rd, 1893: Brotherton.

15 MS. letter April 8th, 1895: Brotherton; *Selected Letters,* 179.

16 MS. letter April 26th, 1896: Houghton. MS. letter April 29th, 1895: Brotherton.

17 *The Letters of Oscar Wilde,* ed. Rupert Hart-Davis, 390 note, 224 note, 776.

18 *Letters,* I. 222. Katherine Lyon Mix. *A Study in Yellow,* 142, 169–70.

19 Edel, 202–3. *Notebooks,* 99.

20 Compton Mackenzie. *My Life and Times,* I. 213–14.

21 *Letters,* I. 169.

22 *Letters,* I. 176–7.

23 *Letters,* I. 180; *Henry James and Robert Louis Stevenson,* ed. Janet Adam Smith, 199.

24 *Letters,* I. 189.

25 Mackenzie, II. 26.

26 Edel. 'The Dramatic Years', in *Guy Domville* (1961), 82–3.

27 *Letters,* I. 228–9. Edel. *Henry James: The Middle Years,* 298. Mrs Henry Huntington: B.B.C.

28 MS. letter January 3rd, 1895: Lamb.

29 *Letters,* I. 239–40.

30 H. G. Wells. *Experiment in Autobiography,* II. 536.

31 *Letters,* I. 233–5.

32 *Letters,* I. 242, Edel, *Guy Domville,* 107.

33 Mackenzie, II. 113–14.

34 MS. Letter to William James, March 28th, 1895: Houghton. *Letters,* I. 245–6.

35 MS. letter March, 1895: Brotherton. *Letters,* I. 122.

36 MS. letter October 13th, 1895: Lamb.

37 MS. Journal of Henry James. July 30th, 1914: Houghton.

38 *Letters,* I. 251.

39 *Letters to A. C. Benson and Auguste Monod,* 35.

40 *Letters,* I. 252. MS. letters, June–July, 1896: Lamb.

41 Mackenzie, II. 151–2.

42 *Letters,* I. 272–4.

43 *Letters,* I. 252–3.

44 Douglas Goldring. *The Last Pre-Raphaelite,* 100.

45 Ford Madox Ford. *Return to Yesterday,* 13–14.

46 *id.* 16.

47 *Letters,* I. 267.

48 MS. letter August 27th, 1897: Lamb.

49 MS. letter September 15th, 1897: Lamb. *Letters,* I. 268.

1 MS. letters September 16th, 20th, 1897: Lamb.
2 *Letters,* I. 269.
3 *Letters,* I. 273–4.
4 MS. letter January 22nd, 1898: Lamb.
5 Further details will be found in H. Montgomery Hyde. *The Story of Lamb House Rye* (1966).
6 Private information.
7 *Letters to A. C. Benson,* 47.
8 MS. letter: Houghton. Partly quoted in *Letters,* I. 289–90.
9 MS. letter to Miss Betham-Edwards, August 16th, 1911; Ashley. Theodora Bosanquet. 'As I Remember Henry James' in *Time and Tide,* 3 July 1954 (Vol. 35, No. 27).
10 *Letters,* I. 290–91.
11 MS. letter June 17th, 1898: Lamb.
12 *Henry James and H. G. Wells,* ed. Leon Edel and Gordon N. Ray, 52–3. *Letters,* I. 303.
13 Wells, *Experiment in Autobiography,* II. 596.
14 MS. letter to Philip Gosse, February 6th, 1919: Brotherton.
15 MS. letters September 23rd, October 5th, 1898: Lamb.
16 *Letters,* I. 312.
17 MS. letter October–November, 1898: Lamb.
18 Diary of Mrs James T. Fields, September 13th, 1898: M. A. De Wolfe Howe, *Memories of a Hostess* (1923), 297–301.
19 *The Awkward Age* (1899) 253, 265.
20 *Letters,* I. 305.
21 *Letters,* I. 310–12.
22 *Letters to A. C. Benson,* 49.
23 Nowell-Smith, 146.
24 *Notebooks,* 268.
25 *Letters,* I. 317–8.
26 MS. letter February 27th, 1899. Lamb.
27 MS. letter March 1st, 1899: Brotherton.
28 MS. letter March 2nd, 1899: Lamb.
29 MS. letter March 7th, 1899: Lamb.
30 MS. letters March 19th, 21st, 1899: Lamb.
31 MS. letter March 29th, 1899: Lamb.
32 MS. letter May 22nd, 1899: Lamb.
33 MS. letter May–June, 1899: Lamb.
34 Mrs Humphry Ward. *A Writer's Recollections,* 325–9.
35 *Letters,* I. 328.
36 *Letters,* I. 324–5.

37 MS. letters July 4th, 9th, 1899: Lamb.

38 MS. letters to Warren, July, August 13th: Lamb; to William James, August 4th/5th, 1899: Houghton. Gay Wilson Allen. *William James* (1967), 399–400.

39 J. Hasler. *The Clare Benedict Collection of Letters from Henry James* (1966), 143.

40 MS. letter to Edward Warren, May 21st–2nd, 1901: Lamb; to William James, May 6th, 1901: Houghton. Obituary notice of Emilie Grigsby: *The Times*, February 12th, 1964.

41 *Letters*, I. 353.

42 *The Letters of William James*. II. 105, 111.

43 Communicated by Percy Lubbock.

44 *Letters to A. C. Benson, 46.*

45 *The Diary of Arthur Christopher Benson*, ed. Percy Lubbock, 46–8.

46 Wharton. *A Backward Glance*, 244–6.

47 B.B.C.

48 Wells, II. 537.

49 MS. letter to Warren, March 19th, 1905: Lamb.

50 A. C. Bradley. 'Henry James as I knew Him' in *John o' London's Weekly*, December 18th, 1936. Bosanquet, *Time and Tide*, July 3rd, 1954.

51 Bradley, *loc. cit.* E. F. Benson. *Final Edition*, 4–5.

52 Mrs Wilfred De Glehn in B.B.C.

53 Simon Nowell-Smith. *The Legend of the Master*, 91–2.

54 B.B.C.

55 Bradley, *loc. cit.*

56 J. Adams. 'The Late Mr Henry James' in the *South Eastern Advertiser*, March 11th, 1916.

57 E. F. Benson, 4.

58 C. Lewis Hind. *Napthali.*

59 MS. Diary of Sir Sydney Waterlow, November 9th, 1907: Berg.

60 Evan Charteris. *The Life and Letters of Sir Edmund Gosse.* See also E. F. Benson. *As We Were* (at p. 327) for Benson's account of how he told this story to one of the 'wantons' in question.

61 Jessie Conrad. *Joseph Conrad and his Circle*, 69.

62 Bradley, *loc. cit.*

63 Douglas Goldring. *The Last Pre-Raphaelite*, 112.

64 MS. letter, October 20th, 1900: Brotherton.

65 Waterlow Diary: Berg. S. P. Waterlow. 'Memories of Henry James' in *New Statesman*, February 6th, 1926. Edel. 'Henry James and Sir Sydney Waterlow' in *The Times Literary Supplement*, August 8th, 1968.

66 Waterlow Diary, February 21st, 1908: Berg.

67 *id.* February 29th, 1908: Berg.
68 *id.* December 14th, 1908: Berg.

CHAPTER FOUR · *The Lamb Household*

1 *Letters,* I. 388–90.
2 *Letters,* I. 392–3.
3 Communicated by Burgess Noakes.
4 Ford Madox Ford. *Return to Yesterday,* 211.
5 Louis Boit. 'Henry James as Landlord', in *Atlantic Monthly.* Vol. 78, pp. 118–21 (August, 1946).
6 Communicated by Burgess Noakes.
7 Wharton. *A Backward Glance,* 243–4, 247.
8 Simon Fleet. 'In Search of Henry James at Rye' in *Modern Age.* Vol. 9, No. 1. (Chicago 1946–65), at pp. 75–6.
9 B.B.C.
10 B.B.C.
11 *Letters,* I. 391–2.
12 *Letters,* II. 135–6.
13 MS. letter, May 24th, 1903: Lamb.
14 M. A. De Wolfe Howe, *Memories of a Hostess,* 298. W. L. Phelps. *Autobiography with Letters,* 551. MS. letters to William James, April 20th, 1898: Houghton; to Warren May 12th, 1901: Lamb.
15 Communicated by Miss C. F. Kingdon.
16 *Letters,* II. 15. An extensive collection of MS. letters from Henry James to James Pinker amounting to 480 is preserved in the Yale University Library; see Alan B. Donovan. 'My dear Pinker: The Correspondence of Henry James with his Literary Agent' in *The Yale University Library Gazette.* Vol. 36, No. 2. (October, 1961).
17 Lady Maud Warrender. *My First Sixty Years,* 172–3.
18 Theodora Bosanquet. *Henry James at Work,* 3–5.
19 *id.* 5–6.
20 *id.* 7.
21 *id.* 6.
22 *Letters to A. C. Benson,* viii–ix.
23 Bosanquet, 12. MS. letter to Violet Hunt, April 1st, 1908: Barrett. Robert Herrick. *The Yale Review,* New Series (1923) xii, 724. ('A Visit to Henry James'), at pp. 735–6. For comparisons of passages in the earlier and later versions of *The American, Daisy Miller,* and other earlier weeks, see Ford Madox Hueffer.

Henry James (1913), 179–92; also Bosanquet 17–19 and Herrick, 737–40. A facsimile of a page of *The American* with the author's manuscript corrections is reproduced in *Letters*, II, facing p. 72.

24 Alvin Langdon Coburn. *A Portfolio of Sixteen Photographs* (1962), *passim*. See also MS letters from James to Coburn: Barrett.

25 Preface to *The Golden Bowl*, at pp. xii–xiii.

26 *Letters*, II. 109–10.

27 MS. letter December 29th, 1908: Brotherton.

28 Communicated by Methuen & Co.

29 Bosanquet, 21–2.

30 *The Letters of William James*, II. 277–8. A copy of *The American Scene* inscribed by the author, 'To William James his incoherent admiring affectionate brother. Lamb House. August 21st, 1907' is in the Clifton Waller Barrett Library, University of Virginia.

31 *Letters*, II. 111–12.

32 MS. letter May 10th, 1909: Houghton.

33 Private information.

34 *Letters*, II. 161, 165.

35 MS. letter March 9th, 1910: Brotherton.

36 *Letters*, II. 166.

37 MS. letter June 14th, 1910: Brotherton.

38 *Letters*, II. 174. *Letters of Henry James to Walter Berry*. No. 7 (September 3rd, 1910).

39 Communicated by Burgess Noakes.

40 MS. letter to Miss Betham-Edwards, August 16th, 1911. Ashley.

41 *Letters*, II. 212–13.

42 *Letters*, 217–18.

43 B.B.C.

CHAPTER FIVE • *Visitors and Visiting*

1 MS. letter July 3rd, 1901: Brotherton.

2 Gosse. *Aspects and Impressions*, 40–1.

3 *id*. 42–3.

4 *id*. 47–8.

5 MS. letter February 2nd, 1907: Brotherton.

6 Thomas Beer. *Stephen Crane*, 321.

7 Beer, 334.

8 Katherine Myon Mix. *A Study in Yellow*, 224.

9 Ford, 30–1

10 MS. letter August 2nd, 1899: Lamb.

11 Lillian Gilkes. *Cora Crane,* 204.

12 *id.* 205.

13 Stephen Crane, *Letters,* ed. R. W. Stallman and Lillian Gilkes, 243.

14 Wells, II. 614.

15 This programme is in the Crane Collection, Columbia University, New York, which also contains five pages of the MS. of *The Ghost:* Crane, 244. An interesting account of the production by John D. Gordan ('The Ghost at Brede Place') appeared in the *Bulletin of the New York Public Library,* LVI (December, 1952), 591–5.

16 Gilkes, 226.

17 Wells, II. 615.

18 Ford, 31.

19 Gilkes, 254.

20 Crane, 288.

21 Wells, II. 567, 577.

22 Leon Edel and Gordon N. Ray. *Henry James and H. G. Wells,* 71–2.

23 Nowell-Smith, 81

24 Waterlow Diary, December 7th, 1907: Berg. See also S. P. Waterlow. 'Memories of Henry James' in *New Statesman,* February 6th, 1926. According to H. G. Wells, the port-wine mark on Gissing's face was a syphilitic scar: Waterlow Diary, January 17th, 1912.

25 *Letters,* I. 398. Edel and Ray, 95. Wells, II. 567–81.

26 Wells, II. 538.

27 Jessie Conrad. *Joseph Conrad and his Circle,* 115.

28 MS. letter with enclosure, June 26th, 1902: Ashley. Information communicated by Mr Victor Bonham-Carter, Secretary of the Royal Literary Fund.

29 *Selected Letters,* 188–9. G. Jean Aubry. *Joseph Conrad Life and Letters;* II. 55–6, 91–2. Ford, 26–7.

30 MS. letter: Brotherton.

31 Ford, 6–7.

32 Henry James. *Views and Reviews* (1908), 226–7, 240.

33 MS. letter to William James. February 6th, 1892: Houghton.

34 *Letters,* I. 278.

35 Max Beerbohm. *Around Theatres* (1953), 245–7.

36 Beerbohm. *Letters to Reggie Turner,* ed. Rupert Hart-Davis, 15.

37 Charteris, 276.

38 Lord David Cecil. *Max,* 154–5. Beerbohm. *Letters to Reggie Turner,* 178.

39 S. N. Behrman. *Conversation with Max*, 201–2.

40 J. G. Riewald. *Max in Verse*, 21–5. The original MS. is in the Houghton Library, Harvard University. A typescript with Beerbohm's autograph corrections is in the possession of the present writer.

41 Charteris, 350–1.

42 J. G. Riewald. *Sir Max Beerbohm* (1953), 127.

43 Beerbohm. *Around Theatres*, 541–3.

44 Violet Hunt. *The Flurried Years*, 86; MS. letter to Violet Hunt, October 31st, 1909: Barrett.

45 Violet Hunt. 'The Last Days of Henry James' in the *Daily Mail*, March 1st, 1916. *The Letters of Oscar Wilde*, ed. Hart-Davis, 64. Douglas Goldring. *South Lodge*, 42. MS. letter to Violet Hunt, April 1st, 1900: Barrett.

46 MS. letters to Violet Hunt, November 5th, 1902; January 5th, 1898; January 28th, 1906: Barrett.

47 MS. letter to Violet Hunt, July 4th, 1903: Barrett. *Letters*, I. 432.

48 MS. letter, November 2nd, 1909: Barrett; Hunt, *The Flurried Years*, 87.

49 MS. letter, November 5th, 1909: Barrett; Hunt, 88.

50 MS. letter to F. M. Hueffer, November 8th, 1909: Barrett; Hunt, 89.

51 Goldring, 101–4.

52 Hunt, 240.

53 W. L. Phelps. *Autobiography with Letters* (1939), 554.

54 Millicent Bell. *Edith Wharton and Henry James*, 161.

55 B.B.C. Jacques-Emile Blanche. *Portraits of a Lifetime*, 237.

56 Percy Lubbock. *Portrait of Edith Wharton*, 69–70.

57 Wharton, *A Backward Glance*, 248–9.

58 Wharton, 250–4, 304.

59 Bell, 139.

60 Wharton, 242–3.

61 Wharton, 233

62 Bell, 153.

63 Bell, 167–8.

CHAPTER SIX · *Chelsea*

1 Benson. *Diary*, 225–6.

2 Rupert Hart-Davis. *Hugh Walpole*, 68.

3 Sir Hugh Walpole. 'Henry James. A Reminiscence' in *Horizon*. Vol. I, No. 2 (February 1940), at p. 76.

4 *Letters,* II. 247.
5 *Letters,* II. 249.
6 *Letters,* II. 255, 298.
7 B.B.C. Bosanquet in *Time and Tide,* July 10th, 1954.
8 *Letters,* II. 256, 259. Charteris, 338–40.
9 *The Journals of Arnold Bennett* 1911–1921, ed. Newman Flower (1932), 57. *Letters,* II. 299, 302–3.
10 MS. letter: Lamb.
11 MS. letter, February 7th, 1913: Lamb.
12 *Letters,* II. 311.
13 *Letters,* II. 317. Hunt, 240.
14 Bell, 191.
15 Bell, 192.
16 *Letters from Max Beerbohm to Reggie Turner,* 222.
17 Hart-Davis, 99.
18 Christopher Hassall. *Edward Marsh* (1959), 375. *Letters,* II. 319–20.
19 MS. letter: Brotherton.
20 *Letters,* II. 321.
21 *Letters,* II. 322–4.
22 Shane Leslie. 'A Note on Henry James' in *Horizon,* Vol. VII, No. 42 (June 1943), at p. 407. Letter mis-dated 1903.
23 *Letters,* II. 324–5.
24 *Letters,* II. 327–8.
25 *Letters,* II. 330.
26 MS. letter August 9th, 1913.
27 *Letters,* II. 361–2.
28 Blanche, 160.
29 *The Times,* May 5th, 1914. *Letters,* II. 379.
30 *The Times,* May 6th, 1914. *Letters,* II. 381.
31 MS. letter, May 1st, 1914: Brotherton.
32 Benson. *Diary,* 273.
33 B.B.C.
34 *London Mercury,* September, 1922 (Vol. VI, No. 35), pp. 495–501; *The Complete Plays of Henry James,* ed. Leon Edel, 811–16.
35 *The Times Literary Supplement,* March 19th, April 2nd, 1914.
36 *Letters,* II. 335.
37 B.B.C.
38 Compton Mackenzie. 'Henry James' in *Life and Letters Today,* Vol. 39, No. 76 (December, 1943).
39 Bradley.
40 William Roughead *Tales of the Criminous,* 252, 256, 257, 260.

CHAPTER SEVEN · *War and Death*

1 *Letters*, II. 398, 400.
2 *Letters*, II. 415.
3 Gosse. *Aspects and Impressions*, 50–1. *Letters*, II. 423.
4 Typescript copy letter Henry James, Jr., to Percy Lubbock, May 20th, 1919: Brotherton. F. W. Dupee. *Henry James* (1956), 249. *Selected Letters*, ed. Edel, 249.
5 MS. letter to Pinker, October 2nd, 1914: Yale. W. L. Phelps. *Autobiography with Letters*, 555. John Bailey. *Diary with Letters*, 152.
6 Logan Pearsall Smith. 'Notes on Henry James' in *Atlantic Monthly*, Vol. 172, No. 2 (August, 1943) at p. 75.
7 *Letters*, II. 495.
8 *Letters of Henry James to Walter Perry*. No. 16 (December 11th, 1914).
9 Henry James. *Within the Rim and other Essays*, 72.
10 *The Book of France (1915)*, edited by William Stephens, was published 'under the auspices of an honorary committee presided over by His Excellency Monsieur Paul Cambon'. The other English members of the Committee included A. J. Balfour, Austen Chamberlain, Winston Churchill, D. Lloyd George, Sir John Simon, Lord Haldane, Sir Frederick Macmillan, Edmund Gosse, Hilaire Belloc, Thomas Hardy, Rudyard Kipling, H. G. Wells, Lady Randolph Churchill, Mrs W. K. Clifford, Mrs Belloc Lowndes and Mrs Humphry Ward.
11 Violet Hunt. *The Flurried Years*, 266–7; 'The Last Days of Henry James' in *Daily Mail*, March 1st, 1916.
12 Communicated by Burgess Noakes.
13 *Selected Letters*, 258–60.
14 Christopher Hassall. *Rupert Brooke* (1964), 187–8. See also Geoffrey Keynes. *Henry James in Cambridge* (1968), *passim*.
15 *Letters*, II. 490.
16 Rupert Brooke. *Letters from America*. With a Preface by Henry James (1915).
17 *Letters*, II. 480.
18 *Letters*, II. 485, 489, 491.
19 Benson. *Diary*, 280–1.
20 Nowell-Smith, 167.
21 *Letters*, II. 495, 498.
22 Charteris. *Edmund Gosse*, 382.
23 J. A. Spender and Cyril Asquith. *Life of Herbert Henry Asquith, Lord Oxford and Asquith* (1932), I. 217. *The Autobiography of*

Margot Asquith, ed. Mark Bonham Carter (1962), 151–3. *Letters,* II. 498–9.

24 MS. letter, June 28th, 1915. Asquith Papers: Bodleian Library, Oxford; Earl of Oxford and Asquith. *Memories and Reflections* (1928), I. 283–4.

25 Spender and Asquith, 216.

26 MS. letter to Pinker, June 29th, 1915: Yale. MS. letter to Gosse, July 9th, 1915: Brotherton. *Letters,* II. 508.

27 MS. letter, July 20th, 1915: Simon Papers.

28 *Letters,* II. 509–10.

29 *Letters,* II. 503.

30 H. G. Wells, *Boon* (1915), 107–8.

31 *Letters,* II. 505.

32 *Letters,* II. 506–8.

33 MS. letter to Miss Betham-Edwards, August 28th, 1915: Ashley. *Letters,* II. 513.

34 Ford Madox Ford. *Return to Yesterday,* 220. MS. letters to Edward Warren, August 19th, 26th, 1915: Lamb.

35 *Letters,* II. 517.

36 The will was executed in Boston, Mass., on December 19th, 1910, and the codicil in London on August 25th, 1915. The original is preserved in the Principal Probate Registry, Somerset House, London.

37 *Letters,* II. 450–1.

38 *Letters,* II. 519.

39 Logan Pearsall Smith, *loc. cit.*

40 Wharton, *A Backward Glance,* 367.

41 Bosanquet in B.B.C. Edel. 'Henry James's "Last Dictation"' in *The Times Literary Supplement,* May 2nd, 1968.

42 Phelps, 556. Mrs William James to Edmund Gosse, December 15th, 1915: Ashley.

43 Christopher Hassall. *Edward Marsh* (1959), 374.

44 James S. Bain, *A Bookseller Looks Back* (1940), 221–2.

45 Virginia Harlow, *Thomas Sergeant Perry* (1950), 349–50.

46 Mrs William James to Edmund Gosse, February 11th, March 4th, 1916: Brotherton.

47 MS. letter, March 4th, 1916: Brotherton.

48 *The Times,* March 4th, 1916.

49 MS. letter, March 4th, 1916: Brotherton.

50 *The Times,* March 7th, 1916.

51 Phelps, 556.

52 The plaque was paid for by the subscriptions of thirty-six residents of Rye and neighbourhood, including Sir Reginald

Blomfield, Lady Maud Warrender, Sir George and Lady Prothero, and Mr A. G. Bradley: *Sussex Express,* October 5th, 1917.
53 Hyde. *The Story of Lamb House, passim.*
54 Bosanquet. *Henry James at Work,* 32.

APPENDIX · *The Lamb House Library*

1 *Catalogue of the Library of Henry James, O.M. at Lamb House,
Rye, Sussex.* In the possession of H. Montgomery Hyde.
2 MS. letter Ruth Draper to Roger Senhouse, October 28th, 1949.
Communicated by Mr Roger Senhouse.
3 Property of National Trust at Lamb House.
4 *id.*
5 *id.*
6 In the possession of H. Montgomery Hyde.
7 *Journals of Arnold Bennett, 1911–1921.* Ed. Newman Flower, at
p. 266.

❦ Select Bibliography

A Bibliography of Henry James by Leon Edel and Dan H. Laurence, 2nd edition, revised, London, 1961, constitutes the fullest bibliography of the writer's own published work. A useful bibliography of literary criticism prepared by Maurice Beebe and William T. Stafford ('Criticism of Henry James: A Selected Checklist') appeared in *Modern Fiction Studies*, Vol. XII, No. 1, Spring, 1966, from Purdue University Department of English, Lafayette, Indiana. *The Legend of the Master*, compiled by Simon Nowell-Smith, London, 1947, contains a comprehensive bibliography of published writings on and about Henry James.

A · *Manuscript Sources*

Ashley MSS. James Correspondence in the Ashley Library of T. J. Wise. In the British Museum, Add. MSS. 4792, 4860, 5739.

British Broadcasting Corporation Sound Archives. 'Recollections of Henry James in his Later Years'. Compiled and introduced by Michael Swan. Produced by Douglas Cleverdon and first broadcast in the Third Programme, June 4th, 1956, from Broadcasting House, London.

Catalogue of the Library of Henry James, O.M. at Lamb House, Rye, Sussex. Prepared by Hodgson & Co. auctioneers of Books, 115 Chancery Lane, London, W.C.2, July, 1931. In the possession of H. Montgomery Hyde.

Gosse Correspondence. Letters to Edmund Gosse and his family. In the Brotherton Collection, Brotherton Library, University of Leeds.

Hamilton Diary. Diary of Sir Edward Hamilton, 1886. In the British Museum. Add. MSS. 48644.

Hunt-Hueffer Letters. Letters from Henry James to Violet Hunt and Ford Madox Ford (Hueffer). In the Clifton Waller Barrett Library, University of Virginia.

James Correspondence. Correspondence of the James Family. In the Houghton Library, Harvard University.

Pinker Letters. Letters from Henry James to James B. Pinker. In Yale University Library.

Warren Letters. Letters from Henry James to Edward Warren. In the possession of H. Montgomery Hyde.

Waterlow Diary. Diary of Sir Sydney Waterlow, 1907–11. In the Berg Collection, New York City Public Library.

Weld Diary. Diary of Mary Weld, 1901–04. In the possession of Miss C. F. Kingdon.

B · *Printed Sources*

ADAMS, HENRY. *The Education of Henry Adams. An Autobiography.* London, 1928.

ADAMS, MRS H. *The Letters of Mrs Henry Adams.* Edited by Ward Thoron. London, 1937.

ALLEN, GAY WILSON. *William James.* London, 1967.

BEERBOHM, MAX. *A Book of Caricatures.* London, 1907.
　　　　　　Fifty Caricatures. London, 1913.
　　　　　　Around Theatres. London, 1953.
　　　　　　Letters to Reggie Turner, Edited by Rupert Hart-Davis, London, 1964.

BELL, MILLICENT. *Edith Wharton and Henry James. The Story of their Friendship.* New York, 1965.

BENSON, A. C. *The Diary of Arthur Christopher Benson.* Edited by Percy Lubbock. London, 1926.

BENSON, E. F. *As We Were.* London, 1930.
　　　　　　Final Edition, London, 1940.

BLANCHE, JACQUES-EMILE. *Portraits of a Lifetime.* Translated and edited by Walter Clement. London, 1937.

BOSANQUET, THEODORA. *Henry James at Work.* London, 1924. 'As I Remember Henry James' in *Time and Tide.* 3/10 July, 1954. (Vol. 35, Nos. 27 and 28.)

CHARTERIS, EVAN. *The Life and Letters of Sir Edmund Gosse.* London, 1931.

CONRAD, JESSIE. *Joseph Conrad as I Knew Him.* London, 1926.

CONRAD, JOSEPH. *Life and Letters.* Edited by G. Jean-Aubry. 2 vols. London, 1927.

CRANE, STEPHEN. *Letters.* Edited by R. W. Stallman and Lillian Gilkes. London, 1960.

DUPEE, F. W. *Henry James.* New York, 1956.

EDEL, LEON. *Henry James. The Untried Years. 1843–1870.* London, 1953.
Henry James. The Conquest of London, 1870–1883. London, 1962.
Henry James. The Middle Years. 1884–1894. London, 1963.

FORD, FORD MADOX. See HUEFFER, F. M.

GILKES, LILLIAN. *Cora Crane.* London, 1962.

GOLDRING, DOUGLAS. *South Lodge. Reminiscences of Violet Hunt, Ford Madox Ford and the English Review Circle.* London, 1943.
The Last Pre-Raphaelite. A Record of the Life and Writings of Ford Madox Ford. London, 1948.

GOSSE, EDMUND. *Aspects and Impressions.* London, 1922.

GROSSKURTH, PHYLLIS. *John Addington Symonds.* London, 1964.

HARLOW, VIRGINIA. *Thomas Sergeant Parry.* Durham, N.C. 1950.

HART-DAVIS, RUPERT. *Hugh Walpole.* London, 1952.

HASLER, JORG. *Switzerland in the Life and Work of Henry James* Berne, 1966.

HASSALL, CHRISTOPHER. *Edward Marsh.* London, 1959.
Rupert Brooke. London, 1964.

HASTINGS, KATHERINE (BAGG). *William James of Albany, N.Y. and his Descendants.* New York, 1924.

HOWE, M. A. DE WOLFE. *Memories of a Hostess.* London. 1928.

HUEFFER, FORD MADOX. *Return to Yesterday.* London, 1931.

HUNT, VIOLET. *The Flurried Years.* London, 1926.

HYDE, H. MONTGOMERY. *The Story of Lamb House, Rye. The Home of Henry James.* Rye, 1966.

JAMES, ALICE. *The Diary of Alice James.* Edited with an introduction by Leon Edel. New York, 1964.

JAMES, HENRY. *The Novels and Tales of Henry James.* 24 vols. New York, 1907–1909.
Views and Reviews. Boston, 1908.
A Small Boy and Others. London, 1913.
Notes of a Son and Brother. London, 1914.
The Middle Years. London, 1917.
Within the Rim. London, 1918.
The Letters of Henry James. Selected and edited by Percy Lubbock. 2 vols. London, 1920.

Letters of Henry James to Walter Berry. Paris, 1928.

Henry James: Letters to A. C. Benson and Auguste Monod. London, 1930.

Theatre and Friendships. Some Henry James Letters. With a Commentary by Elizabeth Robins. New York, 1932.

The Complete Plays of Henry James. Edited by Leon Edel. London, 1949.

Henry James and Robert Louis Stevenson. Edited by Janet Adam Smith, London, 1948.

Selected Letters of Henry James. Edited and introduced by Leon Edel. London, 1956.

Henry James and H. G. Wells. Edited by Leon Edel and Gordon N. Ray. London, 1959.

The Clare Benedict Collection of Letters from Henry James. Edited by Jorg Hasler. Berne, 1966.

JAMES, WILLIAM. *The Letters of William James.* Edited by his son Henry James. 2 vols. London, 1920.

KEYNES, GEOFFREY. *Henry James in Cambridge.* Cambridge, 1968.

LE CLAIR, ROBERT C. *Young Henry James 1843–1870.* New York, 1955.

LUBBOCK, PERCY. *Portrait of Edith Wharton.* London, 1947.

MACKENZIE, SIR COMPTON. *My Life and Times.* 6 vols. London, 1963–1967.

MACCARTHY, DESMOND. *Portraits.* London, 1931.

MCELDERRY, BRUCE R. JR. *Henry James.* New York, 1965.

MARSH, EDWARD. *A Number of People.* London, 1939.

MASON, A. E. W. *Sir George Alexander and the St James's Theatre.* London, 1935.

MATTHIESSEN, F. O. *The James Family.* New York, 1947.

NOWELL-SMITH, SIMON. *The Legend of the Master.* London, 1947.

PHELPS, WILLIAM LYON. *Autobiography with Letters.* Oxford, 1939.

POPE-HENNESSY, JAMES. *Monckton Milnes. The Flight of Youth.* London, 1951.

ROUGHEAD, WILLIAM. *Tales of the Criminous.* London, 1956.

SMITH, LOGAN PEARSALL. *Unforgotten Years.* London, 1938.

TREVELYAN, JANET PENROSE. *The Life of Mrs. Humphry Ward.* London, 1923.

WARD, MRS HUMPHRY. *A Writer's Recollections*. London, 1918.

WELLS, H. G. *Boon*. London, 1915.

    Experiment in Autobiography. 2 vols. London, 1934.

WHARTON, EDITH. *A Backward Glance*. New York, 1934.

❧ Index